ADVANCE PRAISE FOR
CRAZY FOR COLLEGE

"Navigating the college admissions process can be daunting for students and parents alike. In *Crazy for College*, Beth Gelles draws on decades of experience to offer clear, practical advice—along with warmth, humor, and hard-earned perspective. A standout is the Afterword, a bold and thoughtful 'Wish List' of admissions reforms that should be required reading for university leaders and policymakers. This book is an indispensable guide for anyone seeking a saner, more student-centered path to higher education."

–ANDREW MARTIN,
Chancellor, Washington University in St. Louis

"*Crazy for College* is a protein shake for the college admission workout, blending Beth's experience with humor, compassion, and sanity. Offering real-life examples, it is chock full of lessons for parents who not only seek a healthy college search process, but—more importantly—a thriving college journey for their children."

–HEATH EINSTEIN,
Vice Provost for Enrollment Management, Texas Christian University

"*Crazy for College* equips today's parents of college applicants with an invaluable resource to truly understand the complexities of the 21st century college admission process. More importantly, it reinforces what matters most—supporting and loving their children through a process of self-discovery, resiliency, potential setbacks, and the success that ultimately follows. In fact, the journey itself may prove to be just as meaningful as the destination."

–GRANT M. GOSSELIN,
Dean of Undergraduate Admission & Financial Aid, Boston College

"*Crazy for College* provides an antidote to the intensity of the college search process, hitting an ideal mix of advice and wisdom with humor and straight-talk. It's a helpful 'decoder ring' for students and parents alike."

–EMILY ROPER-DOTEN,
Dean of Admissions, Brandeis University

"Reading *Crazy for College* felt like sitting in a living room with Beth Gelles, listening to her stories and hard-earned wisdom about the admissions journey. College admissions today can feel like a high-stakes guessing game—rules keep shifting, competition is fierce, and colleges aren't making it easier. With compassion and a welcome touch of humor, Gelles cuts through the noise and captures the full emotional roller coaster: confusion, stress, hope, excitement. She offers reassuring advice every family needs to hear: your kid is going to be okay, this process isn't about winning or losing, and there's a right-fit college for every student."

–MATT ROSENBAUM,
Former Senior Admissions Officer, University of Chicago

"As someone who works with arts students applying to college, I was happy to see Beth Gelles highlight an often-overlooked opportunity: some colleges invite applicants to submit an arts supplement even if they don't plan to major in an artistic discipline. It's a wonderful chance for a computer scientist to share her love of singing or for an aspiring engineer to showcase their passion for lighting or scenic design. Beth thinks on behalf of students and speaks to the concerns of their parents. I'm crazy for *Crazy for College*!"

–CHRIS ANDERSSON,
Former Director of Admissions, NYU Tisch School of the Arts

"As a grandmother raising two boys who lost their parents, I can't overstate how invaluable Beth and Nancy were in guiding them through the college application process. Their focus on the boys' strengths and interests, and the encouragement and tools they provided, made all the difference. When I later read *Crazy for College*, I recognized that same warmth, wisdom, and practical perspective on every page. I can't recommend it highly enough."

–MICHELLE KNAPP,
Grandmother and guardian of two boys who lost their parents

"*Crazy for College* is an incredibly helpful guide for anyone navigating the college process, including first-generation and low-income students and families who don't always have access to insider knowledge. It brings clarity, compassion, and practical guidance to a system that often feels overwhelming—and reminds readers that behind every application is a young person finding their way."

–SAM WALLIS,
Executive Director, YPIE (Yonkers Partners in Education)

"Even after twenty years in admissions, I found myself nodding and laughing out loud at Beth's insights. *Crazy for College* is a must-read for any parent who wants to survive the college process intact—and sane. With humor, humanity, and expertise, she reminds us to focus on what really matters: our child and our relationship throughout the journey."

–DR. MEGAN STUBBENDECK, Ph.D.,
CEO Arbor Bridge, a leading test prep and tutoring firm

"With warmth, wit, and wisdom, Beth Gelles has written an indispensable guide for anyone frantically seeking a roadmap through the tangled maze of today's college application process. As the spiritual leader of a congregation in a college-crazed community, I am eager to recommend *Crazy for College*, which will take the anxiety of applying down several notches and help parents and students joyfully discover what really matters as they embark on this important journey."

–RABBI JONATHAN BLAKE,
Senior Rabbi, Westchester Reform Temple (Scarsdale, NY)

"After decades as Head of Guidance at Long Beach High School and now as a private consultant, I've seen families overwhelmed by the admissions process. *Crazy for College* is the guide I wish every parent could read from the start. It's wise, funny, and reassuring, like Beth herself. I plan to give this book to every family I work with."

–CAROLYN CUTTLER,
Former Director of Guidance, Long Beach High School (NY)

"*Crazy for College* captures the same blend of humor and heart that guided each of our three children through the admissions process. It's a lifeline for any family, wherever they may be."

–ALEXANDER MACRIDIS,
Father of three college graduates (Yale University), Athens, Greece

"*Crazy for College* is the voice every overwhelmed parent needs in their ear—wise and deeply reassuring. Beth Gelles brings years of experience, humor, and heart to the craziness of college admissions. Her guidance helped both of our sons, two very different students, navigate the process with confidence. This book is a gift to any family trying to make sense of the madness."

–DR. LESLIE SOLOSHATZ,
Pediatrician and mom of two college graduates
(University of Pennsylvania and Boston University), Pittsburgh, PA

"Beth Heller Gelles delivers wise and compassionate guidance to parents on navigating the college process with their teens. Through compelling anecdotes and fascinating commentary, Gelles describes the uncertainty that permeates the college admissions process, often contributing to significant anxiety and distress among applicants and their families. She offers evidence-based strategies to alleviate this stress, providing a blueprint for how to maintain balance, perspective, and joy throughout the process."

–EMILY STERN, Ph.D.,
Clinical Psychologist

"Coming from a huge public school, I often felt like just another number in the college process. Beth and Nancy helped me figure out what I actually wanted in a school, not what I thought I was supposed to want, and that clarity led me straight to the University of Miami. I've never been happier. I found my place, my people, and a path that feels like mine."

–ETHAN,
University of Miami

"Transferring felt like a disappointment at first. I wasn't sure if leaving Wake Forest was the right move or if I'd ever find the environment I needed. Beth and Nancy helped me understand what wasn't working and see what could work. Boston University ended up being the perfect fit. I'm thriving here in every way."

–OLIVIA,
Boston University

Crazy *for* College

The Stories, The Secrets, &
The Shot of Sanity You Need to

MAKE IT THROUGH ADMISSIONS

Beth Heller Gelles

College Admissions Advisor & Co-Founder, Acceptance Ahead, Inc.

CRAZY FOR COLLEGE by Beth Heller Gelles
Published by Inspired by You Books, an imprint of Inspired Girl Publishing Group, a division of Inspired Girl Enterprises
Asbury Park, NJ 07712
inspiredgirlbooks.com

Inspired Girl Publishing Group is honored to bring forth books with heart and stories that matter. We are proud to offer this book to our readers; the story, the experiences, and the words are the author's alone. The stories portrayed within CRAZY FOR COLLEGE are based on actual events. In some incidents, characteristics, names, and timelines may have been compressed or combined to protect the privacy and preserve the anonymity of people involved. The conversations in the book all come from the author's recollections, though they are not written to represent word-for-word transcripts.

This book is written as a source of information only. The information contained in this book should by no means be considered a substitute for the advice of a qualified medical professional. In addition, the publisher and the author assume no responsibility for errors, inaccuracies, omissions, or any other inconsistencies herein. The use of this book implies your acceptance of this disclaimer. Products, books, trademarks, and trademark names are used throughout this book to describe and inform the reader about various proprietary products that are owned by third parties. No endorsement of the information contained in this book is given by the owners of such products and trademarks, and no endorsement is implied by the inclusion of products, books, or trademarks in this book.

ISBN: Hardcover- 978-1-965240-31-1 / Paperback- 978-1-965240-32-8
Written by: Beth Heller Gelles
Editorial & Creative Director: Jenn Tuma-Young
Book Editing and Packaging: Inspired Girl Publishing Group
Jacket Photographer: Andi Schreiber
Library of Congress Control Number: 2026905067
Printed in the USA

To the hundreds of students
I've had the privilege of guiding.
You've reminded me, again and again,
why this work matters.

Table of

Contents

One ACCEPTANCE LETTER, *a* Hundred TURNS

The second the school buzzer rang for my lunch period, I stuffed my AP Calculus binder into my JanSport backpack and bolted. My new Keds squeaked on the linoleum floor as I flew down the stairwell and burst through the double doors. The student parking lot at J.P. Stevens High School in Edison, NJ, was a hodgepodge of hand-me-down Pontiacs and Buicks. We seventeen-year-olds felt lucky to drive whatever we could get our hands on. Anything was better than taking the bus. I had a brown Oldsmobile Cutlass Sierra, passed down to me from my dad. That week, I spent every lunch period racing home to check the mail. It was almost April, and college decisions were trickling in. The 12 o'clock air felt thick with possibility (or maybe just humidity—it *was* New Jersey).

With the windows rolled down, I sped down Grove Avenue, belting along to Whitney Houston's "How Will I Know" blasting from WPLJ, my favorite station. I pulled into my driveway a little too fast, just as the mailman was pulling away. In 1986, college decisions still arrived in envelopes.

The weight of anticipation filled my chest. I flung the car door open, only for the seat belt to snag the pocket of my acid-wash Jordache jeans, yanking me back inside. It was probably the universe telling me, "Hold on! Chill out!"

My eyes locked onto the mailbox. Everything came down to what might be inside. A thick envelope meant possibility. Celebration. A thin one meant the path I'd been picturing might not be mine after all. I finally wrestled myself free from the seat belt's claws and hurried over. In that split second before opening the box, it felt like the whole world was holding its breath alongside me.

The envelope was thick and had my name on it. *Thick!* The return address was marked OFFICE OF ADMISSIONS AND FINANCIAL AID. I melted onto the sidewalk curb, the envelope shaking in my hands as I gathered the strength to rip it open. "Congratulations! I am delighted to inform you..." The rest of the words blurred together. Somehow, my legs carried me inside the house to grab the phone in the den. Hands trembling, I punched in the phone number of the elementary school where my mom taught kindergarten.

"Asher Holmes Elementary School, how may I help you?" a voice chirped on the other end.

"Hi!" I blurted out. "It's not an emergency!" I squealed. "But I need to speak with my mom, Martha Heller."

Minutes felt like an hour before I heard heels clicking on the floor, hurrying toward the phone in the school office.

"Helloooo?" My mom's voice stretched through the phone, each syllable swelling with expectation.

"Mom!" I screamed, surely deafening her. "I got in!"

LIFE BEYOND THAT ENVELOPE

Now, almost forty years later, I can remember everything I felt in that moment. Not just the joy, but the adrenaline rush that felt like a borderline heart attack. Looking back, I might have been a little *too* wrapped up in that envelope, as if it held my entire future in its 9x12-inch grip. I should have slowed down, taken a breath, maybe even opened it inside my house, like a civilized human being. Because thick or thin, those four years of college weren't going to define my life. But I didn't know that then.

As it turned out, college wasn't always rosy. Coming from a big public school in New Jersey where cumulative final exams weren't really a thing, I arrived at Harvard totally unprepared for midterms, finals, and hundreds of pages of weekly reading. I'll never forget getting my first B + on a paper—after years of working hard and earning A's—and thinking, *wait, what?*

Then came the Harvard Marching Band audition. I'd spent three years as *first chair* clarinet in high school, even playing solos in concert band. At Harvard? I was politely told I could play *second* clarinet. Humbling, to say the least.

Little by little, I found my footing, both inside and outside the classroom. I thought I wanted to be a lawyer until I walked into my first government class and realized I could barely sit through seventy-five minutes of rational choice theory. Shakespeare, on the other hand, felt like love at first sonnet. I switched my concentration (Harvard's version of a major), called my dad to reassure him that yes, his daughter would still be employable, and spent the next few years analyzing contemporary fiction and plays instead of Supreme Court decisions.

Still, Harvard could feel cold. The professors often seemed like deities—brilliant, distant, and not exactly interested in mentoring an overwhelmed eighteen-year-old with a Jersey accent.

College knocked me off balance and forced me to find my footing. I battled (and beat) an eating disorder, proving to myself that I was stronger than I realized. I survived Harvard, graduated, and launched myself into the real world, armed with a degree in "English and American Literature and Languages." Then I did what any practical English major does: I got a job in advertising. Clearly, poetry and literary analysis were the perfect training ground for marketing consumer products.

Between late-night ad pitches and weekends with fun, ambitious twenty-somethings in NYC, my life took a wonderful turn: I met a boy. A handsome, blue-eyed boy who matched me in warmth and met me eye to eye. The only catch? He lived in LA, so we dated long-distance for several months. This was before email or texting. We did things the old-fashioned way, with handwritten cards, late-night phone calls, and a three-hour time difference that never cooperated. Eventually, I moved to LA (for love), and somewhere between switching ad agencies and questioning whether I was remotely qualified for business school, I got into Northwestern. We packed up, moved to Chicago, got engaged, married, and after graduation, moved back east to New York, where we settled into city life, work, and, eventually, parenthood.

Two kids later, life threw another curveball: a cross-country move to San Francisco for my husband's job. I traded Manhattan high-rises and four real seasons for a Bay Area "starter" home and wonderful weather, adding a third baby to the mix. I had always been a singer, a pianist, and just plain musical, so taking my own kids to Music Together classes felt natural. Before long, I went from attending classes to starting my own franchise, spending nine years teaching music to preschoolers as "Teacher Beth"—a small-town celebrity but only for those under the age of five.

Then, as life tends to do, it boomeranged us back east, again for my husband's job. This time, something felt different. I didn't know exactly what was coming next, but I was ready for work with more heart. I'd already lived through advertising, business school, multiple cross-country moves, and years of diaper changes. None of that pointed directly to college advising, but the pattern is pretty clear in retrospect. I'd always loved helping people shape their stories. I loved watching someone grow from self-doubt to "Hey, I've got this." It never felt like work. It just felt good.

After meeting my business partner, Nancy, we launched Acceptance Ahead, a private college counseling practice, and somehow, my life had come full circle. The same girl who once hyperventilated over an acceptance letter was now helping *other* kids (and their equally hyperventilating parents) tackle the same nerve-wracking process.

Practically overnight, my kids went from preschool to high school, and I found myself opening the "envelope" with my own three kids (now ages twenty-six, twenty-four, and twenty-one). But, of course, it wasn't an envelope anymore; it was a computer screen and a college portal login. I held my breath as they each clicked "View Decision." The mailbox sprints of my high school years had been replaced by frantic email refreshes and family-wide laptop viewing. At exactly 7:00 p.m. (or some random time only admissions offices understand), we'd huddle around the screen, praying for virtual confetti or a shower of falling leaves to signal an acceptance.

Even with all my additional years and experiences, the nerves around college acceptance never really fade. Every time I hear Whitney Houston's "How Will I Know," I'm instantly transported back to my childhood driveway, staring down that menacing mailbox.

That memory of holding that envelope in my trembling hands is what keeps me anchored in what I do today. It reminds me exactly of how my students feel in those moments of possibility. It also reminds me to tell them what I wish I could have told my younger self: that envelope will not define them. Regardless of whether it's thin or thick, life won't follow a straight line. There will be detours, surprises, wrong turns, miracles, and destinations they never saw coming. Wherever they go and whatever happens next, they've already won, simply by being who they are.

Maybe that's why, all these years later, I ended up here: helping teenagers and their parents find their way through the same swirling mix of excitement and uncertainty. That moment in my driveway was my first taste of how enormous one decision can feel and how much it helps to have someone who gets it standing right beside you.

I didn't know it then, but that mailbox was quietly setting me up for the work I do now: guiding students through their own hopeful, heart-pounding dance...minus the Keds and the Oldsmobile.

WELCOME *to the* MADNESS

TEXT MESSAGE—5:46 p.m. (Thursday evening, mid-chaos—three kids, dinner prep, and garlic bread dangerously close to burning)

"Hi, Beth! Should Amy intern at her uncle's hedge fund this summer or be a camp counselor? Which one looks better on college applications?"

EMAIL—9:18 p.m. (Sunday night, of course)

"I totally forgot I have my Georgetown interview tomorrow at 3. Can you please prep me tonight?"

PHONE CALL—7:07 a.m. (Wednesday morning, before my first sip of coffee)

"Should Alex take the ACT a third time? All his other scores are above 30, but his math score is still at a 24. If he doesn't raise it, should he rethink applying for business? Should we switch tutors?"

IN-PERSON ENCOUNTER—6:32 p.m. (Tuesday evening, pouring rain, dance studio parking lot—a car window slowly rolls down beside me)

"You're Beth, right? I've been meaning to reach out. My daughter's only a sophomore, but can you tell me exactly what she needs to do to get into the University of Pennsylvania?"

This is pretty much a normal week in the life of a college advisor: fielding frantic, last-minute questions from well-meaning parents trying to navigate an admissions process that often feels like a never-ending game of Twister. Blindfolded.

Can you blame them? The heat is intense, and even the most level-headed parents can end up feeling completely lost.

If you feel like you need a lifeline, you are not alone. I promise I get it. I've been on both sides of this madness. As an independent college admissions advisor, I've spent years guiding families through the constantly changing, often baffling process. But I'm also a mom who's crossed this bridge three times with my own kids. I admit that even for me, a so-called expert on the process, I still had my anxious moments. (Thankfully, I discovered that deep breathing techniques help. So does wine.)

The truth is, there's a lot no one can predict, like timing, outcomes, or whether your kid will suddenly mention a forgotten deadline over dinner. But here's what I do know: it all works out.

This book is not just a series of chaotic examples and cautionary tales. It's about how to survive the college application process, stay sane, and find moments of joy along the way. The most important thing? Figure out what excites your child, what they love to do, and find a college that fits *them*. Not what fits the neighbor's kid who plays violin at Carnegie Hall, not your family friend's neuroscience prodigy, and not the debate champ who can recite Supreme Court cases in their sleep. *Your* child.

Brace yourself or grab a cookie. This isn't exactly a guide to the admissions process. It's a conversation that's honest, occasionally uncomfortable, and hopefully reassuring. It's where I tell you what's happening out there and remind you (warmly but firmly) that your child will find their way. You will, too. Just know this: the college process you remember from high school? Ancient history.

WHY YOU NEED THIS BOOK (THINGS HAVE CHANGED. DRASTICALLY!)

If you applied to college before the internet existed, you probably remember filling out a few paper applications, mailing them off, and waiting for a thick or thin envelope to arrive in the mail. Maybe you applied to five or six schools. Maybe you visited a few campuses. The process felt big but bearable.

That version of college admissions is gone. The game has changed. Here's how:

- **One App, Lots of Applications:** The Common App[1] has simultaneously made applying easier *and* more overwhelming. Since students are no longer

---

1 The Common Application (or Common App) is an undergraduate college admissions platform accepted by more than 1,000 colleges. I'll refer to it throughout the book with a mix of gratitude and mild resentment.

required to retype the same basic info ten times, they're applying to way more schools. Twelve, fifteen, sometimes over twenty applications have become the new norm, as students try to cast the widest net possible.

- **More Writing Required**: Colleges, not to be outdone, have responded with a mountain of extra essays. The main personal statement isn't enough. Now, most schools (public and private) pile on their own supplemental essays, anywhere from zero to eight separate prompts depending on the year and the school, and each requires its own answer.

- **Record Numbers of Applicants**: Test-optional policies have turned already competitive schools into full-blown admissions nightmares. Once standardized test scores became optional, students who might not have applied before suddenly thought, "Why not me?" The result? Application numbers have skyrocketed, especially at the most selective colleges. For the most part, the number of spots hasn't increased. Neither has the size of most admissions staff or the speed at which they're expected to make decisions. Acceptance rates, already low, went into a tailspin during the early years of the pandemic, when test-optional policies were widely adopted. While some rates have started to tick back up recently, the overall landscape—especially at the uber-selective schools—remains brutally competitive. One recent exception is Columbia University, which enrolled a first-year class that was about 20% larger than the previous year. It's actively considering permanently expanding its undergraduate intake by a similar margin.[2]

- **Excellence Means More than All A's**: The pressure on students to excel, whether academically, athletically, or as budding entrepreneurs or humanitarians, has never been higher. Colleges claim they value "authenticity," but at times, it can feel like they're looking for students who have started a business, led a nonprofit, and trained for the Olympics. All before junior year.

- **Uneven Playing Field and Moving Targets**: There's no consistency across colleges either. One school wants a graded paper; another wants none. Some *superscore*[3] standardized tests; others don't. Deadlines, requirements, and evaluation criteria vary widely. With every school playing by its own rules, it's no wonder the process feels more like a scavenger hunt than a coherent process.

---

2 Matt Luo, "Columbia Considers Expanding Undergraduate Enrollment by Up to 20 Percent," **Columbia Daily Spectator**, November 21, 2025. **3** "**Superscore**" refers to the practice where colleges take the highest section scores from a student's multiple test sittings (like SAT or ACT) and combine them to create the best possible composite score.

For families across the country and around the globe, this has created an environment of relentless stress and second-guessing. Parents worry they're not doing enough, so they leap into action: booking top test-prep tutors (sometimes when their kid is still in first grade), planning their kids' extracurricular schedules as if they're air traffic controllers, and scrolling college admissions websites at 2 a.m. when they can't sleep.

Too often, families are steered toward what *sounds* impressive, instead of what suits their child best.

That, more than anything, is why I wrote this book.

WHAT THIS BOOK WILL AND WON'T DO

If you're searching for a magic formula that guarantees admission to the most selective schools—now often dubbed "rejective" because of their staggeringly low acceptance rates—you're out of luck. There isn't one.

What you *will* find is an honest, practical, and hopefully funny guide to surviving the college admissions process without losing your mind or your relationship with your kid. It's written by someone who's helped students and families for over fourteen years, and who's lived through it three times herself (I still flinch when I hear the word "submit").

This book might not help you get your kid into Yale. But it will help you keep your cool if they don't.

REDEFINING THE CRAZY

I happen to think that as parents, we're all a little *crazy for college*. But crazy can mean a lot of things. It can mean overwhelmed—like turning your kitchen table into a college command central or debating whether to add "Admissions Whisperer" to your LinkedIn profile. Or it can mean the kind of crazy that makes your heart leap, like when I first fell for my husband's blue eyes.

My hope is that if you begin this book in the first category, you'll finish it in the second. Not anxious and worn out, but more at ease with the process. In the end, it really will be okay. Your kid will land exactly where they're meant to be, and you may even sleep again.

WHO IS THIS BOOK FOR?

Do you live in a hyper-achieving suburb where the line at Starbucks is filled with parents comparing SAT tutors, and you're suddenly grappling with the college admissions chaos for the first time? Or maybe you're in a community where resources are stretched thin, and the public library is hanging on by a thread? Either way, you're not alone. It's about to turn into a wild and crazy ride, but in the best possible way (especially if you take any of my advice).

Did you assume your high-achieving kid's 4.0 GPA and jam-packed resume guaranteed a top-tier acceptance? News flash: not anymore. These days, the most selective colleges want something *exceptional* (we'll get to that). A national award, a published novel, or fluency in multiple languages (preferably, exotic ones). But if your kid doesn't have a trophy case of accolades? Take a breath. This book is here to help you uncover the strengths and stories they already have and steer you toward colleges where they'll not only find their footing but truly soar.

Maybe you live in a big city where parents have been name-dropping Princeton and Duke since the preschool sandbox. Now that your kid is in high school, you can feel the temperature rising as college talk finds its way into every conversation.

You might be in a district where the college admissions process isn't treated like a competitive sport, but it's still confusing and opaque. Your child could be the first in your family to go to college. Or maybe you just want straightforward advice without draining your savings on consultants and test prep.

Perhaps this isn't your first rodeo. You've already launched one or two kids into the college stratosphere. The language hasn't changed so much as the volume. Terms like "test-optional," "holistic admissions," and "demonstrated interest" are everywhere now, and they matter in ways they didn't before. Suddenly, it feels like your child needs more handholding.

And, if you're honest, so do you. The ever-shifting admissions maze can make even the most secure parent reach for a pint of Ben & Jerry's.

Maybe your biggest question is: "Where do we even start without losing our minds?"

You could be here for the stories alone. From parents melting down over SAT scores to helicoptering so hard they should lose their parenting license, this book offers an inside look at today's admissions world.

And if you're already the kind of parent who cares less about prestige and more about helping your child find a place where they'll truly be happy? You're absolutely in the right place (and frankly, your kid is lucky to have you). You'll get practical tips and a reminder that you *can* get through this with your sanity (mostly) intact. Trust me: a surprise snack and a hug go much further than slamming doors ever will.

IT'S NOT JUST PARENTS WHO ARE CRAZY FOR COLLEGE…

I don't want to forget the well-meaning grandparents, aunts, uncles, godparents, and close family friends. This might be you. Thank you for picking up this book to help a student you care deeply about. Some of you are quietly watching from the sidelines, while others are offering opinions at full volume. Some of you may even be helping to foot the bill. But all of you are rooting for a child you love to find a school that feels like home.

Whether you're just getting started or knee-deep in the craziness, this book has your back.

By the time you finish reading, you'll have:

- A clearer understanding of what really matters in the college process and what doesn't.
- Practical and ethical strategies to help your child build a strong, authentic application.
- A roadmap for managing the process and the stress for both you and your child.
- Some much-needed perspective to remind you that this process, while important, is not life or death.
- Repeated reassurance that yes, stress-eating pretzels at midnight is completely normal behavior.

I'M NOT JUST AN EXPERT; I'M A PARENT, TOO:

In this work, I've seen it all: moments of deep sincerity, high hopes, and, at times, sheer panic. To give you a real sense of what this process does to us, I'm going to share some stories. To protect everyone's privacy, I've changed names, schools, and a few telling details. If a story sounds familiar, it's only because the emotions wrapped up in this process—love, fear, pride, hope, frustration—are universal. These experiences—from the heartfelt to the slightly off the rails—are shared with respect and deep appreciation for the families who have trusted us with their children's journeys. I'm never laughing at them; I'm laughing with them. Because, truthfully, in many cases, I *am* them.

When I say I've been there too, I really mean it.

I'm the mom who lost a night of sleep over the thought of my son getting a B (a B!) in gym. Then I took my own advice, reminded myself that one grade wasn't the end of the world, and moved on (by the way, he ended up with an A-).

I'm the mom who drove my daughter to her ACT exam with her favorite breakfast, a confidence-boosting playlist (kicking off with the theme from *Rocky*), and a whispered *Shehecheyanu* prayer[4] in the parking lot. Sometimes, a little tradition and a well-timed toasted sesame bagel with strawberry cream cheese are exactly what a kid needs.

---

4 The **Shehecheyanu** is a Jewish blessing recited to express gratitude for reaching a significant moment or experiencing something new. It is often said during holidays, milestones, or meaningful firsts.

When the world went virtual during COVID, my youngest was crushed that speech and debate tournaments weren't being held in person. We turned our basement into a makeshift studio so she could keep competing with confidence. And when in-person tournaments finally resumed, she realized too late that she had forgotten her lucky pearl necklace. I may or may not have overnighted it to her hotel in Lexington, Kentucky, because hey, those pearls seemed to *work*.

I'm not a Tiger Mom. Really. But when my kids were passionate about something, I showed up. I encouraged them to put in the work. I gave them the space to figure things out and stayed close enough to cheer them on when they needed it. Sure, I expected them to do their homework. Anything lower than a B got an eye roll unless I knew they had studied hard. I let the messy rooms slide, ignored the uncleared dinner plates, and made sure our home was filled with fun, laughter, and plenty of dinner table conversations about their highs and lows of the day, whether they were happy, frustrated, anxious, or just plain tired.

As much as I cared about their academics, I cared even more about raising thoughtful and resilient kids who could weather the hard stuff, laugh at themselves, and head into the world with a strong backbone, a good heart, and the confidence to be exactly who they want to be.

WHY SHOULD YOU TRUST ME?

Looking back, it's almost laughable that I didn't see this career coming.

In 1985, when I was applying to college from a large, competitive public school (with equally large, gravity-defying hair) in Edison, New Jersey, I instinctively knew how to tell my story for college applications. It wasn't because someone coached me. I just knew how to connect the dots.

At Harvard, where I majored in English and American Literature & Language, I sharpened my ability to analyze, write, and best of all, tell a compelling story. After graduation, I spent several years in advertising, managing accounts for big-name brands like Honey Bunches of Oats, Norelco razors, and Crest toothpaste. I suppose graduating from fiber to fluoride was a sign of real career growth.

Back then, I never imagined my work on toothpaste and breakfast cereal would come in handy for anything beyond keeping teeth tartar-free, faces smooth, and mornings sweet. But strangely enough, it did. While I'm not in the business of "packaging" kids for colleges, I do help students uncover what makes them distinct, authentic, and memorable.

Later, I earned my MBA from Northwestern's Kellogg School of Management. As an English major determined to tackle my missing quantitative links, I quickly discovered that some people are born to build financial models, and I was simply not one of them. My sweet spot was writing, editing, and making sure our group projects made sense. While others ran regression analyses, I reworked our class presentations so they told a better story.

When I volunteered as a Harvard alumna to interview high school students—first in New York City and then in Silicon Valley—something fell into place. I loved sitting down with these kids, hearing their stories, and encouraging them to bring their best selves to the conversation.

Over the years, I casually but consistently coached friends' kids, family members, and students, prepping them for interviews, brainstorming essay topics, refining resumes, and polishing applications for private secondary schools. Each time, I felt the same instant joy: watching a kid discover their story and begin to own it.

That work took on deeper meaning when I guided my own three children through the process. I must give a heartfelt shout-out to Scarsdale High School for preparing them so well. The dedicated teachers, world-class curriculum, and tireless leadership (thank you, Principal Bonamo) shaped not only their character but their sense of direction. Watching up close how a great high school can influence a student's trajectory gave me a clearer understanding of how unbelievably different this process looks depending on where a student goes to high school. It also reinforced my commitment to help families, whether they're in a place like Scarsdale with tons of support or doing their best in a setting that's far more limited.

But I didn't put it all together until I met my business partner, Nancy, in a nail salon (a chapter for later, because, of course, the best conversations happen when you least expect them).

That's when I realized that what I loved doing naturally could become something bigger, something that truly helps families through this increasingly crazy process.

FROM OPPOSITES TO ACCEPTANCE AHEAD

When Nancy and I met, we quickly discovered that we clicked—not because we're alike or that we both love chicken salad, but because we balance each other out in the best possible ways.

Nancy, a former lawyer, is hyper-organized, process-driven, and basically the college counseling equivalent of a White House Chief of Staff. She's calm under pressure, always prepared, and somehow keeps everything (especially me) on track. For more than thirty years, she was deeply involved in college admissions, having served as a Cornell alumni interviewer and co-chair of a group that organized interviews and student programs for Cornell alumni across New York City. She's the one who dives into college data, program specifics, and trends, ensuring every recommendation is backed by research.

Meanwhile, I'm the creative half of the duo, the one who can turn a tangle of thoughts into a meaningful story. Nancy, with her sharp eye and straightforward approach, spots what's missing and what needs a rewrite.

While Nancy thrives on efficiency and process, I operate in "controlled" chaos, fueled by pretzels and Diet Coke. Together, we combined forces and launched our college admissions counseling service: Acceptance Ahead.

Thanks to her, I now follow an actual system (yes, with real software!) to track deadlines, drafts, and progress.

She's also the reason we don't blow our entire travel budget on boutique hotels when we visit colleges across the country. While I might be tempted by fluffy robes and a spa, Nancy is a loyal supporter of the Hampton Inn (free breakfast).

Over the past fourteen admissions cycles, we've worked with students from Scarsdale, NY to Seattle, WA, from Atlanta, GA to Athens, Greece, guiding them through the often complex process of applying to college. Every single student we've worked with has reminded us why we love this work. Helping them find their voice and their next step is a privilege we don't take for granted. We've helped students choose the right high school courses, find summer programs, and pursue exciting opportunities that make them forget to check their phones. We've visited over 160 college campuses, getting a sense of what really makes each school stand out. We talk to the students at each one, meet with admissions officers, peek inside dorms, and, of course, taste test the dining hall food. No kidding: bad food can be a deal-breaker.

We don't just guide kids through the mechanics of admissions; we help them build confidence along the way, because that's downright more important than the acceptance letter.

Our goal isn't to mold students into something they're not. It's to help them recognize who they already are and give them the tools to tell their story, silly quirks and all. The strongest applications don't come from stress or self-contortion. They come from students who know themselves and tell it like it is.

THIS PROCESS SHOULDN'T BE MISERABLE

College admissions will always be stressful, but it doesn't have to be demoralizing. There are over 4,000 colleges in the U.S., and most of them are wonderful.

If there's one thing that I hope parents truly take to heart, it's this: your child's college outcome is not a reflection of your love or their potential. It's merely one step on a much longer, winding, beautiful path. What matters most is that they land somewhere they can grow and maybe call home once-in-a-while just to say they're okay and ask how *you're* doing.

The real win isn't in prestige or perfection. It's in helping your student find a place where they can step into independence, take ownership of their choices, and find that one unexpected class or professor who opens a door they didn't know existed. That's what this process is really about: finding the right environment to become who they're meant to be.

So grab a coffee, hide from that neighbor who won't stop talking about their kid's NASA internship, and let's get through this with a little humor, a lot of honesty, and endless gratitude for the kids who make it all worthwhile.

College Admissions Terminology CHEAT SHEET

Before we jump in, here's a quick cheat sheet of the acronyms and buzzwords you'll see throughout the college admissions process. Have no fear. By the end, you'll be fluent (and possibly qualified to teach your own mini-seminar).

APPLICATION TYPES & TIMELINES

EARLY DECISION 1 (ED1) & EARLY DECISION 2 (ED2) These are *binding* application plans. If your child is admitted, they must attend. The only exception is if the financial aid package is genuinely insufficient. But even that isn't simple: families typically need to demonstrate to the college why the financial offer doesn't meet their documented need. It's not just a matter of saying, "This isn't enough," and walking away. ED1 deadlines are usually in early or mid-November, with decisions released in December; ED2 deadlines fall later, often in January, with decisions released in February. ED2 offers students a second chance at a binding option.

EARLY ACTION (EA) A non-binding option that lets students apply and hear back earlier than Regular Decision without committing to attend. Consider it a way to show interest without getting locked in.

RESTRICTIVE EARLY ACTION (REA) OR SINGLE CHOICE EARLY ACTION (SCEA)
A non-binding option that lets students hear back early, but there are usually some restrictions. For example, they are usually prohibited from applying Early Decision elsewhere and may be prohibited from applying Early Action to private schools. This plan is typically offered by schools like Harvard, Yale, Princeton, and Stanford. Because the rules vary slightly from school to school, it's important to read each college's policy carefully, especially if a student is considering multiple early plans.

ROLLING ADMISSIONS Applications are reviewed as they come in. Decisions are released on a rolling basis, so earlier is often better. Once spots fill, they're gone, so early birds really do get the worm (or the concert seat). Think of it like snagging Bruce Springsteen tickets before they sell out.

DEFERRAL When an Early Action or Early Decision applicant is rolled over into the regular decision pool. Not a no, just a *not yet*.

WAITLIST This is the limbo zone. Your child wasn't accepted or rejected. If spots open up (often rare), they might receive an offer. The odds of getting off a waitlist vary widely from year to year. Some years, schools admit dozens of students from the list; other years, it's radio silence.

ACADEMIC PROGRAMS & COURSEWORK

AP (ADVANCED PLACEMENT) College-level courses offered in high school. Strong AP exam scores (usually 3, 4, or 5) may earn college credit or advanced placement and might give your child the possibility of graduating early.

IB (INTERNATIONAL BACCALAUREATE) A rigorous global academic program known for its own curriculum and assessments, and existential essay prompts. Students in IB programs often complete the full diploma or take select IB courses. Also well-recognized by many colleges.

AT (ADVANCED TOPICS) High-level courses created by individual high schools, often to replace APs or go even deeper. These classes are challenging, college-level, and equally respected. Translation: If your kid's taking AT Physics instead of AP, don't panic. Colleges get it.

HONORS COURSES More challenging than standard classes and often weighted more heavily in GPA calculations for schools that use a weighted system.

DUAL ENROLLMENT Students take actual college courses, sometimes at local colleges and sometimes through the high school. They can earn credit and boost academic rigor.

TESTING TERMINOLOGY

ACT/SAT SUPERSCORE Colleges cherry-pick your student's best section scores across test dates. Think of it as a "greatest hits" album.

SCORE CHOICE A policy that allows students to choose which test dates (and sometimes sections) to send to colleges.

TEST-OPTIONAL Students can choose whether to submit standardized test scores. If they don't, colleges will evaluate the application without them.

TEST-BLIND Even if students submit scores, these schools won't consider them at all. They consider everything else in the application.

FINANCIAL AID & SCHOLARSHIPS

FAFSA (FREE APPLICATION FOR FEDERAL STUDENT AID) The form families complete to qualify for federal need-based aid. Opens each fall for seniors. The recently simplified version is more user-friendly than in years past, but it still helps to have your financial documents handy. A spreadsheet and a stash of chocolate (or wine) also help.

CSS PROFILE (COLLEGE SCHOLARSHIP SERVICE) A more detailed financial aid form used by many private colleges to determine eligibility for institutional (non-government) aid. It's even more involved than the FAFSA and digs deeper into your finances, including retirement accounts and home equity. Fun times.

MERIT AID Scholarships based on talent, academics, or extracurriculars, not financial need. Some schools are very generous, while others—especially highly selective ones— offer little to none.

NEED-BLIND VS. NEED-AWARE:

- *Need-Blind:* A college does not consider a student's financial situation when making admissions decisions.

- *Need-Aware:* A student's financial need may be considered, especially in borderline admissions cases. At these colleges, applicants who do not apply for financial aid are treated as "full pay," which can sometimes make them more appealing to the institution.

APPLICATIONS & PLATFORMS

THE COMMON APPLICATION (AKA COMMON APP) Used by over 1,100 colleges and universities, it allows students to apply to multiple schools through one central application.

COALITION APP Used by about 170 colleges. It was created to increase access for students from historically underrepresented backgrounds and includes tools like a digital locker.

NAVIANCE/SCOIR College planning tools many high schools use to help students explore schools, track deadlines, and compare GPA/test scores to past applicants. Names are anonymous. (Kind of like Tinder for college stats but with fewer awkward first dates.) The platforms do more behind the scenes; they're also the application management systems that schools rely on to send transcripts, recommendation letters, and counselor reports to the colleges.

ESSAYS & COLLEGE LISTS

PERSONAL STATEMENT (MAIN ESSAY) A 650-word essay submitted to all schools through the Common or Coalition App. It's the student's opportunity to share a meaningful story and express who they are beyond their high school transcript.

SUPPLEMENTAL ESSAYS Shorter, school-specific responses that often include questions like "Why do you want to attend this school?" or "Describe a community you belong to." These essays help colleges understand how a student might fit on campus and how much thought they've put into their application.

COLLEGE LIST (REACH/TARGET/LIKELY) A student's list of schools, ideally balanced across Reach, Target, and Likely colleges. A *Reach* is any school that's hard for that specific student to get into. Reach is always relative and not only for top students applying to highly selective places. *Targets* are solid academic matches where admission is plausible, and *Likely* schools are ones where the student has a strong chance of getting in. Think of the list as a well-balanced diet: some protein, some carbs, and a slice of cake just in case.

OTHER TERMS COLLEGES LOVE TO TOSS AROUND

YIELD The percentage of admitted students who choose to enroll. Colleges obsess over this number because it affects their rankings and reputation.

YIELD PROTECTION When a school waitlists or rejects a highly qualified student because they assume the student won't attend if admitted.

HOLISTIC ADMISSIONS A review process that looks beyond grades and scores. Admissions officers consider the full picture: extracurriculars, essays, recommendations, context, character, and more.

DEMONSTRATED INTEREST Showing how much a student wants to attend a particular school. Some colleges track visits, opening of emails, event attendance, and genuine display of affection from students—anything short of sending baked goods (and please, don't do this!). It can influence admissions decisions, especially at smaller or mid-sized schools.

GAP YEAR A year off between high school and college, used for travel, work, service, or personal growth. Also known as "the year your teen finds themselves." Many colleges openly support this option. Harvard and Princeton encourage it, and Florida State helps fund one through its gap-year fellowship program.

FIRST-GENERATION STUDENT A student whose parents did not complete a four-year college degree. Many colleges offer specific support and resources for first-gen students.

DIVERSITY, EQUITY, AND INCLUSION (OFTEN CALLED DEI) Programs and policies designed to support a diverse student body, promote equitable access, and foster an inclusive learning environment. How colleges organize and describe this work varies by institution and can change over time.

MISCELLANEOUS STUFF TO CONSIDER

HOOKS Traits that give students an admissions boost (legacy, athlete, first-gen, underrepresented background, development case).

LIKELY LETTER An early (unofficial) heads-up that an acceptance is coming.

DEMONSTRATED FIT An emerging term referring to how well a student aligns with a college's mission, values, and academic offerings. It's the softer cousin of Demonstrated Interest.

Vocabulary lesson accomplished! Now that we're speaking the same language, let's get to it. No flashcards required.

Part One

Let the College Crazy Begin

CHAPTER 1

Seismic Changes: WHAT'S ROCKING COLLEGE ADMISSIONS

Picture this: It's 1985, and I'm sitting cross-legged on the charcoal blue shag carpet of my childhood living room, hunched over a typewriter (yes, a typewriter!), with a can of TAB at my side and an unopened pack of Twinkies within arm's reach. I'm hunting and pecking away at my college essays as if it's an Olympic sport. Fun fact: I hadn't yet taken the typing class that my mom forced me to take in senior year instead of band. Thanks, Mom, for making my future life 1000% easier. But the real brainstorming? That happened under the shade of an oak tree at nearby Roosevelt Park, where I spent hours scribbling ideas on a yellow legal pad, trying to muster up the one dramatic story I thought would miraculously win over the hearts of the admissions gods.

Just me, a pencil, and a pad. No laptop, no Common App, no Google Docs. If you applied to college before 1995, you probably remember how blissfully simple it was: you visited a handful of schools, filled out some paper applications, and then waited by the mailbox.

For teacher recommendations? I casually asked my 11th-grade English teacher and my 9th-grade French teacher, and that was that. But today? A rec from a 9th-grade teacher and two humanities teachers? Acceptable but definitely not preferred (*more on that in Chapter 12*).

THE MODERN ADMISSIONS MAZE

These days, applying to college feels like navigating Disney World with a broken leg, crutches, and a blindfold, only to end up stuck on "It's a Small World." For the fourth time.

One of the craziest shifts since the last century? The sheer number of applications kids submit, which has flooded every admissions pool.

Back in my day, applying to five or six schools felt ambitious. Today? Twelve, fifteen, or wait for it...twenty-plus is the norm. In the 2024-2025 cycle alone, students submitted more than 8.5 million applications through the Common App, a six percent increase from the prior year.[5] 8.5 million! That's an average of about seven per student. Among high achievers, that number often climbs well into the double digits.

You'd think technology would make things easier, right? With platforms like the Common App, submitting applications should be as simple as scrolling through your Instagram feed. But no. Many applications come with a mountain of essays.

"What's your favorite book?" Summarize in 150 words.

"Most meaningful activity?" Check.

"A difficult conversation that changed your perspective?" Check.

"A letter to your future roommate?" Check.

"An idea for a class, podcast, TED Talk?" Check, check, check.

Please don't get me started on the infamous *Why us?* essay, which can range from a short fifty words to a grueling 500, depending on the school. Because, of course, every seventeen-year-old, already drowning in AP classes, standardized tests, away sports games, and play rehearsals, has loads of time to conduct extensive research on the pros and cons of every college on their list.

(Note to admissions committees: I am begging you to stop the madness!)

ACCEPTANCE RATES, A.K.A. *THE HUNGER GAMES*

Speaking of madness...let's talk about acceptance rates. According to the National Association for College Admission Counseling (NACAC), the *average* college acceptance rate has hovered around 70-73% in recent years, a statistic that surprises many families.[6]

So why does it feel so brutal? Because at the most highly selective colleges—the ones that dominate headlines and dinner table conversations—acceptance rates often fall in the single digits, sometimes between 4-10%. That disconnect fuels the panic. Applying to college can feel less like submitting an application and more like auditioning for *Survivor.*

5 Common App, **End of Season Application Trends Report, 2024-2025,** https://www.commonapp.org/files/DAR/deadline-updates/Common-App-End-of-Season-Report_24-25.pdf **6** https://www.nacacnet.org/selectivity-acceptance-rates-at-4-year-colleges/ National Association for College Admission Counseling, "State of College Admission 2020 Report," NACAC, 2020.

A few years ago, Nancy and I visited a small liberal arts college during reading season. We didn't witness this room ourselves, but we heard all about it: an exhausted admissions officer had turned her office into a spaceship cockpit. Her laptop and desktop were illuminated, empty Starbucks cups streamed across her desk, and a pillow and blanket were on standby. She'd already plowed through thirty-two files that day, with thirty more to go.

Admissions officers are underpaid, overworked humans reading thousands of applications each season. Now picture their mindset: reviewing one application after another on glowing screens at 7:30 a.m. with their first cup of coffee in hand (lucky applicant), or slogging through new essays at 4:00 p.m., when the blue light from their laptop is the only thing keeping them awake (not-so-lucky).

Many of these officers earn around $50,000 a year (often less), and turnover is high as they hop from college to college in search of better pay. They spend long, exhausting hours debating whether an applicant's efforts to rebuild a school in the Dominican Republic are more impressive than being captain of the Model UN team. Most college admissions offices are filled with young staffers in their early to mid-twenties, trudging through reading periods that stretch into late nights and weekends.

SHOT OF SANITY

> *While the system can feel frustrating from the outside, most admissions officers care about students and want to make the best decisions they can. They're merely doing it under intense pressure and with way too much coffee.*

If the odds feel stacked against you, that's because they are. The admissions process has officially become *The Hunger Games*, minus the gore but with the same level of drama.

VARSITY BLUES, PANDEMIC WOES, AND THE TEST-OPTIONAL GAME CHANGER

Just before the pandemic, a scandal rocked the entire college admissions system. Con artist Rick Singer proved that if you were wealthy and morally bankrupt, you could fake a rowing resume for your non-athletic child and bribe your way into a prestigious school.

I'll never forget when the *Varsity Blues* news broke. It was 2019, and I was sitting in a jury duty holding room, glued to my phone, as text after text popped up. College admissions would never be the same. The investigation exposed the ugly truth: some families were leveraging their privilege to snag spots that equally talented (but less connected or wealthy) kids had legitimately earned. As a college counselor who'd watched students pour their hearts into their classes, activities, and essays, I felt a mix of fury and heartbreak. It wasn't just unfair; it was a slap in the face to every honest kid I'd ever worked with.

Just as the dust was settling, the pandemic hit, and with it, the college search process was flipped on its head. College tours? Canceled. For most students, the college search process became a purely virtual experience. Families who had carefully planned their visits to schools were left creeping through ghost-town campuses, trying to gauge a school's vibe from deserted quads and locked buildings without live students around, formal tours, or information sessions.

Colleges raced to patch together virtual tours and online info sessions, but no amount of upbeat tour guides on Zoom could match the feeling of being there in person. Nancy's youngest son, like thousands of others, applied to schools on campuses he'd never set foot on. It became a surreal and frustrating reality that made an already stressful process even more punishing.

One young woman, Caroline, from a boarding school in the UK was wooed by the palm trees and laid-back vibes on a virtual tour with the University of Miami. She applied Early Decision sight-unseen and got in. When she arrived that August, she texted us photos of the "resort-like" pool outside of her dorm, more stunned by sun-soaked oomph than anything she'd glimpsed on her laptop screen. Four years later, she called it the best leap of faith ever.

Another student, Ariadne from Greece, applied Early Decision to the University of Chicago, having never even visited the U.S. When she arrived, she was wowed by the Gothic beauty of the Main Quadrangles. Though she initially felt small in comparison to towering stone archways and the academic intensity, she soon found her place, thriving in the Core Curriculum and debating philosophy late at night with new friends.

Standardized testing took a hit, too. Students could no longer gather in testing centers. Almost overnight, most colleges shifted to test-optional policies to accommodate the global crisis. But the movement itself wasn't entirely new. A small but growing number of schools including Bowdoin, Wake Forest, and Wesleyan had already gone test-optional in the years leading up to 2020.

What COVID did was light a match. Suddenly, nearly every college was on fire. According to FairTest, as of 2025, more than 2,015 four-year colleges and universities—over 80% of U.S. institutions—have adopted test-optional or test-free policies for undergraduate admissions.[7]

What started as an emergency response quickly became a game changer, especially for students with strong grades but weaker test scores. But test-optional didn't fade away once the pandemic subsided. Even after access to testing was restored, it stuck around, reshaping the admissions landscape in a much bigger way. Suddenly, students who might have once held back, including those who couldn't afford extensive test prep or who simply didn't test well, felt they finally had a fair shot at applying to more selective schools.

Applications went through the roof, and the colleges weren't exactly complaining. More applications meant more fees, lower admit rates (since they still had the same number of dorm beds), and a boost in perceived prestige.

What began as a necessary health and safety measure lingered long past the pandemic because, frankly, it worked in colleges' favor. But was it really benefiting them in the long run? We'll circle back to that later.

DIVERSITY IN ADMISSIONS: THE PUSH, THE BACKLASH, AND WHAT CAME NEXT

Meanwhile, another major shift was happening in admissions. In the wake of George Floyd's murder and a national reckoning with racial injustice, colleges made a more intentional push to build racially and economically diverse student bodies. Schools ramped up efforts to find more diverse applicants by expanding outreach to underserved high schools, community-based organizations, and lower-income areas, rather than just waiting for students to knock on their door.

And then came June 2023.

The Supreme Court struck down the use of race as a factor in college admissions, effectively ending affirmative action as we knew it. The ruling landed just as many schools were beginning to turn the tide. Since then, they've had to pivot. Most are still deeply committed to enrolling students from all kinds of backgrounds; they're just figuring out new ways to do it.

---

7 FairTest. *"Overwhelming Majority of U.S. Colleges and Universities Remain ACT/SAT-Optional or Test-Blind/Score-Free for Fall 2025."* The National Center for Fair & Open Testing. https://fairtest.org

While nothing in college admissions stays simple for long, the current administration has warned colleges that even seemingly "neutral" diversity efforts like race-conscious scholarships or certain outreach programs could put them on shaky legal ground unless they pass a much tougher test. In other words, "race-neutral" now comes with a legal asterisk. Yikes. Schools are being pestered to prove their admissions processes don't rely on race or even the faintest hint of it, adding yet another layer of complexity to this constant madness.[8]

Now, admissions officers are looking more closely at things like zip code, school environment, family income, first-gen status, and the personal stories students share in their applications. Will it be enough? Truthfully, no one knows yet (and if they claim they do, they're bluffing). What is clear is that the rules are in flux again.

But wait. There's more...

Enter a renewed focus on holistic admissions, the latest buzzword that sounds like a trendy cocktail with a mystery ingredient. Colleges claim they're evaluating the whole student, but what they're really after is depth and commitment.

This doesn't mean every applicant needs to be an academic powerhouse, a social activist, an athlete, and an artist all at once. But it does mean that students who go deep in one or two areas (and show real excitement and grit) tend to stand out. Crafting a college application today isn't about being a superhero who can fight, fly, and cure cancer on weekends. It's about a student sticking with what excites them and finding ways to make an impact, big or small.

This approach can often be a relief. It means that a perfect SAT score or a knock-your-socks-off activities list isn't the only path to admission anymore. A student who spent summers caring for siblings, traveling to assist aging grandparents in a different state or country, or holding down a part-time job might now have those experiences valued as much as test scores and titles.

Of course, the flip side is that holistic can feel ridiculously vague. When everything counts, nothing feels clear. But when it works the way it's meant to, it gives admissions officers room to see the full story behind the numbers.

Lauren Sefton, Associate Dean of Admission at Rhodes College, explains holistic review in a way that makes sense. She compares an application to a cupcake. The academic record is the base—essential and the thing that must hold everything up. The frosting is what makes a student memorable: their voice, how they spend their time outside the classroom, the glimpses of curiosity, character, humor, or grit that show up in essays and

---

8 Associated Press, "Trump Orders Colleges to Prove They Don't Consider Race in Admissions," **AP News**, August 6, 2025, https://apnews.com/article/9fe070750d31879b24800032a01w59d.

recommendations. And the sprinkles? Those are the extras no one can fully control like demonstrated interest, particular talents or successes, or shifting institutional priorities.

Her point is simple. Every school likes a different cupcake. What looks extraordinary at one college may barely register at another. Holistic review is about seeing the human being behind the bullet points.

KIND OF CRAZY

It's EASIER *than* EVER *to* FAKE BEING REAL

Just when admissions offices start asking for realness, along comes a tool that can fake it all: artificial intelligence.

Tools like ChatGPT can spit out essays in seconds. They're eloquent, articulate, and, well...utterly impersonal. More and more students are tempted to let AI do the hard part: telling their story. But colleges (and advisors like us) can often tell when something feels off. The voice doesn't sound like a teenager. The essay says everything and reveals nothing. The drafts don't match their earlier writing, which might read more like a seventh-grade English paper than a perfectly polished college essay.

And colleges are responding. Some schools have even started using AI detectors or asking students to certify that the work is their own. Yale has published an explicit AI policy warning students that submitting AI-generated content as their own can be treated as application fraud and may jeopardize their admission or enrollment. Duke publicly announced it had stopped assigning numerical ratings to essays (and test scores) because AI made style-based scoring unreliable. They now read essays for content instead of "writing quality." [9] The Common App requires applicants to affirm their work is their own, and students must sign a page. In an age where almost everything can be programmed, honesty and originality matter more than ever.

HOPE ON THE HORIZON

With all the commotion of the last few years, there's still reason to feel hopeful. The

---

9 Kate Murphy, "Duke Admissions Will No Longer Score Writing and Test Sections, Citing AI," *The News & Observer,* February 13, 2024.

story is starting to take a new direction. More students (and yes, even their parents) are realizing that success isn't about where you go. It's about what you do once you're there: taking advantage of professors' office hours, jumping into new clubs, landing internships, and saying yes to the kinds of experiences that can change their trajectory. We encourage families to look for colleges that offer hands-on learning and open doors to real-world opportunities. Maybe even a place where their child will meet someone who shares their love of puns and late-night existential conversations over pizza.

For some students, the next step isn't college right away. Gap years—structured time off to work, travel, learn a new language, or dive into new interests—have gone mainstream, with participation up 10% since the pandemic, according to the American Gap Association. Other students are starting at community colleges and then transferring, pursuing apprenticeships, launching small businesses, or joining service programs like AmeriCorps. The old "straight to college" track is now often replaced by routes that leave more space for growth and sanity.

It's no longer considered taboo to take time to recharge and expand your perspective after a packed schedule of challenging high school classes and extracurriculars.

Here's another promising development. A recent Hechinger Report article noted that many colleges, faced with a shrinking pool of high-school graduates (a trend often called the "enrollment cliff"), are starting to ease the admissions process rather than complicate it. Some are waiving fees, offering "direct admissions" to qualified students without requiring a full application, or inviting students to apply with a few short clicks. The narrative is no longer about students needing to contort themselves to impress colleges. Colleges realize they need to meet students halfway, and in some cases, literally court them.[10]

Sure, the admissions process can still make your head spin. However, more students are stepping into the driver's seat with clarity and confidence. They're adapting and finding their way through a system that often doesn't make sense.

With the right support and some necessary laughter, they'll come out of this process a little stronger, a lot more self-aware, and remarkably ready, not just for college, but for everything that comes next.

---

10 Jon Marcus, "Colleges Ease the Dreaded Admissions Process as the Supply of Applicants Declines," *The Hechinger Report*, February 5, 2025, https://hechingerreport.org/colleges-ease-the-dreaded-admissions-process-as-the-supply-of-applicants-declines/

CHAPTER 2

HOW *to* STAY SANE *when* YOUR KID APPLIES *to* COLLEGE

You *will* get my son into Stanford!" the dad bellowed from the couch, fists clenched, ready to step into a boxing ring. "If I'm paying you, then you will make it happen!" I could hardly believe it. He wasn't even a client yet; this was just a consultation. His entitlement and inability to process reality were staggering, as if he believed we somehow had the power to bend college admissions to his will. Momentarily paralyzed, I shot Nancy a look, a desperate plea for rescue.

Without missing a beat, Nancy slammed her laptop shut. The decisive *snap* cut him off mid-rant. She stood up, looked him in the eye, and calmly stated, "This meeting is over. We don't work with families who make unrealistic demands. And we certainly don't make promises that are unethical."

For a second, I thought the dad might literally explode: his face went through a spectrum of reds, from strawberry to fire engine. I braced myself for combustion. But then his wife jumped in: "Please, Hank, stop it! You're making a scene," she whispered, as if her politeness could erase his rudeness. "He's just...stressed."

Meanwhile, their son sat staring at his shoes, mortified. My heart went out to him. No kid should have to sit through a parent's meltdown. I wondered what his father thought his kid might learn from this moment. The message was loud and clear: this dad thought his son's future was something that could be bought or bullied into existence.

Fifteen minutes after they had left, Nancy and I bolted out of the building and into the bar across the street. We plopped into the barstools and toasted to our survival.

The college admissions process has a way of throwing the most grounded parents off balance. Everyone wants the best for their kid, but the pressure and what-ifs can twist instincts. Fast.

THE STRESS AND STRUGGLES ARE REAL

Unfortunately, these dramatic displays aren't isolated incidents. We've had a student show up in distress after a heated argument in the car (complete with scratching) because her mom insisted that she'd "better get her act together in art class" to have a shot at her first-choice school. We've heard about parents pushing their kids into seven-day SAT boot camps during those last precious weeks of summer before junior year, convinced it's the golden ticket to admissions glory. A well-constructed and well-timed plan for test prep? Great. But full-on marathon training while everyone else is plunging into the town pool? Let's just not.

On the other hand, we've seen parents who don't care where their child goes to school, but they can't help from dropping hints about their awesome memories from Wharton or casually mentioning hopes for Harvard, right in front of their child. As soon as we kick off the discussion about the college list, those chill attitudes unravel into expectations that weigh heavily on their kids.

I'll never forget the time, many years ago, when a mother pulled us aside after a consultation, her voice trembling with hope and desperation. She lived in a modest apartment and worked overtime to give every privilege she could to her only child. It was clear she hoped college was another thing she could earn for him. "Please, just get my son into Dartmouth," she whispered in my ear, clutching my arm, as if she were sharing information from the C.I.A. "I'll give you $5,000 if you make that happen."

We didn't take the money or work with her, of course. But I still think about that mother and her son, hoping they found the right path. Her story is a poignant example of how this process can make even the sanest people lose perspective. And the irony? We couldn't influence an admissions decision even if we wanted to. The offer wasn't just inappropriate; it went against everything we stand for.

Often, the trouble starts when parents, so used to protecting their kids, try to shield them from any form of disappointment, including their own. Like the dad who managed to engineer an entire resume for his daughter, transforming a slightly above-average student into a prodigy who had published four papers in scientific journals and started a charity that raised thousands for senior citizens. Sounds impressive, right? Except when we asked the student to summarize her research, she nervously babbled an explanation that even she clearly didn't understand. When her Common Application essay arrived in our inbox for review, it sounded suspiciously like the work of a Pulitzer Prize-winning novelist, along with a resume fit for a 52-year-old scientist. We knew something was off. After a gentle but firm conversation with the dad and the student, we decided to part ways. Some battles aren't worth fighting.

We also can't forget the mom from Baltimore who insisted her son had raised over $50,000 for a community baseball field by selling socks. We'd helped him only with essays, but when he logged on to submit his applications, something was off. He mentioned selling just a handful of pairs and didn't seem aware of any major fundraising effort. Even more telling, he couldn't navigate the Common App at all. He grew flustered, shouting for his mom to come help, and it became painfully clear that he hadn't filled out a single part of the application himself. That meeting ended with a vow. Nancy and I wouldn't work with his younger siblings. We can guide students through essays and self-doubt, but we cannot undo bad ethics.

Then there was the Colorado mom who needed to be on every Zoom, every email, every text. Her son was fantastic; he was diligent and beyond capable. But every time we asked him a question, she jumped in to answer for him. By spring of junior year, it was obvious that if we didn't step in, she'd be the one applying to college, not him. Therefore, we did what we had to do: we played her exit music. Not literally. Though that would have been fun. In May of junior year, when we start our application process, we told her son (and all of our students) the same thing: it's *your* turn now to take the reins. From that point on, our meetings became student-only. To her credit, she backed off. Guess what? Her son thrived.

We will always remember the Massachusetts dad who turned college admissions into a full-time job. His son is a kind, enthusiastic student who lights up when talking about fitness and nutrition, and he will likely flourish no matter where he ends up. But his dad approached his schooling like a luxury renovation: always upgrading in search of perfection. After his son earned two B's, he pulled him from public school and enrolled him in a smaller private one. When that didn't meet his expectations, he moved him yet again in search of something better. This boy is now at his third high school.

Another dad often met with us alone, asking which teachers his daughter should target for recommendations, whether she should cram over the summer to skip a level in Spanish, and if it was too early to prep for college interviews that didn't yet exist. One Thanksgiving, he proudly announced they had finalized her college essay topic...a year before the application was due. We often joked that he was the one applying. But lately, we haven't been laughing. This is exactly why we tell parents. Please let your child take the lead.

Is it about getting into the most selective school? Or is it about finding a place where your child will genuinely be happy, feel challenged, supported, find friends, stretch, and grow? When we as parents keep that perspective, our kids are able to relax and breathe. When this happens, they ironically do even better.

My mom taught kindergarten for over twenty-five years, and I remember one thing she said frequently: "Kids pick up on everything." High school students know when their parents are disappointed or compare them to the neighbor's kid. If you can remember that the real goal is raising a healthy, confident young adult who isn't afraid to take risks and grow, you've got it. It's not about helping with "getting in" but about helping our kids grow up and letting them fly.

KIND OF CRAZY

STOP *the* INSANITY BEFORE *it* STARTS

You may not be this parent...yet. But here are some warning signs that you are about to turn into one.

The thought of your kid getting into college occupies your brain more than your own job does.

The "C" word slips into at least half of your conversations, including with your hair stylist, receptionist at the dentist's office, or strangers in a restaurant ladies' room.

You've already started researching summer programs from computer science to dramatic arts, even though your child is only in third grade.

You plan family vacations around destinations that "just happen" to be near prestigious universities.

These stories are proof of the incredible pressure parents can unintentionally put on their kids. We've seen students second-guess themselves at every turn, afraid to disappoint the adults around them. Others check out completely, overwhelmed by expectations they never agreed to in the first place. When the process becomes more about proving something than discovering something, where is the joy? That's when we know it's time to take a breath and help both parents and kids regain sight of the bigger picture.

Regaining that perspective starts with us, the parents. We see our kids' stress and instinctively jump to their defense, sometimes when a simple, "Hey, make sure you reply next time," would do. We've even had parents email to explain why their child missed reminders, worried that we were being too firm. One father told us that school had just started, his son was playing fall lacrosse, and there were tests and homework. All true. But every senior we work with is equally busy.

Part of our job is to remind families that accountability is part of growing up. This process isn't just about getting into college; it's also about learning to handle responsibility and the occasional disappointment that comes with life on campus.

Seeing your child the way their teachers, coaches, and admissions officers see them can be uncomfortable, but it's essential. You may have to accept that they procrastinate or that they're moody at dinner. The admissions season is full of uncomfortable moments like unanswered emails, essay rewrites, tight deadlines, and disappointing news. The best thing you can do is help your student face those moments with honesty and calm instead of rushing over to rescue them. When parents model perspective, kids will learn to stand back up after they stumble (and they—and we—all do). This skill will undoubtedly serve them far beyond this process.

WHEN PARENTS GET IT RIGHT

Not every story ends with spreadsheets and stress. Some of our favorite families have reminded us what poise and perspective look like, especially when things aren't so easy.

One mom in Pittsburgh stands out. Her daughter, Valerie, struggled for years with depression and self-doubt before finally coming out. From that moment, she seemed lighter and more herself. Her mom was so proud that she asked Nancy and me to watch Valerie's "coming out" video. Together, they searched for colleges that would welcome her identity. Valerie found her home at Occidental College, where she thrived academically and socially.

Then there's a remarkable mom from Miami—one of the most grounded, dedicated parents we've ever met. Her son, an avid rock climber, lives with a chronic neurological condition that made daily routines challenging. She never tried to shield him from his limits or inflate his accomplishments. Instead, she focused on helping him find a place where he could both manage his health and keep doing what he loved. He found his community at the University of Vermont, where he climbed (literally and figuratively) higher than anyone imagined. Now, that same mom is supporting her younger nonbinary child with the same mix of adoration and respect. Her only wish? That they find a welcoming college community, and they did. At Oberlin College.

These are the parents who get it. They listen and learn. I want to literally hug them because they're the best reminder that this process, at its core, is about growth and love.

Love your child unconditionally no matter what. Be there at any time of day for support. Listen to your child when they want to talk, but please remember there's no need to talk with your child about college 24/7.

Try not to judge any school. Try not to judge your child. Remind them over and over again that their worth is much more than a college acceptance. Show up for them no matter when, where, or what. Celebrate the wins and the losses. Even rejections deserve recognition because they build resilience and all those other life skills that matter far more in the long run. Growing up in today's tumultuous world is hard enough. Add in the stress of college applications, and these kids deserve as much love and compassion as we can give them.

SOME TIPS FOR KEEPING YOUR COOL IN THE ADMISSIONS PROCESS

BE REALISTIC All the parental scheduling, pestering, and chauffeuring in the world won't buy your kid an extra point on the SAT or suddenly turn a B+ into an A. No amount of well-intentioned "advising" from the sidelines can replace steady support. Be patient with your child's mistakes and procrastination. Please remember: a well-rounded college list with a healthy combination of "reach," "target," and "likely" schools is a smart and sanity-saving move.

MODEL INTEGRITY Let your child's real achievements shine, even if they're not quite Nobel Prize material yet. Show them that integrity matters most and that you're proud of who they are, not just what they accomplish. Of course, character and kindness count, too. If they hold the door for someone, send their grandma a heartfelt thank-you note, or empty the dishwasher without any prodding, please celebrate that, too. It's far more impressive to raise a *mensch*[11] than for your child to earn a perfect SAT score.

COMMUNICATE OPENLY The admissions process can feel like it's consuming every conversation, but kids need a breather from all the college *mishigas*.[12] Every now and then, it's okay to press pause and be a family again. Things like pizza night, rewatching *The Office* for the eleventh time, and going for a walk all count. When you check in with your child, mix it up: ask how they're feeling and what made them laugh today. Or casually drop off their favorite snack with no agenda (trust me, snacks work wonders).

BE SUPPORTIVE, NOT CONTROLLING This is your child's journey, so let them take the wheel—even if you're silently gripping the imaginary side emergency brake. A well-timed hug or an "I'm proud of you" text goes a much longer way than a reminder about deadlines.

FOLLOW YOUR CHILD'S LEAD Some kids lock into the college process like it's their full-time job. They spend their free time researching schools, touring campuses virtually, making spreadsheets, and reminding you of deadlines. Others bolt from the dinner table the moment someone utters a word that sounds like college.

Both are normal.

Some kids need a gentle push; others need to be reined in before they burn out. Think of when your child learned to walk: some take their first steps at eight months and others at fourteen. They all get there. The same applies here.

You can even watch the first Harry Potter movie with them, then agree to save the rest for another night. If they're avoiding everything and rewatching the whole series in one sitting, it might be time to set a limit and help them refocus.

If they're out with friends until late Saturday night and then spend all of Sunday in bed, help them carve out a window for work later in the day. The point is to meet them where they are and help steer them back on track.

CELEBRATE THE SMALL STEPS ALONG THE WAY Your child took their first ACT? Survived their first college tour without rolling their eyes too much? Submitted their first application? These are huge moments. Honor them with a pancake breakfast, or at the very least, a "holy crap, you did it!" high-five.

---

11 *Mensch* is a Yiddish word that means a good, honorable person. It's basically someone who remembers to thank their teachers and doesn't leave the shopping cart stranded in the parking lot. **12** *Mishigas* is a Yiddish word that signifies craziness, nonsense, or the general chaos of life. It's often used with affection to describe the whirlwind of emotions, expectations, and everyday absurdities we all get swept up in.

FOCUS ON GROWTH, NOT JUST RESULTS Remind your child that each experience—every acceptance, rejection, deferral, and waitlist limbo—is part of their growth. College is just one chapter and not the whole story.

Your influence as a parent is powerful. Be their cheerleader, offer unlimited hugs, and try your best to keep your sense of humor intact. The best outcomes often come from simply being there, listening, encouraging, and reminding them they are loved no matter where they end up (and yes, I love my kids unconditionally, but if they have a giant zit in the middle of their forehead, I'm still going to point it out. That's love, too).

Love and laughter will get you far, but the hardest test for most parents comes next: expectations.

CHAPTER 3

Great Expectations: HANDLE WITH CARE

There's a reason I keep a mega-sized bottle of Pepto Bismol within arm's reach before and after some of our college list meetings with students and their parents. The process of crafting a realistic college list that balances hopes with actual chances can be gut-wrenching. Literally. Breaking the news to parents that certain colleges aren't just reaches but completely out of reach is the hardest part. That's when my stomach churns out noises so intense that they could be mistaken for the sound of engines revving at the start of the Indy 500.

Before we meet with families, Nancy and I have our own "pre-meetings." We talk through the student's profile, consider what's realistic, and most importantly, figure out how to share that information with kindness and care. We know it won't always land easily.

We've been doing this long enough to know that the toughest part of our job isn't the students; it's gently managing their parents' expectations. We love the parents. Really. But also...

Too often, it's the parents who show up to our "let's build a preliminary college list" meetings armed with a lineup of top-tier schools like Princeton, Dartmouth, and Wharton.

The problem? Their child's profile doesn't align with those schools.

That's okay.

Plenty of happy, successful people did not go to Princeton.

HOPES AND REALITY CHECKS

These conversations aren't easy, because they're rarely just about college. They're about long-held hopes and years of imagining a certain path—all wrapped up in one decision.

They're also deeply personal, because at the heart of it all is a teenager who wants to prove that they're capable, and, more than anything, make their parents proud.

We know there are thousands of wonderful places where students can thrive. But helping some families see beyond a short list of name-brand schools? That's often the toughest part. Fortunately, there are tools that can help broaden the search. Websites like BigFuture, Niche, and Scoir's Explore feature allow families to build balanced lists based on size, location, majors, and acceptance data. Even the Department of Education's College Scorecard can provide a helpful reality check when it comes to outcomes and affordability.

Every year, without fail, we end up in several meetings with parents who seem completely unfazed by the statistical realities of college admissions. They nod along as Nancy and I explain acceptance rates, as if we're reading them the weather report in a city they've never visited. "Oh, a 3% acceptance rate? That sounds chilly." What they often fail to grasp is that a 3% admit rate really means a 97% rejection rate. Sometimes flipping the equation helps it click. Other times, they simply stare back, unconcerned, as if those odds apply to *other* people but certainly not to their children.

It makes perfect sense. Numbers don't always win when they're up against a parent's love and enormous belief in their child's potential. But part of our job is to help families widen the frame and see the many great possibilities beyond the small handful of brand-name schools that dominate dinner talk. We also want to make sure each student has real options in the end. That means keeping the list realistic and balanced, especially since there's a limit to how many applications most teens can complete before they hit a wall.

For families conquering this process on their own, the key is maintaining balance and self-awareness. A good list usually includes an assortment of schools: a few reaches, several targets, and at least a couple of options where admission is very likely. Parents can start by asking a few honest questions: Is my child's GPA and testing (if any) in line with what this school typically admits? Does the school's culture match my kid's disposition? Could the academic pressure here be overwhelming for my student? The goal is to make sure the process ends with choices that feel both realistic and exciting.

Every child is special in their own way. They all have something valuable to offer to a college community and the world beyond. We've become experts at helping kids find that "specialness" and making it shine in an application. But at the most rejective schools? That level of "special" needs to be *objectively outstanding*, the kind that makes an admissions officer sit up in their chair and think, *Wow! We don't see this every day.* Not just the kind of special every parent (understandably) sees in their own child.

What many families don't realize is how truly extraordinary some of the competition is. We try to provide context, offer examples, and gently share what we've seen. Some parents understand immediately. Others need time. Some, no matter how gently we try, never quite get there.

Later in the book, we'll break down how colleges in fact view extracurriculars, from the everyday to the exceptional, and what separates a "good kid" from a genuine standout.

We get it. It's hard to be objective when it's your kid. But the more clearly parents can view their child through the lens of an admissions officer, the more grounded (and less painful) the whole process tends to feel.

CASE STUDIES IN SKY-HIGH EXPECTATIONS:

Every year, we meet parents who are so convinced their child is such a lock for a top school, they are convinced something has gone terribly wrong if things don't go their way.

Here are some of my personal favorites:

THE YALE-STANFORD MOM

"She's an excellent student. I think Yale should be at the top of her list, right?" the mom asked in earnest.

Deep breath. Big sip of Pepto.

Her daughter played the saxophone—not competitively, not in Carnegie Hall, but enough to hold her own in the school band. She was a capable student with solid (though not straight-A) grades and strong test scores that put her in a good range, if not the highest tier. She dreamed of becoming a journalist, though her experience was still in the early stages: a few articles for the school paper and a personal blog she updated when she had the time. She was curious and full of promise. But in a pool where some students had already published op-eds in *Teen Vogue* or launched podcasts with real audiences, her journalism resume was in its infancy.

"You are a fantastic young adult," I said warmly, smiling at the student. "I just want to make sure I have the fullest picture. Is there anything about your academics or extracurriculars that hasn't come up yet?"

I paused, then added, carefully, "At these schools, students are often bringing something very distinctive to the table like national writing awards, published research, or projects that have reached a wider audience. Is there anything along those lines we might highlight?"

"Okay, then what about Stanford?" the mom blurted out.

Cue the Pepto. That was also a school with a 97% rejection rate.

THE BROWN LEGACY DAD WHO MAY HAVE LIVED UNDER A ROCK

One dad was so sure his daughter would follow in the family tradition at Brown. "Northwestern is her safety," he declared confidently.

(FYI: No such thing exists anymore. Maybe in 1985, but not today.)

His daughter? She had mostly A's, a few B's and had taken a solid, though not the most rigorous, course load at her high school. She had a broad mix of activities: president of the Climate Change club, a theater kid, and active in LGBTQ+ rights as an ally. She was a kind, engaged, socially conscious student, but not the next Malala.

We carefully built a well-balanced college list for her, one with reach schools, plenty of great options, and, most importantly, a strong safety net to ensure she had choices in the end. Part of our job is to protect students from the heartbreak of a pile of rejections. Parents often insist, "I know these are all moon shots!" But trust me. When those decisions roll in, reality still stings.

Every year, we see families who swear they're just "taking a shot" at those ultra-selective schools. "We know it's a reach! She just wants to try!" they say with a casual shrug. But something psychologically happens between hitting "submit" and decision day. Hope creeps in. Since they applied, maybe—just maybe—there's a chance?

Then the rejection lands, and suddenly, it feels personal. "How could they not see how amazing she is?" We knew it was coming. They knew it was coming. But human nature is a funny thing. It's easy to talk about how unlikely it is to win the lottery. It's much harder to accept that it probably won't be your child, and that the odds really, truly aren't in their favor.

Despite plenty of data points supporting the breadth of our recommendations, this family wouldn't budge. Alas...this girl faced more rejections than necessary in the end.

Yet fate has a sense of humor; she ended up at the University of St. Andrews in Scotland, a perfect escape from her dad's Ivy-or-bust dreams. Last I heard? She's thriving.

HARVARD FOR THE HECK OF IT

We're currently working with a family whose son, Kyle, has near-perfect grades in the most rigorous courses and a one-and-done perfect SAT score. But when it comes to extracurriculars? There's not much yet. No real involvement beyond the classroom, no leadership roles, and no strong sense of what lights him up.

He's also hesitant to dive into anything new. Most of our suggestions are met with polite nods...and not much follow-through.

Still, his parents are taking him to tour Harvard, Princeton, and Yale. Just because.

"We know they're long shots," the mom emailed. "But if he really likes them, it's worth applying. You never know."

She's not wrong. Occasionally, it *is* worth applying. We are not in the business of destroying dreams. We love a bold reach when it's thoughtful and supported by a balanced list. But when there's no clear match between a student's academic and extra-curricular profile and what these schools are looking for, applying "just to see" can set everyone up for disappointment.

Honestly, it feels like we're stuck in that scene from the movie, *Dumb & Dumber*. Jim Carrey's character asks the beautiful woman he's after if he has a shot. She hesitates, then says, "Well, maybe one in a million." Instead of being discouraged, he beams: "So you're saying... I have a chance?"

That's what this can feel like for some parents. Even if they understand the odds, that teeny, tiny spark of hope flickers. Whether they mean to or not, that mindset trick-les down to their kids. Yet when the "no" arrives? It hurts.

DERANGED OVER DARTMOUTH

One mom was convinced her son was a shoo-in for Dartmouth (her alma mater) because he had started his school's first mock trial team.

"He has tremendous initiative!" she gushed.

But when we asked what inspired him, he hesitated. Then he admitted that she had organized the team, managed the spreadsheets, scheduled the training sessions, and handled logistics. His biggest contribution? Bringing doughnuts to team practices and cheering them on. He hadn't racked up any significant wins to objectively highlight his rebuttal skills; he had simply helped create a nice club atmosphere.

He may have enjoyed being part of the team, but without clear achievements to point to, Dartmouth wasn't exactly a guarantee.

While we applaud any effort to build a school community, at the most rejective schools, "impact" needs to be both clear and measurable. Colleges want to see evi-dence of follow-through and influence. That might mean mentoring younger students, earning recognition or awards, expanding a club's membership, exceeding fundraising goals, or leading a project that creates a noticeable difference in the community.

THE HARSH REALITY:
WHAT IT REALLY TAKES TO GET INTO A TOP COLLEGE

These parents aren't delusional; they're just not aware of how insanely competitive college admissions has become.

I understand. Every parent wants to believe their child is special.

When my daughter was two years old, she won Artist of the Month at ArtForms, a child-centered art program in San Mateo, California. I was convinced she was an artistic prodigy.

Never mind that her painting looked like a Crayola crime scene. I was already envisioning her first exhibit at the Guggenheim.

It's what we do as parents. We see brilliance in the smallest moments and assume the world will recognize it, too.

However, college admissions officers aren't your kid's parents. They're not looking at your child through the lens of unconditional love; they're looking at tens of thousands of applications from high-achieving students, each with their own impressive credentials.

Quite frankly, even after all these years, we're still blown away by the sheer level of achievement some seventeen-year-olds have amassed.

One student from a strong public high school in Atlanta skipped two grades, earned a perfect SAT score, and conducted international award-winning research in environmental sustainability—analyzing data on renewable energy use and creating a community outreach project to promote solar access in low-income neighborhoods. In her spare time, she played violin in a youth orchestra and organized care packages for cancer survivors. There's more, but I'll stop. Despite her extraordinary resume, she was deferred by Princeton, waitlisted by Harvard, and ultimately admitted to MIT, Caltech, Yale, and Stanford (where she is a happy student).

Then there was the three-time national speech champion from a public school in Chicago—a student with perfect grades and test scores (and later, a National Merit Scholar), who somehow packed an entire universe into her high school days. She spent evenings and weekends dancing tap, jazz, hip-hop, you name it. She also found time to bake treats for hospital workers during COVID, advocate for children with disabilities at her high school, and chair a student-run nonprofit offering free, fun classes for middle schoolers around the world. She took three languages at school while teaching herself new ones and mentoring younger students who saw her as both a role model and a solid source of support. She applied early to Princeton and got in.

You get the picture.

Most students don't need to operate at that rarified level of achievement to bring something valuable to the table. The vast majority have plenty to offer, in ways that will serve them well wherever they end up.

That's why parents need to approach this process with realistic expectations and an open mind. College admissions today are brutal and often defy logic. What used to be a straightforward formula—good grades, solid activities, strong teacher recs, a compelling essay—has morphed into a nerve-wracking game of musical chairs with far more players than seats.

This is where school counselors and private advisors (if parents hire them) can be invaluable. They've worked with hundreds of students, tracked trends, and seen firsthand who gets in year after year. For families trying to get a sense of those trends on their own, there are a few helpful tools. Platforms like Scoir, Naviance, and College Kickstart provide scattergrams, admission data, and predictive modeling based on historical results from a student's own high school or national data sets. More importantly, they bring a level of objectivity that's nearly impossible for a parent to have when it comes to their own child.

I get it. These are your kids we're talking about. But if you think your student is eligible for a highly selective college, here's the reality check you need before you dive in.

1. Almost perfect grades and test scores

That's just your ticket to play. Almost everyone applying to these schools has them. They'll get your student into the admissions room but not necessarily into the conversation.

2. Extracurriculars that show depth and distinction

Leadership, initiative, impact, and recognition all matter. However, at the most selective schools, it's not about how many activities your student does; it's about how meaningful they are. Admissions officers are drawn to pursuits that feel both personal and uncommon.

A student who speaks multiple languages and continues learning on her own? Rare. A student who launches a community campaign to support minority-owned businesses and ends up on national television discussing how to publicly confront racism? Personal and unforgettable.

3. Institutional priorities

They're real. Every college has its own behind-the-scenes agenda. One year they may need a French horn player, another year, more Classics majors or students from North Dakota. Yes, colleges really do aim to represent all fifty states, but this is not a reason to uproot your family.

4. The element of luck

Two nearly identical students can apply—same grades, same activities, same test scores—and yet, one gets in while the other is waitlisted or rejected. Why? Sometimes, there *is* no why. There's no secret formula, no equation that adds up. It's literally a dollop of randomness in every yes and no. That's the hardest truth for many parents to swallow. But remember that a rejection isn't a verdict on your child's worth; it's a reminder that no one controls this process completely.

KIND OF CRAZY

THERE ARE *so* MANY DIFFERENT PATHS *to* SUCCESS

Here's a little perspective to calm everyone's nerves: there are nearly 4,000 four-year colleges and universities in the United States. That number doesn't even include the hundreds of two-year and specialty programs where students can absolutely blossom. In October 2024, about 63% of recent U.S. high school graduates were enrolled in college.[13] The vast majority of them find a place that's a great fit for them.

Yes, the headlines about single-digit acceptance rates make this process sound nuts. But the good news is, there are so many wonderful schools and so many different paths to success. Your child will land somewhere that values who they are, not just what's on their resume.

A GUIDE TO OBJECTIVELY ASSESSING YOUR OWN KID

This is hard. Even as a college counselor, I wrestle with it myself.

If anyone asks about my three kids, I'll happily gush. In my completely unbiased opinion, they are wonderfully capable humans with bright, promising futures ahead of them. (Hey, I'm their mom! It's my job to believe in them, just like every other parent.) Maybe they'll become exactly what I imagine. Maybe they'll take a completely different path, and that will be equally meaningful. I don't know how it'll all play out. None of us do.

College applications aren't built on hope alone. The path we picture isn't always the one our kids are literally on. Interests develop. Priorities change. What matters most is helping them apply as they are right now, not who we imagine they'll become.

---

13 U.S. Bureau of Labor Statistics, *"College Enrollment and Work Activity of Recent High School and College Graduates—2024,"* news release, April 22, 2025, https://www.bls.gov/news.release/hsgec.nr0.htm

Before declaring your child to be the perfect candidate for an uber-selective school, try this:

THE OBJECTIVITY TEST

Can You Assess Your Child Like a College Admissions Officer?

1. **If this weren't your kid, would their application wow you?** Try to imagine you're reading it as a stranger, not as a proud parent.

2. **Are their interests truly self-driven, or are they pursuing activities just because they look good on a college application?** Colleges can tell the difference between passion and performance.

3. **Do their activities line up with what they love and paint a clear picture of who they are?** Admissions officers look for a thread that connects a student's interests and how they've chosen to spend their time.

4. **Will their teachers gush about them in their recommendations, or simply say nice but forgettable things?** Parents don't see these letters, but you can usually sense how invested a teacher is. At parent-teacher conferences, are they the kind who lights up when talking about your kid? Or do they squint and mumble, "Oh, I think your daughter sits over there"?

5. **Are you maybe, even a tiny bit, projecting your own hopes and ambitions onto them?** We've all been guilty of this one.

6. **Are you already picturing the college bumper sticker on your car?** No judgment. It happens to the best of us.

7. **Are you seeing your kid for who they really are or just the version you've built up in your head as impressive and flawless?** Reminder: colleges want the real one.

If you hesitated on any of these, congratulations! You're a normal parent.

It's only natural to want the best for your child, but your role isn't to mold them into a "perfect candidate." It's to help them find a college where they'll succeed for real, not just one that makes for impressive small talk at family reunions or at the office water cooler. For parents, that means moving from steering to supporting. Ask what's resonating instead of wondering what's impressive. Try to quiet the background noise—the rankings, the carpool gossip, your inner voice whispering, "But what about Yale?" The best gift you can give your child is space to figure out what feels right and the trust that they'll get there in their own time.

THE PARENTS WHO RESTORE MY FAITH IN HUMANITY

For all the ambitious, spreadsheet-wielding, Ivy-or-bust parents we've encountered,

I've also met some of the most grounded, wonderful, and wise families along the way.

These are the parents who ask:

"Where will my child be happiest, not just academically, but emotionally?"

"Where will they grow into the person they're meant to be?"

"Will the social and campus vibe make them comfortable?"

"Will the curriculum and required courses be a good fit?"

Fun fact: most of these wonderfully non-neurotic parents are not from New York. Many hail from the laid-back Midwest. We absolutely adore them.

They're realistic, open to suggestions, and meet their child where they are, not where they want them to be. They explore schools they've never heard of with curiosity instead of skepticism. When we make recommendations, they don't roll their eyes. They listen. Some even take notes!

Over the years, we've had countless moments where we suggested a school we *knew* would be a great fit, one the family barely recognized. With a little trust, an open mind, and maybe a campus visit, the student fell in love...and ultimately, ended up there.

The lesson? Be open. Listen to the matchmakers. You might be surprised at where your child finds their perfect fit.

Then there are the unicorns. These are the parents who rarely join our meetings. They hand us a check and say, "Here's my kid. I trust you."

Imagine that.

These parents remind me that the purpose of this process is raising a kid who feels confident in their own path. They understand that letting their child step into the lead, with proper support, is one of the best ways to foster growth and independence.

The growth we see in students throughout this process? It's incredible. It's one of our favorite parts of the job. We watch these young adults evolve as writers, thinkers, communicators, organizers, planners, and decision-makers, and sometimes in the span of a few months. It's rewarding. I often get misty because, in so many ways, I feel like these kids are my own.

SHOT OF SANITY

At the end of the day, most kids find their way to the college that is right for them—not because of all the spreadsheets and late-night stress, but often in spite of them.

And me? I'll still be here, restocking my emergency supply of Pepto Bismol and pretzels, and cheering for every kid I've worked with (and probably a few I haven't).

College admissions may be unpredictable. But parental love, hope, joy, and grit? Those are the constants I count on every time.

Part Two

Laying the Groundwork

CHAPTER 4

SLOW *and* STEADY WINS *the* RACE *(if you time it well)*

When our family moved from California to New York in the summer of 2011, we didn't just haul furniture. We brought chaos, hope, way too many boxes, and our three beloved pets: Yankee the golden doodle, Sweetie the guinea pig, and Tuffy the Russian tortoise. With kids entering seventh, fifth, and first grade, there was no way we were leaving anyone behind.

To make the move more of an adventure and less of a prison sentence, we decided to drive across the country. All five of us crammed into a Ford Explorer stuffed with enough food to feed a small army. Oh, and the entire itinerary was planned by our kids, because what could possibly go wrong? What started as a cross-country drive became a two-week odyssey of roller coasters, quirky roadside attractions, stops at every state's welcome sign for the obligatory photo op, and questionable dining choices. We braved the Top Thrill Dragster, the country's fastest roller coaster (in 2011) at Cedar Point in Sandusky, Ohio, enjoyed an alarming amount of cheese in Dell, Wisconsin, and indulged in what were allegedly "the best" fries at Joe's in Pocatello, Idaho (spoiler: they were just okay).

Meanwhile, our pets experienced their own travel saga. Yankee enjoyed a luxurious stay at Woofgang's (think Ritz-Carlton for dogs) back in California, while Sweetie and Tuffy bunked with our ever-generous friend Hilary. Once we were settled in Scarsdale, it was time for them to make their grand journey.

Getting three animals across the country was no small feat. United Airlines had strict rules, especially for exotic pets like Tuffy. While Yankee and Sweetie needed only standard veterinary clearance, Tuffy required a special exam to confirm he was fit to fly. Apparently, "Russian tortoise" raised some TSA eyebrows.

On the day of his big arrival, my husband Jeff, dressed in a full suit on a sweltering July day, stood in a cavernous warehouse next to the airport, watching crates of heavy cargo roll by on forklifts. Finally, a freight elevator creaked open, and there was Tuffy, riding solo in a tiny cage, looking like a king.

Jeff made a show of dramatically lifting the lightweight cage, nodding at the workers as if to say, "Yep, tough cargo."

We still laugh about Jeff's moment as a forklift hero. But what really stuck with me was how carefully we had to plan each stage of our move, especially Tuffy's. His journey couldn't be rushed. Each step had to happen in the right order.

We didn't pack up our lives before it was time. We let our kids finish the school year, say their goodbyes, and close one chapter before starting the next.

That's what I wish more families would remember when it comes to college.

Kids should be kids for as long as they can. Let them enjoy middle school before worrying about high school. Let them enjoy high school before being consumed by the college pressure cooker.

Our cross-country move confirmed what I already knew: the weather in California is better (sigh). But it also reminded me that transitions work best when they're done thoughtfully, one phase at a time.

College planning should be no different.

ADMISSIONS ISN'T A SPRINT; IT'S A MARATHON

Most families assume that the students who get into the most competitive colleges are the ones who burst onto the scene with a strategically plotted four-year master plan created before they even hit high school. In our experience, that's rarely the case.

The students who navigate this process in the healthiest ways aren't usually the ones who start mapping out their future in middle school. They're the ones who simply stay curious, take small steady steps, and let their interests unfold organically. There's no secret formula and no single "right" path. It's about having an open mind and the willingness to grow along the way.

Nancy and I love helping families break this process into manageable, bite-sized steps. Not all at once. And please: no college talk dominating the dinner table in ninth grade. We encourage a gentle, thoughtful approach that gives students room to develop on their own timeline.

KIND OF CRAZY

The PERILS *of* STARTING *too* EARLY

One of the patterns we see regularly? Families eager to jump in early, convinced that earlier means better. Believe me, it doesn't.

Some parents reach out to us when their child is in middle school.

That's too early. Kids need time to grow before turning college into a full-time job. Let them be twelve. College can wait.

I was reminded of this recently while reaching into the freezer section at Trader Joe's for a Roasted Garlic & Pesto pizza. A woman tapped me on the shoulder.

"Aren't you Beth Gelles? The college advisor?" She was clutching a box of cauliflower crust pizza like it was a life raft. "My daughter is in eighth grade, and she's already won poetry awards. Can we chat about college?"

Eighth grade. Poetry awards. College.

Crazily, she's not alone. Just this week, a mom of a tenth grader reached out to start building her daughter's college list. Another family wanted to plunge into essay coaching in August, before their son had even started his junior year.

We get it. Your kid is busy. There are rehearsals, recitals, tournaments, games, practices, and you're just trying to stay one step ahead.

But starting too early doesn't always bring peace of mind. More often, it leads to stress, second-guessing, more pressure, and a longer, more grueling trek for your child *and* you. It's better to walk at a steady 3.0 pace on the treadmill and reach the full three miles than to hop off gasping after the first five minutes. (I say this from experience; I rarely run three miles in under thirty-five minutes.) Same goes for college prep.

No student benefits from diving in too early. They need time to grow into the kind of person colleges are sincerely hoping to meet. That means not just someone who looks good on paper, but someone you'd honestly enjoy talking to (or singing Taylor Swift with) on a long car ride.

That's why the early years of high school should be about building a strong foundation: academically, emotionally, personally, and socially. It's easy to zoom in on grades and goals, but it's just as important that your student feels grounded and okay in their everyday life. When that happens, the rest tends to follow.

THE EARLY HIGH SCHOOL YEARS: FINDING THE RIGHT BALANCE AS EARLY AS FRESHMAN YEAR

Ninth grade is a big leap. New building, new schedule, new teachers, and a locker that might not open on the first try. While colleges view freshman year as a transition, it still counts, and it's the perfect time to build strong habits without turning it into a frenetic race to get ahead.

Encourage your child to take courses that set them up for success over four years. Colleges want to see strength in the core subjects: English, math, science, history, and foreign language. But that doesn't mean loading up on every advanced class right away. The right balance looks different for every student. Parents can help by checking in regularly and not focusing solely on grades. Aim for a course load that encourages growth without causing constant anxiety.

Do freshman year grades count? You bet. They're on the transcript, they factor into the GPA, and colleges will see them. But equally telling is how a student responds when things don't come easily.

We once worked with a student who struggled in English her first semester. Her confidence took a hit, but instead of giving up, she asked her teacher (and friends she trusted) for help. Slowly but surely, she found her voice. By senior year, she was editor-in-chief of the school newspaper and headed off to college to study Communications. Grades matter, but growth and self-advocacy matter more.

Freshman year is also about exploration. Whether it's debate, soccer, theater, or something completely offbeat (like building your own canoe or producing podcasts), the goal is for students to find activities they get a kick out of doing. Parents can help by encouraging little risks like trying a new club or showing up to a meeting solo.

TENTH GRADE: BUILDING CONFIDENCE AND CONSISTENCY

By sophomore year, it's time to take off the training wheels. Students know the ropes, teachers expect more, and it's time to turn good habits into steady routines. Colleges will look closely at these grades, but sophomore year is also the "sweet spot." There are no major standardized tests yet, and still enough room to figure out what makes a student tick.

Encourage your child to continue challenging themselves in core classes while finding their academic rhythm. This is a great time to notice what ignites genuine interest, whether that's a deep dive into biology, a fascination with world history, or the creative rush of a design class.

Outside the classroom, less is often more. If your student joined clubs or teams in ninth grade, help them think about ways to strengthen those commitments: mentoring younger students, organizing an event, or securing leadership roles each new year.

This is also the year to start thinking strategically but calmly about testing and summer plans. A low-stakes diagnostic SAT or ACT in the spring gives a handy baseline without stress. A meaningful summer experience like a job, class, or community project can build maturity. Parents can support by nudging (not pushing), listening often, and helping them prioritize what lights them up along with their effort.

The early high school years aren't about getting everything right. They're about helping your child learn how to juggle, stumble a little, and still get back up. All three of my kids were on their high school's Speech & Debate team, and I always told them I was prouder of the losses than the wins. It takes more resilience to keep showing up after a tough round than to party after an easy victory. When kids feel supported and not pressured, they start to take healthy risks and grow into confident, curious juniors who are ready for whatever comes next.

Before we jump into the upper-class years, it's worth pausing to talk about something that can make or break the high school experience: friendships and belonging.

THE SOCIAL SIDE OF HIGH SCHOOL

We spend a lot of time talking about academics and extracurriculars, but we don't talk nearly enough about the social side of high school and how much that affects everything else.

Friendships change. Sometimes gradually or sometimes all at once. It can be unsettling for kids who are used to having a stable group of friends. We've worked with students who walk into the cafeteria and suddenly feel like they have no idea where to sit or who to join.

One student had always been part of a close-knit friend group. But once high school started, his friends gravitated toward sports. He joined the football team, but he spent most of the season on the bench. Eventually, he realized he didn't even like football, and trying to fit in made him feel worse. He switched gears and found community in Model UN, where he finally felt like himself again.

Another student watched her longtime friends drift toward a more popular crowd. She tried to join them but felt out of place. After some gentle and persistent encouragement from her mom, she signed up to help backstage in the school theater program. That's where the light bulb finally went off and the stage lights came on. There was no need to impress anyone. For the first time in months, she felt like she belonged and had loads of fun.

As parents, it can be hard to watch your child go through these transitions. The best thing you can do? Let them know it's okay if friendships change. It's perfectly fine if they don't find their people right away. That takes patience, time, trial, and error.

High school can be brutal at times. Sometimes worse than middle school. Academically, socially, and emotionally, it's challenging to grow up, be yourself, make good choices, and get through each day unscathed. Good friends are often what keeps kids grounded, and they remind each other who they are and what's important, especially after a bad test, a break-up, or just a "meh" day. It's important for parents not to put pressure on kids about having a group of friends. Sometimes, having one or two loyal, wonderful friends is all it takes to get through high school—and even life.

Parents should try not to jump in to fix every conflict or friendship hiccup. Ask questions. Listen. Remind your child that no friendship is perfect and try not to overreact when they share something uncomfortable. At times, a kid just needs to vent. Other times, it's more helpful to ask, "What do you think you should do?" than to solve it for them.

It also helps when parents model healthy friendships themselves. If your teen sees you making time for people who make you laugh or feel inspired, they'll start to understand what real friendship looks like. Try complimenting your own child for being a good friend, too. It's a two-way street. High school is when kids learn how to build trust, compromise, make mistakes, recover from disappointment, and still have fun along the way.

After everything students have weathered in recent years, especially the isolation and disruption of COVID, building a sense of connection is more important now than ever. When Nancy and I talk with students, we go beyond checking in about their grades and activities. We often ask, "How is the social scene for you?" Because no matter how strong a transcript looks, a student who feels down or isolated is going to struggle.

When students feel happy, they're more likely to take healthy risks, whether that's speaking up in class, trying a new club, or running for a leadership role they thought they'd never get. That's the kind of growth colleges notice. It often shows up in the activities section of the Common App as new leadership roles or a stronger purpose in what they love to do. It's also what helps kids feel like they're really coming into their own.

JUNIOR YEAR: WHEN THINGS GET REAL

For many families, junior year is when everything kicks into high gear. Classes get tougher. Teachers start casually dropping the word "college" into conversations. Plus, the looming cloud of standardized testing rolls in.

The intensity feels real and for good reason.

Junior year is the last full academic year colleges will see before students apply, which gives it extra weight. However, that doesn't mean it has to become a year-long grind-fest. One of the biggest stressors? Standardized testing. Between mock exams, test prep, and trying to find an open test site (some states really do run out of seats, so book early!), the whole thing can feel overwhelming and fast. That's why we suggest starting test preparation for the ACT or SAT in late summer before junior year begins, even if it means sacrificing a few pool days.

The key is to not overdo it. Pick one test (SAT or ACT), prep with purpose, and aim for a first sitting between fall and winter. More tests don't always equal better results. Although test-optional policies surged during COVID and remain firmly in place at many colleges, we recommend that every student prep for at least one standardized test and see how it goes. A good score never hurts, and that first result gives families a clearer sense of what's possible as they begin to build a college list. And the PSAT? It's not always a crystal ball for what's ahead.

Still, junior year is not an all-or-nothing make-or-break year. A tough class, a bad quiz, even a lower grade in something like AP Chem won't derail everything. Admissions officers are human. They're not looking for perfection; they're looking for effort, curiosity, resilience, and progress.

What's the best way for your kid to survive this year? Slow and steady, keep their eye on the stuff that counts, and trust the process. Oh, and ideally, they should get some sleep, too.

THINKING ABOUT VISITING COLLEGES? TAKE IT ONE STEP AT A TIME

College visits can begin as early as winter of junior year, but early spring works equally well, especially if you want your child to see what life is really like on a campus buried under three feet of snow and slush. We've seen students feel giddy on a tour in March trudging through gray snow and wind tunnels, or grinning ear to ear in a torrential downpour. If the vibe still clicks for them at that school in that kind of weather, it's probably the real deal.

> *Whatever you do, try not to let your kid fall in love with a school that's entirely out of reach based on their academic profile. We've seen the heartbreak, crumpled tissues, slammed doors, and dramatic proclamations of "But this is my dream school!"*

How can you tell if a school is out of reach? Most high schools use online tools like Scoir, Naviance, or MaiaLearning to show where past students with similar grades and test scores have been accepted, deferred, or denied. You can also check a college's Common Data Set, which breaks down the academic profile of admitted students and shows how much weight the school gives to factors like grades, test scores, and essays. It's a reality check and a source of hope, giving you concrete data from both your school and the colleges themselves.

One student came back from a visit to Vanderbilt positively glowing, to be clear, this was not a trip we recommended. She'd bought herself a pair of cowboy boots and announced with full conviction, "This is my school!" Her excitement was real, and we didn't want to shatter it. But her transcript didn't exactly align with Vanderbilt's admit rate in the single digits. We knew it wasn't going to be an easy path.

We managed to help her take a step back and figure out what she truly loved about the school—the community, the energy, the Southern vibe—and together, we found other colleges that captured that same spirit. Southern Methodist University (SMU) quickly rose to the top of her list. She could still rock her cowboy boots, but this time at a place where she could grow into herself.

How do you help your child stay excited and hopeful, while keeping their feet and their expectations firmly on the ground?

KEEP DATA IN PERSPECTIVE

Context is key. Just because one student with a perfect SAT score got into a reach school doesn't mean the same thing will happen for the next. Maybe that student was a legacy, with a parent who went there.[14] Or a recruited athlete. Or maybe their grandpar-

---

14   "Legacy admissions" refers to giving special consideration to applicants who have a parent or close family member who attended the institution. While the practice is still used at many colleges, several schools and a few states have recently limited or ended it as part of broader efforts to promote equity in admissions.

ents happened to build the new science wing.

Admissions can be unpredictable, and no two applicants bring the exact same story to the table. Use the data to guide your child's list, but don't let it be the final word.

SPRING FORWARD (WITHOUT FREAKING)

By spring of junior year, it's time to start thinking about college essays. Not writing. Not panicking. Just thinking. And no, this doesn't require an existential crisis. Students do not need to have their entire life story figured out.

Instead, encourage them to jot down small but meaningful moments, like the time one student accidentally gave a customer $75 instead of $7.50 in change, or when another completely froze during a solo at the school winter chorus recital. These kinds of real-life stumbles often lead to great essays.

That's why we use late spring and summer to not only brainstorm but also draft and refine essays. By the time senior year rolls around, they'll have a head start and a solid personal statement, not just a blank Google Doc and an impending sense of doom.

They'll thank themselves (and you) when they walk into Day 1 of senior year feeling prepared while many of their classmates are in full-blown panic mode, juggling the 650-word Common App essay they haven't started with fall classes, papers, tests, and extracurriculars.

CHOOSE WISELY: COURSE RIGOR STILL MATTERS

One more thing to keep in mind during spring of junior year: selecting senior year courses.

Some admissions officers have told Nancy and me that the first thing they look at is the senior year schedule. They want to see that students are still challenging themselves appropriately and maintaining or increasing the level of rigor they've shown in previous years.

As your child is choosing classes this spring, keep in mind: colleges really do pay attention. Senior year still counts.

SENIOR YEAR: THE GAME PLAN

Senior year is either where all the hard work pays off, or where students succumb to senioritis, daydreaming of TikTok stardom instead of finishing their applications.

Here's how to help your child keep things on track:

1. Strategy Meeting in Late Summer: Sit down to finalize the Early Decision

(ED1), Early Decision II (ED2), Early Action (EA), Rolling Admission, and Regular Decision (RD) plan, because "I'll figure it out eventually!" is not a great strategy. If you have the resources and your child has the time, consider revisiting two or three schools in early fall. A quick return visit can make all the difference in deciding which one feels right for an ED choice.

2. **College Essays:** Finish all remaining supplemental essays by December 1st. Believe me: no one wants to be writing "Why Wake Forest?" while everyone else is opening holiday gifts, watching movies, and drinking hot chocolate on winter break.

3. **Keep Grades Up:** Just because the finish line is near, doesn't mean it's time to coast. Colleges check final transcripts, and a sudden drop in grades can turn deferrals into rejections or an acceptance into a "warning" letter. We've seen students who've worked incredibly hard for three years suddenly hit a wall in the fall of senior year. Between applications and the monumental pressure, they crash. Hard. Think skinned knees, even concussion-level nose dives. Encourage sleep, breaks, and reality-checks. A student who paces themselves will end up in a much stronger place than one who burns out before December. Until those acceptances are locked in, senioritis is not an option.

4. **Most Important Reminder?** Your kid is going to land somewhere great. It may not be the school they dreamed about since ninth grade, but it'll be a place that gives them room to stretch, stumble, and figure stuff out. Maybe they'll even find better tacos than they had at home.

TUFFY'S TRANSITION AND YOUR CHILD'S

Looking back, I sometimes think about our cross-country move, and yes, Tuffy the tortoise's slow and carefully coordinated journey. Nothing about that transition was rushed. Every part required planning, patience, a few headaches, and the trust that we'd get there in one piece.

That's how the college process should be, too. Not a mad dash but a thoughtful, step-by-step path that gives kids space to grow into themselves.

We don't want students sprinting toward a version of success that doesn't make sense. We want them entering senior year curious, not burned out. They should be engaged in their favorite classes, surprised by new clubs, trying whatever the school cafeteria is serving that day, and building friendships that make them feel like they belong.

That kind of growth doesn't happen all at once. It happens slowly, in the in-between moments: a tough teacher, a new activity, a friendship shake-up, a failure that turns into something better.

I want to say this again. Kids shouldn't be thinking about college before ninth grade. They need time to be middle schoolers—to be silly, to goof, to discover what lights them up without wondering if it's "application-worthy." With so much road ahead, there's no need to floor it.

SHOT OF SANITY

Let your kid take a few detours. Let them try the wrong club or even the weird elective. Let them figure it out in their own time.

They don't need a four-year master plan. They don't need a forklift. They just need room to move forward: slow and steady. Like Tuffy. Like all of us. And maybe someone waiting at the finish line with a snack and a hug.

A SLOW *and* ROADMAP SCHOOL

- Freshman year counts, but it's about building a foundation, not a frenzy.
- Help your child build habits early: stay organized, ask for help, challenge themselves without overload.
- Encourage involvement but not excess. A few real interests are more important than a jam-packed resume.
- Remind your child to keep a running list of classes, clubs, and awards. It'll save time later.
- Use summer for low-pressure exploration: a class, job, volunteering, time with family are all good ideas.
- Read. Read. Read. It builds curiosity and better writing.

- Sophomore year counts even more, but there's still room to breathe.
- Encourage focus on core subjects. Steady progress is the game—not perfection.
- Enjoy the "sweet spot" year. No major tests! Let them experiment and figure out what they enjoy.
- Try a low-stakes diagnostic SAT or ACT in spring, just for a baseline.
- Nudge them to take on small leadership roles in the clubs or teams they love.
- Summer can be a continuation of what they love or a time to try something new: a job, class, or volunteer experience that feels genuine.

STEADY *for* HIGH
(one year at a time)

- This is the year colleges look at most closely, so help your child balance rigor and sanity.
- Choose one test (SAT or ACT), plan early, and get it done by summer if possible.
- Visit a few colleges. Spring break is ideal (and yes, still cold on the east coast).
- Keep cheering on the things they truly care about. Colleges recognize growth and commitment.
- Plan a meaningful summer: college applications, internships, research, or projects that stretch their curiosity and independence.

- Finalize the college list and application strategy (ED, EA, RD).
- Aim to finish essays by December 1st. Holiday break is for hot chocolate, not Common App stress.
- Keep grades steady. Colleges often look at first quarter grades before everything else.
- Don't succumb to senioritis! This is real.
- Remind them (and yourself) that this is still high school. Savor each moment, because the next chapter will come soon enough.

CHAPTER 5

GRADES, GROWTH, & *what* REALLY COUNTS

Let's play a game. I'll tell you about two students, and you can guess which one had the stronger college application.

First, meet Samantha. Her parents were absolutely convinced that more APs meant more points on her college applications. By junior year, she was taking so many weighted courses that her backpack needed its own chiropractor. Exhausted, she could barely keep her eyes open during our 6 p.m. essay brainstorming session. Her transcript captured it all: a scattering of C's, a few B's, and the occasional A–.

When we gently suggested she scale back her rigor, her mom half-smiled but emphatically stated, "She needs to take as many AP classes as possible! Colleges will see how hard she is working."

"Yes," I replied, "but they'll also see her grades."

Then there's Evan. He didn't load up on as many APs, but he built a schedule that worked well for him. Freshman year, he jumped into an ambitious lineup and quickly realized that "rigor" wasn't the same thing as "right fit." We encouraged him to drop down a level in math and science, and his mom agreed. Almost immediately, Evan's confidence (and his sleep) returned. He started enjoying his classes again, even cracking jokes at family dinners. Over time, he added more challenging courses by choice, and his grades trended steadily upward.

He's now at the University of South Carolina, where he manages to love both his classes and the football games, though not always in that order.

So, who do you think had the stronger application? (Spoiler: it wasn't the one with the heavier backpack.)

While you're trying to keep things in perspective, there's one topic that tends to rattle even the calmest parents: grades.

At some point, every family stumbles into the eternal GPA debate.

"Is it better to get a B+ in an Honors or an AP class, or an A in a regular class?" If I had a dollar for every time I've been asked this question, I'd have built my own college by now.

Our go-to answer is: "Get the A in the harder class!" This usually gets a laugh, but the reality is far more nuanced. Colleges expect students to challenge themselves, but they also value strong grades. That doesn't mean a student should load up on the hardest possible schedule only to end up drowning in B's and C's. Nor does it mean they should take all regular-level classes and try to get all A's solely to protect their GPA.

In other words, colleges care about both what your student takes and how they do. The goal is a transcript that shows steady challenge and solid performance.

As Kenneth Bonamo, Principal of Scarsdale High School, a nationally recognized public school known for its academic rigor and excellence, told me:

"The diminished role of standardized test scores (although that seems to be getting reversed slowly) has intensified anxiety around grades, leading some students to choose courses that may not be challenging enough just to increase their chances of getting a top grade."

This kind of anxiety shows up everywhere: in course selection, family conversations, and those late-night GPA calculator sessions when everyone's just trying to feel some sense of control. "If I get over a 90 on my next test, this will boost my grade to a 91.3, right?" Meanwhile, a parent is double-checking the math.

It's completely understandable. But when students choose easier classes to protect their averages, they often miss out on the kind of learning that creates real growth. Yes, colleges can usually tell when a student is playing it too safe.

UNDERSTANDING THE TRANSCRIPT'S REAL STORY

It's important to understand how colleges evaluate transcripts. Too often, parents come to us late in the game, usually at the end of junior year, in a mild (or not-so-mild) panic, and we'll see transcripts with a mix of B's, maybe a few C's, often in notorious grade-killers like Honors Physics or AP Chemistry.

Ideally, parents should take a thoughtful look at the transcript at the end of each year, beginning in ninth grade. Is your child fascinated by the Revolutionary War but tangled up in equations? Excited by chemistry labs but puzzled by poetry? Those themes tell a story that colleges will eventually read. It helps to recognize them early and discuss them calmly, not mid-dinner or the night before a big test.

Use what you see to help guide course choices each spring. When families start mapping out classes for the next year, one question always comes up, and it's a big one: "But isn't it better that she challenged herself?" a mom will ask, her eyes desperate for reassurance.

It depends.

Not every student needs to take every AP class under the sun to impress colleges. However, that doesn't mean they should avoid rigor either. The smartest approach? A balanced combo of challenging courses, especially in their stronger areas, while staying strategic enough to avoid classes that cause nightly meltdowns or that look of, "I swear we never learned this."

Here's what colleges look for:

- **Overall performance**—This isn't just about course difficulty, but how well the student handled it.
- **Growth and trajectory**—Did they improve over time? Stay consistent? Crash and burn?
- **School context**—Colleges compare students to their peers. They'll check the high school profile to see what was offered and whether a student challenged themselves relative to their classmates.

Finding that magical place between challenge and success is what really makes a transcript sing.

WHY THE STUDENT TRANSCRIPT IS THE HOLY GRAIL

The high school transcript is like the Holy Grail of college admissions. For all the fuss about the other elements that colleges screen for—SAT scores, recommendation letters, extracurriculars, and perfectly polished essays—I'm here to tell you that the transcript is *the* single most critical piece of a student's application. It's usually the first thing colleges look at. Admissions officers treat it like an important artifact by poring over every semester and scrutinizing each grade and course choice. It's the most direct evidence they have of a student's performance over time and one of the best predictors of how they'll do in college.

They scan for patterns: how a student challenged themselves, where they improved, and what they seemed to love (or avoid).

Parents don't need to analyze every grade, but it helps to understand how colleges view it. Two students from the same school might both have a 3.8 GPA. One earned it through tough classes and steady progress; the other skated through easier courses. Same number but very different story, particularly at schools where GPAs aren't weighted.

And speaking of GPA...

The SCHOOL PROFILE *is the* CROWN JEWEL *of* CONTEXT

How do colleges truly assess a student's academic choices? That's where the school profile comes in. While students stress over the number of APs they take, admissions officers take a broader view and assess rigor based on a school's course offerings.

Think of the school profile as the cheat sheet that helps colleges interpret a student's transcript. It helps colleges fairly evaluate an academic journey, whether the student's high school has dozens of AP classes, only a select few, or a full IB curriculum. Some smaller schools or those with limited budgets simply can't offer the same breadth of advanced courses or hire extra teachers to teach them, and that's fine. Without the school profile, admissions officers would be left guessing and comparing apples to oranges. Even worse, they might mistake a student's choices for a lack of ambition rather than a reflection of what was available.

One of our students attended a large, competitive public high school in New Jersey where over fifteen AP classes were offered, starting as early as ninth grade. She took only four. Another student attended a tiny high school in rural Connecticut with just twelve kids in his entire grade and only three AP courses total. He took all three.

On paper (okay, on the computer screen), both students had four or fewer APs. But context matters. A lot. Colleges saw those numbers through the lens of each school's offerings. Without that lens, it's like comparing sushi to Chinese takeout: completely different menus.

If you're curious, most schools post their profile online (check under "School Counseling" or "College Office"). If yours doesn't, ask the counselor for a copy.

WHEN A 3.87 ISN'T QUITE AS IMPRESSIVE AS IT SOUNDS

"Well, Sydney has at 3.87654321!" a mom might proudly declare. But please wait a minute, Sydney's mom.

Most high schools calculate a GPA by including grades from the core classes English, history, science, math, foreign language and non-core/elective classes like art, gym, music and that one semester of criminal justice. While there is certainly value in high school electives and non-core required classes, colleges pay more attention to performance in the core subjects when reviewing an applicant's transcript. Many colleges use their own system to recalibrate the GPA to include only those core academic courses. Others simply weigh them more heavily in the review process. Either way, a high GPA that's boosted by easier electives doesn't always carry the weight parents think (by the way, the eighth decimal point won't tip the scales in Sydney's favor).

Adding to the tension over grades? Many high schools have implemented rolling grade books, which give students and parents access to the student's weekly (or even daily) quizzes and assignments. Checking these grades daily is like checking social media "likes" every five minutes; it's stressful and not productive.

This is why a simple glance at the GPA doesn't reveal as much as examining each line on the transcript. Think of the transcript as a story, one that hopefully reveals consistency, resilience, and growth. It shows whether a student has stretched beyond their limits or played it safe, whether they've maintained high performance across all subjects, or sparkled in a select few.

The numerical GPA? It's just one chapter in that story, not the whole plot.

A FEW REAL-LIFE STORIES

Take Tommy, for example. His leadership on and off the basketball court made him a natural mentor for younger kids. He lived for basketball, whether he was running drills with his team, coaching younger players, or daydreaming about his next game. But between practices, tournaments, and watching highlight reels, his grades in ninth and tenth grade took a nosedive.

Maybe his parents tried a classic negotiation: "Bring those B's up, and we'll talk about that extra screen time." Or perhaps they went with a heartfelt plea: "We just want you to have options for college, that's all!" Whatever the turning point, something fell into place. Tommy started spending more time on his schoolwork, and his grades climbed during junior and senior year.

Admissions officers love to see this kind of upward trajectory, because it signals maturity, follow-through, and a student who's finally found his footing—not just on the court.

That growth, however, needs to stick. A few strong semesters followed by another dip in grades? That's not a trend; that's a roller coaster. While a sudden drop might be fun on a ride at Six Flags, colleges are looking for a steadier climb that reflects sustained academic progress day in and day out.

SHOT OF SANITY

As a parent, it's easy to get caught up in the numbers. But academic growth isn't just about better grades. It's about helping your child discover where they thrive, what truly interests them, and how they respond when things get challenging.

Take Alan: a compassionate student, he always pictured himself going into journalism. He enjoyed writing and staying on top of current events. But when his father was seriously injured in a car accident, everything changed. Watching the incredible work of his dad's physical therapists, Alan realized his future wasn't in writing, but in helping people move and heal.

That turning point showed up on his transcript. For the next two years, he loaded up on AP Biology, AP Human Anatomy, and AP Psychology. He began shaping his activities around physical therapy, too. His courses told a clear story of growth and direction.

This paid off. Alan was admitted to the University of Michigan's School of Kinesiology, ready to keep exploring how science and compassion intersect.

Meanwhile, Molly was a natural storyteller with a deep love for literature and history. But science was never quite her thing. Her transcript reflected that; it was full of A's in English and history, but science dragged down her GPA like cement shoes. In hindsight, Molly probably would have been better off by challenging herself where it counted most and easing up in areas that didn't come as naturally. Her parents had their hearts set on Northwestern for her, but Molly's record told a different story. She was a student who came alive when learning by doing, not memorizing formulas. Eventually, she landed at Northeastern University, where the focus on hands-on learning and co-ops fit her beautifully. She's now thriving in a communications program that blends storytelling and media, a reminder that the right match matters far more than the reach.

If your child realizes that stepping down a level or changing direction helps them flourish, that's not a setback. Colleges value this self-awareness just as much as raw talent.

WEIGHTED GRADES ARE DIFFERENT PIZZAS

Here's where things get murky. With approximately 24,000 public high schools across the U.S., there's no universal grading system.[15] This means transcripts can look drastically different from one school to the next. Some high schools use weighted GPAs, while others don't. Some label courses clearly as Honors or AP, while others list them as generic numbers, leaving it unclear what level of rigor a student took on.

To complicate things further, not all schools even offer AP or Honors classes, and what's considered a challenging course load at one school might look very different at another. Seasoned admissions officers know this and take the high school's profile into account when reviewing applications. But for students and parents, it can be frustrating to decipher how rigor is measured in the college admissions process.

A college dean at Scarsdale High advised my friend's daughter to take Honors Calculus instead of Advanced Topics (AT) Calculus. Scarsdale, known for its exceptional academics, doesn't offer AP courses. Instead, its most rigorous classes are labeled AT (Advanced Topics), designed to challenge students with college-level material in a way that prioritizes true understanding over test preparation. Colleges familiar with Scarsdale's curriculum recognize the depth of these courses, thanks in part to the school profile, which ensures admissions officers understand the level of rigor available to students. This student was reassured by her counselor that having a solid foundation in Calculus was more important than simply enrolling in the highest-level course.

Even with context, grading systems vary so widely that the numbers can tell very different stories. In some schools, advanced courses like Honors, AP, or IB classes get extra weight in GPA calculations. For instance, an A in an AP course might be worth 5.0 instead of the standard 4.0, reflecting the tougher coursework. This rewards the students who are taking more rigorous classes, which can boost their GPA and class rank. Others stretch the 4.0 to a 15-point scale, while some stick to letter grades, or a 1-100 system. Because why make this simple?

Another important fact: not only do most colleges not take the GPA on the transcript at face value, but many colleges recalculate the students' GPAs according to their

15 National Center for Education Statistics (NCES), "Fast Facts: Public Secondary and High Schools," 2021, https://nces. ed.gov/fastfacts/display.asp?id=84

own formula. Some eliminate the weighting so they can compare all applicants on an even playing field. Others stick to evaluating core academic courses, ignoring any extra points from gym or electives. It's like comparing two different slices of pizza from Greenwich Village in NYC: both are great, but the crusts don't taste the same.

THE CHALLENGE OF CLASS RANK

When I attended J.P. Stevens High School, a big, diverse public school in Edison, NJ, college pressure was very real, especially in the competitive classes.

Four-year college, two-year college, and vocational school were all respected paths, but for many, Rutgers University was the natural choice, an excellent in-state option just fifteen minutes down Route 1.

Then, there was class rank to consider.

Starting in tenth grade, we received our ranking each quarter, delivered in a sealed envelope, like it contained top-secret medical results. You'd sit there in home-room, heart pounding, debating whether to open it immediately, or wait until no one was watching. Would it be good news? Bad? A life-altering catastrophe?

Your rank fluctuated based on course rigor, with weighted grades for Honors and AP classes. By senior year, the pressure felt off the charts—at least, for me.

Thankfully, in recent years, the practice of ranking students has been on the decline. According to the National Association for College Admission Counseling (NACAC), over 50% of high schools no longer include class rank on transcripts.

This shift reflects an important truth: a single number doesn't define a student's potential or tell their whole story. Finally. Progress.

These days, fewer kids are defined by a number in a sealed envelope, and that's progress worth raising a glass to.

MAP OUT THEIR HIGH SCHOOL PATH

It's smart for your child to plan their four years of classes strategically, but remind them to stay flexible. Interests evolve, and sometimes that Honors Physics class that sounded great on paper really isn't.

Having a preliminary roadmap helps kids stay on track and ensures they're ready for advanced courses when the time comes. Equally important? Electives. These aren't just "filler" classes: they're opportunities to explore real interests, veer off the usual path, and add a little surprise to a student's academic story. Encourage your child to take them as seriously as the core subjects because you never know when that random photography class or creative writing workshop will turn into something bigger.

One of our students signed up for forensic science on a whim. She was so captivated that she spent the following summer diving deeper into the field, eventually volunteering with her local police department. She went on to study criminal justice at the University of Delaware and later applied to law school.

Another student took AP Psychology because it was the only class that fit her schedule. Within weeks, she loved learning how children think and behave. During *Senior Options*, a six-week internship program offered at her high school, she conducted research for a child psychologist and discovered this was the kind of work she wanted to pursue. She went on to study psychology at Emory University and is now earning her PsyD.

Then there was the student who took Latin purely to boost his SAT vocabulary. We laughed, but he ended up falling in love with the language and the stories behind it. He applied to a competitive summer program in Italy, where he studied Roman history and culture up close and later majored in classics at Haverford.

Stories like these are wonderful reminders that electives can open unexpected doors. But while students explore, they also need to stay strong in the academic fundamentals that colleges care most about.

A few key guidelines:

- **Science matters.** Ideally, students should take all three core lab sciences—Biology, Chemistry, and Physics—at some point in high school. If their school offers APs, it's perfectly fine to take AP Bio, AP Chem, or AP Physics instead of two or all three. What's essential is covering all three bases.

- **Calculus is (still) king.** For reasons beyond human understanding, many colleges continue to see calculus as a marker of academic strength. It doesn't have to be AP or even honors-level, but if a student can get there by senior year, it can give their application a nice boost. (Full disclosure: I hated calculus and still have the occasional nightmare where I'm supposed to be taking the AP exam, but I'm completely lost in the hallways and absolutely panicked.)

- **Stick with a language (but don't make them suffer).** Completing four years of the same foreign language in high school is ideal for admissions. Middle school language may place a student into a higher level, but colleges like to see four years of continued study once high school begins. However, if Spanish has your kid yelling *¡Ay, caramba!* or French feels more *merde* than magnifique, it's okay for them to shift gears.

GRADES, GOALS, AND KEEPING YOUR COOL

Above all, the goal is balance. Push where it matters, explore where there's genuine interest, and leave a little wiggle room to change course if needed. A schedule like that shows colleges your kid is both serious about learning but hasn't lost their curiosity. Or their sanity.

The transcript should reflect their best work. That means picking courses that match their strengths and interests, where they can stay engaged, challenge themselves appropriately, and earn the strongest grades they can without burning out. Getting into college is a marathon, not a sprint.

So, the next time your child is tempted to calculate their GPA down to the eighth decimal point or spiral over that B+ in Honors Spanish, help them remember the bigger picture. A transcript should show growth, highlight their potential, and prove that they can push themselves without completely losing it.

In the long run, high school (and yes, even college) is just one chapter.

CHAPTER 6

WHAT YOU DO AFTER 3 O'CLOCK:
why extracurriculars matter

When one of our students, Rohan, launched the Indian Culture Club at his high school, he thought a few friends might show up and learn a little about Diwali and Holi. He asked his mom to make samosas for twelve students. But those twelve told twelve more, and so on...and so on. Three weeks later, fifty kids showed up, each hungry and curious. Rohan's mom suddenly had a part-time job frying samosas, and the club was cooking (literally). By spring, they'd helped raise money for the rural school where he'd volunteered the previous summer, and soon, the students were hosting their own culinary nights.

Not bad for an idea that started with twelve samosas and a little initiative.

Dr. Seuss wisely said, "You'll never get bored when you try something new. There's really no limit to what you can do." He probably wasn't picturing high school students air frying samosas, but the message still fits: curiosity often leads to wonderful surprises.

Extracurricular activities are where the magic often begins in high school. They're not about padding a resume. They're where your child can try new things and figure out where they want to spend their energy. Sometimes they'll stumble into something they love; other times, they'll discover what's not for them. Both lessons matter. While extracurriculars have always factored into the college process, the focus has evolved. It's less about quantity and more about quality.

WHAT COLLEGES REALLY SEE

When so many students have similar grades, test scores, and course rigor, activities have become the real differentiator. They show character. They reveal what excites a student and what matters to them. Colleges are asking "Who is this student beyond the numbers? How will they add value to our community? What kind of roommate will they be? What will their peers learn from them?"

FROM BUFFETS AT THE SIZZLER TO A CHEF'S TASTING MENU

Once upon a time, admissions officers wanted "expert dabblers." These were the kids who could juggle band practice, mock trial, Hands Across America events, and sports practice, all while making it home in time to watch *Miami Vice*. Today? Admissions offices are trying to build a well-rounded class at their college by seeking "angular" students who go deeper into two to three areas of interest. Bottom line: trying to be everything to everyone doesn't work anymore.

Whether you applied to college fifteen years ago, thirty years ago, or (a-hem) longer, you probably remember the words "well-rounded" bouncing around the guidance counseling office like a colorful beach ball. Back then, college admissions folks wanted students who were sort of like the perfect plate at the Sizzler's buffet: a little salad, some rib-eye steak, a scoop of Jell-O, and maybe even a slice of pizza.

I still laugh when I think of my own Sizzler buffet resume from high school. I tried everything, not because of college expectations, but because I wholeheartedly wanted to explore. I was a band geek: piano in jazz band, clarinet in concert band, and xylophone in our 140-person marching band, because I couldn't walk and play clarinet without crashing into a trombonist (thank you, Mr. DeNicola, the most wonderful band teacher, for believing in my musical skills but recognizing my marching limits). Even my older brother would pause his daily sibling torment to practice his trumpet alongside me while I played piano. We still make time to play together today, thankfully, minus the sibling squabbles.

Musical theater was also my thing; my favorite was *Anything Goes*, where I fully embraced my inner diva as Reno Sweeney. I stayed busy in other ways, too, from leading French Club (mostly for the croissants) to participating in Model UN, where our team traveled all the way to the international conference at The Hague to proudly represent...*drum roll, please*...Guinea. I will also never forget those late-night study marathons fueled by trips for coffee to the local Dunkin' Donuts. Shout-out to my mom, who chauffeured me at 11 p.m. in her nightgown because New Jersey doesn't give teens licenses until they're seventeen.

While admissions officers have always had their eyes on national debate champions and teenagers winning the Regeneron Science Talent Search awards, back then, they were looking for well-rounded students who could plug into campus life in a million ways, like joining the orchestra, writing for the college paper, and still showing up at 8 a.m. to give tours to prospective students. My mile-long resume back then checked every box.

WELCOME TO 2025: DEPTH OVER BREADTH

Flash forward to today, and my Sizzler buffet approach would likely get a polite "thanks, but no thanks" from selective schools. At top-tier colleges—think Ivy League, Stanford, MIT, Duke, Northwestern, and their equivalents—admissions officers aren't looking for students who dabble in everything. They're hungry for something more focused, more distinctive. Think less "all-you-can-eat buffet," and more "chef's tasting menu."

If I were applying today, I'd have to double down on one, two, or three activities. Maybe I'd channel everything into music and compose more than the four songs I recorded on my cassette tape recorder. Remember those ancient devices? Perhaps I'd lean more into theater, producing a student-written play. The key now is building a narrative that shows initiative and impact. Not a laundry list.

HELPING KIDS TAP INTO THEIR INTERESTS

Sometimes, it's helpful to find that "signature dish" early, but kids shouldn't feel like they're being forced into a hobby when they're fourteen. Push too hard, and that flicker of excitement can fizzle.

Whether they stick with something or continue experimenting, what matters most is that they feel supported while figuring out what really lights them up.

The goal isn't to create the next Ben Platt or Ariana Grande; it's to let their interests develop naturally.

We always remind our students that the smoothest college admissions experiences come to those who've spent high school paying attention to what excites them and why. By the time they apply, they have a real story to tell about who they are and what they'll bring to campus.

Freshman year is the ideal time to test the waters. Encourage your child to dip their toes into the smorgasbord of activities, inside or outside of school. The goal? To find the thing they won't shut up about at the dinner table or on the bus ride home. Have them wander through the club fair. Maybe they'll check out Model UN, join Speech & Debate, or sign up for Yearbook. Interested in coding? There's a robotics team. Love music? They can audition for the school play even if their only prior acting experience involves dramatically faking an illness to skip religious school. Some activities will stick, some won't, and that's all part of the fun.

FINDING FOCUS: QUALITY OVER QUANTITY

Sometimes, students spread themselves a little too thin, but that can be a normal part of the process. Nancy and I recently met Amara, an earnest eleventh grader from a strong public school in Westchester County, New York. Her activity list was three pages long, packed with performing arts, science research, chess championships, Youth Court volunteering, and a summer internship in venture capital. Impressive? Sure. Cohesive? Not so much. It felt like that random Sizzler buffet instead of a list of special entrees.

"Who are you, and what do you want to be?" I asked her in my best college counselor-therapist voice.

She laughed, but the truth was, her list was exhausting.

I asked the kinds of questions that usually help cut through the noise:

- "Which activity makes you lose track of time?"
- "What day of the week do you look forward to the most and why? Do you have a club or an activity that meets on that day?"
- "If you could do anything on a Saturday (no judgment), what would it be and why?"

Parents usually watch their child's face light up, and just listening to their child's answers is a game changer.

After an hour of candid discussion and brainstorming, we helped her zero in on her love of chess and a budding interest in business. By the time we ended our session, she had an exciting plan to launch a chess workshop series for kids. It became more than teaching strategy; it was an opportunity to gain real-world experience running a business. She couldn't wait to tackle pricing and figure out a marketing plan. Picture the overzealous parents in Westchester County, New York lining up to have their kids master chess. She finally got it: less is more. Thankfully, her parents did, too.

When I explained that colleges weren't looking for the longest list but the most authentic one, her parents admitted that part of the reason she'd done so much was because of them. They'd been listening nonstop to what everyone else's kids were doing, from coding camps to field hockey travel teams. They didn't want her to fall behind.

The Sizzler buffet can be tempting when everyone around you is piling everything onto their plates. But the students who stand out are the ones who pick a few dishes, savor them, and share them with others.

PROGRESSIVE INVOLVEMENT

Once your child finds something that lights them up, your job is to encourage them to keep at it. Colleges notice when students show follow-through and growth. They love seeing how a kid goes from a curious freshman to the one running the show.

Here's how that can evolve:

- **Yearbook Staff:** A student might start as a staff writer in ninth grade, become a section editor in tenth, take on managing editor responsibilities in eleventh, and, by senior year, lead as Editor-in-Chief.
- **Robotics Club:** They could begin as a builder in ninth grade, design the robot in tenth, lead a project team in eleventh, and in twelfth grade, become captain of the team while securing sponsorships. Some students also mentor younger kids or students from under-resourced schools.
- **Athletics:** Progression might look like moving from JV to varsity, growing into a team leader, and even organizing a charity game to fund equipment for underserved schools.
- **Community Service:** They could start as a volunteer with Habitat for Humanity as a freshman, lead supply drives in tenth grade, and by senior year, spearhead large-scale projects as chapter president.
- **Business:** A student might join DECA in ninth grade to learn the ropes of competition, then launch a small baking business sophomore year to test their marketing skills. By junior year, they're working at a local bakery, moving up from frosting cupcakes to handling customer orders: real-world experience that shows initiative and probably smells amazing, too.

- **Arts:** Maybe they begin in the ensemble of the school musical, work their way up to larger roles each year, and branch out into community theater. By senior year, they're running a mini-backyard theater workshop for younger kids and helping them perform in front of family and friends.

Colleges don't expect students to do everything; they want to see dedication, growth, and creativity. It's not about where they start—it's about how far they go.

THE IMPORTANCE OF SCHOOL INVOLVEMENT

Being part of the school community counts big time. If a violin prodigy never joins the school orchestra, admissions officers might raise an eyebrow. "Impressive talent but do they only play solo?" Colleges don't just want achievers; they want contributors. Joining a club, leading a team, even showing up for yearbook staff meetings all matter. It shows a student isn't simply building a resume: they're building a community.

SOME IDEAS FOR EXTRACURRICULARS

Not every activity has to be groundbreaking.

Most colleges want to see students doing something they care about. That can be performing in a school play, designing a logo for their school's teams, organizing coat drives in the thick of winter, or showing up every week to coach a Little League team.

If your child isn't really involved yet, that's fine. Some kids pour their energy into academics, others need downtime, and some are still figuring out what makes them tick. As long as they're curious and kind, they're doing fine.

Your child doesn't need to start a nonprofit, captain a team, or cure diabetes to impress anyone. For most colleges, steady involvement and real enthusiasm within an existing club, team, or job is more than enough. If your child hasn't found their thing yet? That's okay, too. It may take a little more time for something to click. When it does, it's fun to watch. Here's what that can look like in action.

We've worked with students who:

- Organized a living room concert featuring elementary school kids performing alongside them to raise money for cerebral palsy research.
- Developed a scheduling app to help students keep track of classes, clubs, and assignments. This became a hit with teachers, too.
- Created a sustainability campaign that began as an infatuation with butterflies and turned into a curriculum teaching elementary students about ecosystems.
- Launched a youth mentorship program after realizing they loved guiding

younger students through Model UN.

- Built a backyard summer karate camp that started as a fun way to pass the time during quarantine and turned into a multi-week adventure.

Traditional jobs or sports also carry weight if there's a deeper story behind them. The student who taught hockey at a local arena and then launched a free clinic for younger kids? That's leadership. The student who spent summers earning money serving pizza, and then used the experience to start a financial literacy blog for teens? That's initiative.

KIND OF CRAZY

WHEN PASSIONS COLLIDE

The best extracurriculars often come from combining two seemingly unrelated interests. My own daughter loved American Sign Language (ASL) and dance. During quarantine, she became fluent in ASL. (What else was there to do besides bake banana bread and watch Netflix?) Later, she found a summer job teaching dance to deaf campers at Gallaudet University. It was the perfect mix of what she loved, and it stood out to admissions because it was real and unmistakably her.

Another student we coached loved dogs, but his mom didn't think walking their family pet daily was college material. We disagreed. He always talked about starting his own business, so he began walking his neighbors' dogs, recruited friends, and turned it into a thriving enterprise. Within a few months, he'd saved over $1,000 (folded bills tucked into his beloved Yankees cap) and learned the basics of entrepreneurship. His story wasn't just about walking dogs. It was about initiative and problem-solving. He just needed someone to give him the green light.

If you can help your child connect their interests, no matter how random they seem, they'll end up with a story that's as personal as it gets and way more fun to tell.

A WORD ABOUT COMMUNITY SERVICE

Worried your kid hasn't done enough community service? You're not alone. Many kids (and parents) don't realize that there are more opportunities to give back beyond volunteering at soup kitchens or donating to clothing drives. It's not just about racking up the hours; it's about putting heart into something that feels personal.

The best community service grows out of a student's own interests and strengths. If your child loves knitting, encourage them to make warm scarves for a local shelter. If they love music, they could play for an audience that could use some joy, like for kids at an after-school community center, or residents in a nursing home. If advocacy excites them, maybe they organize a donation drive or speak on behalf of a cause that hits close to home, like a disease that has affected them or someone in their family. We love when there's a meaningful backstory behind a student's drive.

MAKING THE MOST OF SUMMERS

Summers are a golden opportunity for students to explore, experiment, and sleep past 6:30 a.m. Before ninth and tenth grade, when interests are still taking shape, the goal isn't to curate a perfect resume: it's to test things out. Maybe that means signing up for a week-long "Life as a Medical Student" program, where they scrub in and dissect a cadaver. Maybe they take a linguistics class online or enroll in the "History of Hip-Hop." Maybe they attempt a Python bootcamp and then realize unequivocally that they do not want anything to do with computer science. It's all part of the process.

A meaningful summer doesn't have to come with a big price tag. Sometimes, a good old-fashioned job can be every bit as rewarding. Maybe even more so. One of our students in the Bay Area, Charlie, was hired as a tennis instructor, teaching both small group and private lessons at the very academy where he once trained. On his drive home, he'd pass neighborhoods where many kids had little or no access to tennis; some had never even picked up a racket. That bothered him. He approached the Academy Director and helped launch an early-evening program for kids from those under-resourced areas. The following summer, he took it further, creating a competitive league so those young players could keep playing and believing they belonged on the court.

Another student, Harris, began volunteering at his town library in Colorado and loved watching the excitement on young kids' faces as they raced into the preschool section. Eager to share that joy more broadly, he organized a book drive to support libraries in underserved communities. His parents happily schlepped him around town collecting book donations. Soon, there were mounds of books stacked in his living room—much to his tidy parents' chagrin. Undeterred, Harris developed his own inventory system, proudly tracking every title. Later, he landed a job at a local bookstore to keep promoting literacy and a love of reading right in town.

There's something refreshingly real about a good old-fashioned summer job. Whether it's babysitting, lifeguarding, pumping gas, or ringing up sandwiches at the local deli, these experiences build confidence. Getting dressed for work (even in a slightly scratchy uniform with a name tag), showing up on time, and earning a paycheck? Great! A summer job teaches independence and how to tolerate customers and bosses who are less than delightful. Admissions officers see it the same way.

When I spoke with Gary Ross, Senior Vice President for Admission and Financial Aid at Colgate University, he put it plainly:

"So many families stress about finding the 'perfect' summer opportunity to add to a student's college application. Some companies profit from that worry with slick marketing that convinces families colleges want to see the programs they're selling. Don't fall for it. Instead, consider flipping burgers at the local McDonald's or a mom-and-pop diner, or stocking shelves at a neighborhood grocery store. As someone who reads thousands of applications each year, I'm always glad to see students accountable to a real boss, expected to show up on time, and held to real performance standards."

It's a helpful reminder that responsibility and showing up still count, often more than anything designed to impress.

Some families negotiate a compromise: one-part academic enrichment, one-part adventure. Maybe your kid takes an online finance course or interns at a start-up for a few weeks, then spends the rest of the summer hiking at a national park, gaming with friends, or roaming the mall in search of bubble tea and new sneakers. It doesn't have to be all work and no play. What matters more is balance and remembering they're still a kid.

If you're stressing about planning the perfect summer? Don't be. This isn't a resume contest. Growth can happen anywhere: in a lifeguard chair, behind the counter at the local ice cream shop, or figuring out the train schedule for their first summer commute into a nearby city.

By the summer before twelfth grade, it's helpful to start tying things together. If business is on their radar, taking an investment or marketing course or gaining some practical experience through a job or starting a small business could be a smart move. Future scientists might want to pursue research opportunities that span multiple summers, culminating in a project they can showcase before senior year. The most important thing? Don't let your kid over-orchestrate summers as if they're a Broadway production. The goal is to encourage their curiosity, allow for some misses, and help them find experiences that make them want to get out of bed in the morning, and maybe even feel, dare we say, a little grown-up.

THE BIG PICTURE

Whether your child is starting something new, mixing unexpected interests, or sticking with a long-time favorite, their activities should feel like them. Colleges want to see what they've done and why it matters to them. Encourage your child to take the lead and leave their mark. If they need reassurance, remind them that every generation figures it out in their own way. Back in the '80s, we didn't need a meticulously crafted resume to succeed. We just needed big hair, a packed extracurricular schedule, and a little luck not to crash into the trombones.

CHAPTER 7

SOS *for* PARENTS *who* NEED *a* LITTLE BACK-UP

The dogs were barking. Someone was yelling for clean socks. A few doors slammed in the background. It was the first week in October. I had picked up the phone only seconds earlier, but I already knew this wasn't going to be a quick call.

"I have triplets!" the mom announced, out of breath. "They're seniors. None of them have started their essays. We don't even have a college list. Please! Can you help?"

When Nancy and I arrived two days later, the house told the story before she did. There was a friendly kind of chaos, the kind that comes from a family living a very full life. Notebooks and papers were stacked on the kitchen table, and two dogs greeted us like we were long-lost relatives.

The triplets were kind, funny, and bright. But they, too, were visibly overwhelmed.

Within minutes, Nancy and I had turned their home into a college-admissions relay race. One of us sat with a triplet to build a college list while the other began brainstorming essay topics. The third was tasked with researching schools, filling out his activity list, and refilling everyone's drinks (non-alcoholic, of course). Three hours later, we'd pulled off a small miracle: three paths forward, two happy dogs, and one calmer mom.

Let's just say, we were glad she didn't try to manage the process solo.

IT'S OKAY TO ASK FOR HELP

Parents who can juggle back-to-back Zoom meetings and carpool chaos without blinking mysteriously lose all composure once the applications start flying.

This process can undo even the calmest among us. That's why having a little help matters.

Many families find that having someone guide the process helps keep things calm and organized. Others prefer to tackle it on their own, and with a clear plan, that can absolutely work, too. This book is here for both.

If you are already working with an advisor, consider this book as a bonus resource. After all, not every advisor has the same strategies or approach (and definitely not the same mantra about eating Wheat Thins to manage the stress).

What's undeniable is that this process—with its web of deadlines, essays, test scores, course choices, summer plans, financial aid forms, and a continually changing admissions climate (phew!)—can humble even the most loving, competent, color-coded-spreadsheet-carrying parents.

Over the years, I've had parents approach me at the car wash, in dressing rooms (hello, Bloomingdale's), and yes, even in airport security lines. My husband and kids once had to intervene mid-conversation so we wouldn't miss our flight.

One mom was convinced her eleven-year-old son was the next Bill Gates due to his love of selling lemonade on their street corner. I still think about that kid sometimes and wonder if he ever expanded into a neighborhood-wide delivery service or a special line of organic juices.

Then there was an old friend from sleepaway camp who resurfaced years later, not to reminisce about Color War, but to gush about her son, a gifted orator already winning school speech contests and starring as Aladdin...in fourth grade. She wanted to discuss his best path toward college. Yup.

Meanwhile, in Scarsdale cocktail party circles—where the competition typically starts before kindergarten—the tone about my work fluctuated from dismissive to desperate. Some parents prided themselves on not needing help. "Oh, I'd never hire a private college advisor. Such a waste of money. My kid is a strong writer. We can figure it out on our own."

Fast forward to September of her kid's senior year, when I picked up the phone to a different tone, "Beth, I'm sorry to bother you, but I'm drowning. Desperate. Can you *please* help?"

Calls like that are far more common than you'd think. By late summer, even the most methodical parents can start to come undone. Often, their coping mechanism is... overcompensation.

We once worked with a dad who ran his son's college process like he was competing in the Russian Olympics. He sent daily essay quotas and motivational emails to him (and to us) that could rival a halftime pep talk in the NBA playoffs.

By mid-August, he wanted Theo to write and submit all twelve college supplements (about thirty essays). We gently explained that essays get better with breathing room and that maybe he should spend some time at the local pool before senior year hit.

His son, believe it or not, took it all in stride. He was bright, easy-going, and determined. He admitted his dad treated homework, sports, meals, and family Monopoly night with a "training" plan. Eventually, Theo wrote a poignant essay about how he finally stood up to his dad and found his own voice.

Theo didn't need a coach like him or even us. He simply kept at it, steady and sure, until he got there. On his own terms.

Then, right when we need it most, a family shows up and reminds us that this process can be calm and even joyful.

This year, it was the parents of twin boys.

They were two of the kindest, most genuine kids we've ever worked with. The kind who email thank-you notes after every meeting. The kind who talk about their teachers, siblings, and their parents with warmth and respect. They're not straight-A superstars. But they're hard-working, leaders at school, and the kind of young men you'd want your own kids to be friends with (or maybe marry!).

Their parents didn't need us in the same way some families do. The boys could have handled the process perfectly fine on their own. But their mom wanted to preserve her sanity and make sure someone else was pushing them to stay organized. She trusted us and trusted her kids. Guess what? It worked beautifully.

HELP IS OUT THERE FOR EVERY PRICE

Most students in the U.S. don't have access to private advisors who offer personalized guidance. That's the reality. The good news? You don't need one to navigate this process successfully.

There's a common misconception that private college advisors are only for wealthy families or students chasing Ivy League dreams. Not true. A good advisor helps students from all backgrounds find schools that fit not just on paper, but in real life. But if hiring an advisor isn't in the financial cards, don't panic.

There are plenty of ways to get great guidance without spending a dime (except okay, maybe on this book).

- **School counselors:** Many high school counselors are incredible. They're knowledgeable, compassionate, and fully invested in helping your child find the right schools. They know your student, they understand your student's world, they know the admissions landscape, and they often work miracles under impossible time constraints. While they might be stretched thinner than the last smear of peanut butter in the Skippy jar, don't underestimate the insight they can offer, especially if you take the time to connect with them early and often (shout-out to the amazing Scarsdale High School Deans, Jennifer Morgan and Nancy Thompson, who guided all three of my kids with warmth and wisdom).
- **Online resources:** Websites like CollegeVine, Khan Academy, and the Common App's free essay guides can be incredibly helpful.
- **Community-based programs:** Organizations like QuestBridge, ScholarMatch, and CollegePoint offer free support for students from lower-income backgrounds. Many cities also have Community-Based Organizations (CBOs) that provide tutoring, test prep, and college advising at no cost. A little research into what's available locally or online can go a long way. Nancy and I have had the privilege of working closely with YPIE (Yonkers Partners in Education), an extraordinary local organization that supports students in Yonkers through every stage of the college process and beyond. From interview prep to essay coaching to long-term mentorship, YPIE is the kind of place that changes lives, and we're super proud to cheer these students on.
- **Pro bono advising:** Many private college counselors (including us) take on a small number of pro bono students each year. We also work with students who have extenuating circumstances that make paying for college or a private advisor feel out of reach. It never hurts to ask.

WHAT ETHICAL ADVISORS DO

Of course, even with these resources, applying to college can still feel like a full-time job, which is why some families choose to work with an advisor.

A great advisor isn't just an essay editor or a college list custodian. We're also part-therapist, part-project manager, and when necessary, part-Nag-in-Chief. For many parents, having someone else be "the reminder person" can take a huge weight off their shoulders.

We've worked with families in every emotional state: teens overwhelmed by the pressure, parents unsure how involved to be, and the occasional feud about whether the Common App essay should open with a quote or a joke (tensions definitely run high).

A great advisor helps your child make smarter choices about their mental health. That's because we guide them toward their real interests and help them stay true to themselves. We'll remind them that they are much more than a standardized test score or a number on a transcript. Our job is to help them find the places where they'll feel like they belong and find the kind of campus where they'll even look forward to Mondays.

There are plenty of advisors who take a tutoring-style approach. They meet with students weekly, in person or virtually, to micromanage every step of the process including researching schools, planning out extracurriculars, and writing and tweaking their essays alongside them. That works for some families.

But that's not our style.

We believe students should take ownership of the process. As a theater fan, I explain it this way: the kids are the ones on stage, telling their story. We're the ones behind the scenes, helping with the hair, the makeup, the lighting, the cues, and making sure they're ready when the spotlight hits.

That's pretty much how it should be.

KIND OF CRAZY

What ETHICAL ADVISORS DON'T DO

College advisors can't (and don't) "get your kid in" anywhere. That's not how this works. If an advisor tells you otherwise and claims to have special connections or insider pull at elite colleges, run the other way. Fast.

There's also a growing corner of the industry specializing in working with kids as early as eighth grade. They sell families on the idea that if a child follows a hyper-strategic, well-choreographed plan, it will lead straight to an acceptance letter from a name-brand college.

Some even promote $300,000 luxury admissions tours via private jet to visit the Ivies. If that doesn't scream privilege and pressure, I don't know what does.[16]

---

16 Ruthanne Terrero, "$300K Luxury College Admissions Tour Includes Private Jet, Ivy League Visits," *Luxury Travel Advisor*, July 23, 2025, https://www.luxurytraveladvisor.com/private-jets/300k-luxury-college-admissions-tour-includes-private-jet-ivy-league-visits.

I'll cut to the chase:

- No private advisor has special "insider" access to admissions decisions (yes, we've all seen how the *Varsity Blues* scandal story played out).

- At the most selective schools, admissions folks typically don't meet with private counselors to discuss individual students. They want the process to be entirely student-driven.

- Admissions offices are often staffed by talented, thoughtful people, but many are also young, starting out in their careers, and frequently moving on to new roles. Although we meet them during campus visits (which we do, often), it's hard to maintain a long-term relationship with any one rep. Within a few years, they've usually darted off to another college or another career entirely.

Bottom line: colleges want real students, not robotic applicants who spent four years chasing an admissions strategy instead of their actual interests. Remember, there is no one recipe that guarantees admission to a student's dream college.

How do you know which colleges will see your child for who they are and not just for how well they fit a formula?

That's where real, firsthand knowledge comes in.

Nancy and I have visited over 160 colleges. We love touring large universities, small liberal arts colleges, urban campuses, rural gems, and everything in between. When we visit, we explore the campus, student centers, and cafés, chatting with students about their experiences. If an admissions officer is available, we'll sit down to learn more about the school's unique programs and academic culture so we can better guide our students. We never rely exclusively on schools' websites or online guides. We go, we see, we ask questions (and yes, we eat somewhere on campus to check out the food).

We've walked on campuses from sunny California (Stanford) to northern Michigan (University of Michigan), down to southern Florida (University of Tampa and USF), and across the heart of the country, at schools like Oberlin, Denison, and the University of Cincinnati. Our students apply to a wide range of colleges—from those that specialize in learning differences, like Lynn University and Curry College, to the most selective universities in the country.

How can you possibly match a student to a school if you've never met the prospective match? Would you trust a real estate agent who hasn't set foot in the house she's recommending? Of course not. Yet every year, families pay thousands of dollars to "experts" who haven't visited many of the colleges they're discussing. Firsthand knowledge isn't everything, but it can make a real difference.

Here's what sets ethical advisors apart:

- We help students discover schools that are a genuine fit—not just the ones with the most recognizable names.
- We remind families that a "dream school" is any place where a student will feel supported, inspired, and able to grow (with over 4,000 colleges and universities in the U.S., there are more possibilities than most families realize).
- We encourage parents to take a step back so their child can engage with the process and maybe even enjoy parts of it, instead of fearing it.
- We believe students should lead this process and not be dragged through it by adults.

When the stress inevitably hits (and I promise you it will), it's the advisor who's there to keep the momentum going, reassure your child, inject some laughter, and deliver a little tough love when necessary. Instead of this process taking over your household like a second full-time job, you can get back to being the loving parent you know you are (at least 85% of the time) and leave the logistical headaches to us. Fun fact: I've played the piano most of my life, but I hired someone else to teach my kids. Less arguing for everyone.

FINDING THE RIGHT ADVISOR

We always encourage parents to interview multiple college advisors before committing to one. Just like with college, the connection must feel right. You wouldn't pick an orthopedic surgeon for a knee replacement without doing your research, right? Same goes for this process. Finding the right advisor is about more than credentials. It's about trust.

Start by doing your homework (yes, like your kid). Not all advisors are created equal. Some are ethical, experienced, knowledgeable, and are rooting for your kid. Others? Well, let's say they're better at marketing themselves than guiding students.

Finally, ask yourself the most important question:

Do you actually *like* this person?

This is someone who will be prodding, encouraging, and occasionally, offering a reality check. If their vibe is off, trust your gut and keep looking. It's about chemistry. If you wouldn't want to sit next to them in the bleachers at your kid's track meet, maybe they're not the right person to guide your family through this process.

Whether you work with an advisor or go it alone, the goal is the same: to find a college where your child can grow academically and socially, feel supported, and enjoy the experience. You don't need to map out every turn. It's key to stay present, take a few breaths when things get nutty, and remind yourself that nobody's getting an award for *Most Efficient College Process.*

When INTERVIEWING *an* ADVISOR, HERE'S WHAT *to* ASK:

- **"How do you help students build a balanced college list?"** If the answer is, "I specialize in getting kids into Ivy League schools," that might sound impressive, but it's not the right fit for every family. Make sure their approach aligns with your goals.

- **"How do you support students with essays?"** If they say, "I write them," that's your exit music.

- **"How involved should parents be?"** A great advisor won't encourage helicoptering or outsourcing the process to Mom and Dad.

- **"How many colleges have you personally visited?"** If an advisor relies only on websites and rankings, that's worth noting. Seeing a campus in person gives valuable insight into the student experience. There's no substitute for experiencing the energy and vibes in person.

- **"Will my child be working with the same person the entire time?"** Different firms handle this differently. Some assign one advisor for overall strategy and another for the writing process. Others keep everything with a single counselor. Neither model is inherently better. Families should know who their child will interact with and whether that setup works for them. What matters is that the guidance feels cohesive, and your student feels supported.

- **"Do you do your own editing?"** Some firms use outside or "ghost" editors. That might be fine, but you deserve to know how the process works before signing on.

Part Three

On the Road
(Literally and Figuratively)

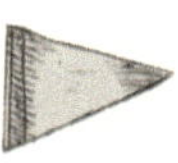

CHAPTER 8

KEEPING YOUR COOL *while* BUILDING *a* COLLEGE LIST

Before you can pack the car for campus tours or debate the perks of an urban environment versus a rural campus surrounded by cows, you need one non-negotiable thing: a college list. This is where the rubber meets the road, despite the sporadic bumps on the ride. I always tell parents that the college list is a "living, breathing" document, much like a teenager's mood swings or their always-in-flux Starbucks order. It will undoubtedly change. The list will evolve based on school visits, academic performance, and the occasional existential crisis about whether they want to pursue business, psychology, or suddenly become a classics major with a minor in astrophysics.

Building a realistic college list is part strategy, part negotiation, part art, and yes, part therapy. The goal isn't to create a list that will impress everyone in your book club. It's about finding places where your kid will be genuinely happy, in real life, on a Tuesday in November when it's raining cats and dogs and they have two papers due by 5:00 p.m. A well-balanced list provides options—real choices—so they aren't left with one lonely school acceptance that feels like their only choice.

Once the list is in good shape, the next step is figuring out how to send applications into the world: where to apply early, where to take a leap, and how to keep everyone (mostly) sane in the process. That's what I call the "launch."

UNDERSTANDING ADMISSIONS REALITIES (NO, THAT'S NOT A SAFETY)

Back in the stone ages, students had a few "reach" schools, a few "target" schools, and at least one "safety" where admission was practically guaranteed. That era is dead, buried, and unlikely to be resurrected any time soon.

The term "safety" has now been rebranded as "likely," which sounds friendly enough, except that by 2025, that concept is wobbly at best.

Thanks to yield protection (aka colleges trying to admit students who have the highest likelihood of enrolling), even schools that once accepted nearly every qualified student are playing hard to get.

Here's what that means:

- Perfect grades and test scores don't guarantee anything if the college thinks you're applying to the school as a backup.
- Schools track demonstrated interest: if you haven't visited or at least clicked on one of their emails, they may just ghost you.
- Students with 4.0 GPAs and top scores are being waitlisted or rejected at schools that used to welcome them.

This doesn't mean students should give up hope; it just means they need to be smart. Instead of fixating on old definitions of reach, target, and likely, the real question should be: "Where does my child have a strong chance of admission and a real shot at being happy?"

As Jay Jacobs, Vice Provost for Enrollment Management at the University of Vermont, reminded me:

"Building a balanced college list really needs to be the first, and probably the most important, step in the process. When that list is done, a student should genuinely feel they could be happy and comfortable on any of those campuses. Think about both academics and extracurricular life, and above all, be realistic—that's the hardest part for most students and families. If a list is packed with schools that admit fewer than 25 or 30 percent of applicants, there's no guarantee that any of them will say yes. A school that admits such a small slice of its applicant pool simply can't be considered a 'safety.'"

He's right. A realistic list doesn't dampen dreams. It gives students real choices and a little peace of mind in a process that can feel anything but peaceful.

EMOTIONAL ATTACHMENT VS. REALITY: TIMING MATTERS

It's so easy for students to fall in love with a school before they've done the hard work of figuring out whether it's a good fit academically, socially, or financially. Sometimes, well-meaning parents accidentally make this worse. "We're in town anyway, so let's go walk around the Princeton campus!" might seem harmless, but it may set many students up for heartbreak later.

Maya fell head-over-heels for USC, visited four times before junior year, decked herself out in Trojan merch, and practically memorized the "Fight Song." But when her SAT scores came in, they weren't exactly in USC's ballpark (a school's middle 50% SAT range is easy to find on its website or sites like BigFuture and Niche). You can imagine the tears that followed in our office that day.

Before engaging with us, Ethan's parents took him on a twenty-five-school college tour (yup, you read that right), hitting all the Ivies and their equivalents. By tour number eighteen, they were so exhausted they could barely remember which campus they were on. Crazily, they were convinced they were checking the right boxes.

Unfortunately, Ethan's GPA and test scores weren't anywhere near competitive for the schools on his list.

By the time they landed in our office, they had crisscrossed the country multiple times, spent a small fortune on hotels and flights, and still didn't have many viable options on his list. Together, we reworked Ethan's list based on his academic profile, and, yes, we sent them on yet another round of visits (but this time, to schools where he had a real shot). He ended up thriving at a small, welcoming liberal arts college in Pennsylvania. Later, his parents admitted they wished they had focused on fit and not fantasy.

Often, the issue isn't the number of schools on the list but the logic behind it that goes sideways.

Let's talk about the family of Charlotte, a bright aspiring scientist at a large STEM high school outside Washington, D.C. Her parents, both professional musicians, were convinced—based on virtual info sessions and deep internet dives—that their daughter would get more generous financial aid from a small liberal arts college in rural Pennsylvania than from an Ivy League university. We gently explained that wasn't necessarily true. Both offered strong aid programs, but the difference came down to endowment, size, institutional priorities, and the specifics of each family's financial picture. Still, her dad remained adamant that he'd unlocked a secret that others had missed. Of course, the best-intentioned parents can get swept up, hearing what they want to hear instead of what's true. When so much feels uncertain, a little wishful thinking can go a long way.

We see it all the time. Parents pick up half-truths from college tours, Facebook groups, or their cousin's son's roommate. *Oy veh!*[17]

---

[17] *Oy veh* is a Yiddish expression that roughly means "oh dear" or "here we go again." It's often expressed with a dramatic sigh of exasperation or disbelief.

Right when we think we've seen it all, another email lands in our inbox.

"Hi Beth & Nancy! Oliver is doing great. He now has an SAT score (1290) and is taking it again in December, hoping to get closer to 1500. He's also no longer interested in business. Now he's looking into engineering programs. We've started a list of schools and already visited a few: Duke, Northwestern, Michigan, and Tufts."

One small (okay, huge) issue: engineering is one of the toughest programs to get into. Anywhere. Oliver has strong grades, but with a 1290 SAT, the schools they visited are *serious* reaches. The odds of his SAT score increasing 200 points are slim. The real kicker? His mom planned the whole tour before checking in with us. We see this often. Families mean well but often get ahead of the data. Our job is to keep dreams and reality in the same time zone.

TIMING YOUR COLLEGE VISITS

Hold off on visiting schools that might be long shots for everyone until you have a clearer understanding of where your child stands academically, usually by mid-junior year. Before then, it's a guessing game. Otherwise, it's like planning your dream vacation before checking if your passport has expired.

If Harvard is on your child's list? Do. Not. Start. With. Harvard.

If your kid has only a remote shot, kicking off college tours with the most selective school in the country is like trying on the most expensive wedding dress first. After that? Everything else might pale in comparison.

Start with colleges that are realistic based on your child's current profile. Let your student build confidence in the process before walking onto a campus where admissions rates hover around the single digits.

The goal isn't to label schools as reaches or safeties. It's to build a balanced list of places that feel right, stretch your kid just enough, and still offer strong odds of success.

The last thing you want is for every other school to feel like a consolation prize.

Common College List Mistakes: HELPFUL *vs* HIJACKING

Many of these instincts come from a good place. The issue isn't caring or wanting to protect your child. It's when those instincts crowd out your student's voice, curiosity, or growth.

Parents, we love you. However, we've seen some interesting behaviors over the years. Here are some warning signs:

THE SPREADSHEET PARENT A parent who emails a color-coded Excel file with acceptance rates, test scores, a probability graph, and "thoughts" (spoiler: they're the parent's, not the kid's), but has no clue if their child actually *likes* these schools.

THE PRESTIGE CHASER A parent who builds a list solely based on the top twenty and considers any school outside of it as "less than."

THE NOSTALGIC PARENT A parent who wants their child to attend their alma mater. Minor details like their kid not being qualified or the school being a terrible fit don't matter.

THE "WHATEVER THEY SAY GOES" PARENT A parent who wants to be hands-off and "supportive," so they let their teen call every shot. Not always the best approach when a kid needs a reality check.

THE OVERLY PROTECTIVE PARENT A parent who removes co-ed campuses or schools known for a big party scene. Wanting a campus that feels safe or aligns with family values or religion is completely valid. The trouble comes when fear, rather than fit, drives the entire list.

THE VALUES-FOCUSED PARENT A newer type we're seeing. These parents care deeply about the social and political climate on campus. Some avoid schools in states with restrictive reproductive rights or conservative policies; others steer clear of campuses where their child's faith or political views might feel unwelcome. These concerns are real and valid. The key is finding a place that reflects your family's values while still keeping space for your student to encounter new ideas and perspectives.

THE TRAILING PARENT A parent who can't quite let go—even after move-in day. Some rent apartments near campus, tag along on study-abroad programs, or call professors to "clarify" grades. It all comes from love (I think), but there's a fine line between being supportive and Velcro-ing yourself to your child. As *The Atlantic* recently noted, we're now in the age of the "trailing parent."[18]

18 Russell Shaw, "When Helicopter Parents Touch Down—At College," *The Atlantic*, November 2, 2025, https://www.theatlantic.com/family/archive/2025/11/trailing-parents-college-helicopter/681999/

BUILDING A COLLEGE LIST THAT ACTUALLY WORKS

It's easy to get swept up in the idea that there's one perfect college out there. But the best college lists aren't built for bragging rights. They're built for your kid.

Scarsdale High School Principal Kenneth Bonamo has watched this scenario unfold with hundreds of families and offered this perspective during a recent conversation with parents of juniors:

"The pressure on our students, as always, is intense, but the most important thing to remember is that most of them thrive regardless of the school they attend. Whatever we can do to help minimize the fixation on a small list of schools will do a world of good for countless students."

We couldn't agree more.

Rankings might seem useful, but they're often based on things like faculty salaries, endowments, alumni-giving rates, or how many students study abroad. None of that tells you whether your child will feel comfortable, motivated, or seen on that campus. We always encourage families to look beyond the numbers and pay attention to what feels like a true match.

Forget rankings and acceptance rates for a minute. Focus on who your child is and where they'll thrive. As Anne Brewer, Senior Associate Director of Admissions at Dickinson College, told me:

"After more than a decade in admissions, I've seen the landscape shift in ways no one could have predicted. It's more complex and competitive every year, but one thing hasn't changed: students who begin with self-reflection, who understand their values, imagine their ideal learning environment, and seek a community that supports them, are the ones who find the right fit. The college process is about more than getting in. It's about discovering where you can grow, contribute, and thrive—and using your college years to become an engaged learner and an impactful member of the world beyond campus."

She couldn't have said it better. The best college lists grow from the inside out, not from the rankings down. Forget the *U.S. News* list. Aim for the "my kid really loves it here" list. Families who approach the process that way often end up discovering schools they might never have considered before.

Education writer Jeff Selingo makes a similar point in his book *Dream School*. Students do best when they choose colleges that fit who they are and what they want to learn, rather than chasing the most recognizable names.

In recent years, we've noticed a new trend. More students from New Jersey, New York, and Massachusetts are expanding their search to seriously consider schools they might not have looked at five years ago, especially in the South. The University of Alabama, Clemson, the University of Georgia, the University of South Carolina, and Auburn University have all seen an uptick in visitors from the Northeast. Once families experience these campuses in person, many walk away wondering why they weren't on everyone's list from the beginning.

We visited Auburn on a recent trip to Alabama and were struck by the beauty of the campus, the friendliness of the students, and the contagious school spirit. Auburn consistently ranks in the top ten for happiest students, as the welcoming tour guides were eager to let us know. Five different students stopped to point us in the direction of the student center. We loved visiting Toomer's Corner, where students "roll" the trees with toilet paper after big wins. Although we were there as visitors for a day, we felt right at home.

We spoke with Grace Morris, an admissions advisor at Auburn, who's seen this trend firsthand. "We're seeing more students from the Northeast who are looking for something different," she told us. "They want warmer weather, a strong sense of community, and a little Southern hospitality. Auburn offers all of that, along with academic strength and a campus culture that makes people feel like they belong."

Students are realizing that spending four years in an environment different from what they've always known can be refreshing and not intimidating. Auburn and its peer schools are showing up on more college lists for a reason.

We've worked with many families who began with the usual list (what Nancy and I jokingly call "the hit parade")—think Penn, Cornell, Northwestern, Michigan, Tulane, Tufts, Syracuse, Vanderbilt, WashU, NYU, Wisconsin, and Boston University—only to watch their child show real excitement on a completely different kind of campus. One student fell in love with a school because, in her words, "everyone just seemed kind." Wow. Imagine a student being drawn to a community where kindness mattered. That speaks volumes about her character.

By winter or spring of junior year, it helps to start narrowing in on what really matters. Here's what we recommend focusing on:

1. SIZE, LOCATION, AND WEATHER

Before you dive into stats and spreadsheets, zoom out and envision the life your child wants to wake up to every morning.

- Does your child thrive in small, discussion-based classes where professors know their name? Or are they picturing themselves tailgating next to a 100,000-person stadium football game and painting their face in their school's colors?
- Student body size? 1,500 students? 5,000? 50,000?
- Urban, suburban, or rural? Do they want the energy of a city, or the charm of a traditional campus bubble?

- Weather? Some kids *think* they can handle Northeastern winters until they're trudging to class in a blizzard and vowing to move back home the second after they march through graduation.

2. ACADEMICS & MAJORS

A school can be Instagram-perfect, but if it doesn't offer what your student needs, it's probably not the right fit.

- Does the school have your child's major? You'd be surprised how often families fall in love with a college, only to realize it doesn't offer what their kid wants to study. No business major? No nursing track? No thanks.

- Are general education (Gen Ed) requirements flexible, or set in stone? Some students love academic freedom (Brown, Rochester, and Hamilton), while others prefer a structured curriculum (Columbia and Chicago, we're looking at you!). Make sure the academic setup matches how your child learns best.

- How easy is it to switch majors? Surveys show that a huge number of students do. One Forbes Advisor poll in 2024 noted that 36% of students change their major at least once, while others estimate it's as high as 80%.

- What's the advising and support system like? Will your child get real guidance, or will they be left navigating course registration as if they're tributes in *The Hunger Games*?

3. CREDITS, COURSE ACCESS, AND GRADUATION REALITY CHECKS

It's not just about what a college offers on paper. It's about how things work once your child is there.

- **AP and IB Credit:** Some schools give generous credit, letting students place out of introductory courses or jump ahead. Others take a less generous approach and treat those scores like nice extras, not real currency. If your child is hoping their hard work in high school will buy them some breathing room, please check each college's policy.

- **Course Access:** Your child might be excited about classes like "The Psychology of Decision-Making" or "Taylor Swift and the Politics of Pop Culture,"[19] but the big question is whether they can register for the classes they need to graduate. At some schools, it's easy. At others, students wake up at dawn, juggle multiple devices, and frantically refresh their screens like they're tracking a delayed flight on Thanksgiving weekend.

---

19 Princeton University offers "The Psychology of Decision Making and Judgment" (PSY 260), and Binghamton University offers "Pop Culture (Taylor's Version)," a course focused on Taylor Swift's influence in music and celebrity culture.

Before committing, explore the college's website. Look under "Academics," "Advising," or "Registrar" for details about course registration and access. Many schools also post course catalogs online, which can show how quickly classes fill or whether they're restricted to certain majors. For the inside scoop, ask current students. They'll tell you whether getting into that Taylor Swift seminar is a breeze or a bust.

- **Graduating in Four Years:** You would think this is the norm but not always. Look at each school's four-year graduation rate and what it takes to stay on track. Delays can come from scheduling snafus and limited course availability. There's nothing like waiting three semesters before getting into "Intro to Bio." Sigh.

4. FINANCIAL FIT

Prestige is cool, but so is being able to afford dinner.

- Does the school meet full demonstrated need?
- Do they offer merit scholarships?
- Would attending require selling a kidney? (Kidding. Mostly.)

Before falling madly in love with a school or banishing it based on its price, it's worth checking out the financial aid section of each college's website. Most have a Net Price Calculator that gives families a ballpark estimate of what they might have to pay after aid and scholarships *(see Chapter 14 for a closer look at how to make college affordable)*.

5. SOCIAL SCENE & EXTRACURRICULARS

At this point, you're still in the early research phase, whether that's poking around online or walking on a real campus. The goal is to get a feel for what clicks and what doesn't.

- Do students stick around on weekends, or does the campus become a ghost town?
- How important is Greek life? Some schools are frat-central; others barely have a Greek system.
- Does the school have clubs, activities, and resources that match your child's interests?
- How important are sports? A student who thrives in a big sports culture may not be happy at a school where the biggest athletic event is an intramural badminton match. On the flip side, if your child couldn't care less about sports, a university where Game Day is the highlight of the week may not be the best fit.

- Is the campus genuinely inclusive? For LGBTQ+ students (and for any student who wants an open, welcoming community), it's worth paying attention to the campus culture and support systems. Are there active LGBTQ+ clubs or resource centers? Do students describe the school as affirming and safe? Does the campus feel like a place where your child can show up as themselves? For many kids, this is one of the most important factors in finding a school that feels like home.
- Is a co-ed campus the right fit or would an all-women's college better support your child socially and academically?
- Does the school have faith-based or religious communities (such as a Hillel, campus ministry, or chaplaincy) that your child could connect with if they want to?

6. HOUSING

When evaluating housing options, it's worth reading the fine print early. A few things to keep in mind:

- **Guaranteed Housing:** Some colleges and universities, like Franklin & Marshall, Colby, University of Dayton, and Fordham guarantee housing for all four years. Others, like Auburn and the University of Florida, don't guarantee housing for freshmen. If your child has their heart set on living on campus, it's worth checking the fine print early.
- **Application Timing:** At schools like University of Texas at Austin, Pace, and Stony Brook, students are allowed to apply for housing before they receive an admissions decision. At schools where housing is limited or first-come, first-served, applying early can make a big difference.
- **Availability and Competitiveness:** At some schools, juniors and seniors may be hustling for off-campus apartments due to limited housing. Even at a handful of schools (like Cornell), many students feel obligated to secure housing a full year in advance.
- **Living-Learning Communities:** Many colleges offer themed housing where students with similar interests live together. Examples:
  - Middlebury College has interest-based housing like outdoor leadership and social justice themes.
  - Virginia Tech has over twenty living-learning communities centered on topics like engineering, the arts, and leadership.
  - Michigan State University offers residential colleges that integrate academic and residential life.

7. CAREER OUTCOMES & ALUMNI NETWORKS

Four years fly by, but what happens after graduation?

- What's the job placement rate?
- Do they have strong internship pipelines?
- Are there active alumni networks that help students land jobs?

Schools like Northeastern, Endicott, and Drexel offer built-in co-op programs that provide real-world experience before graduation. Others rely on traditional summer internships. Colleges love to brag about employment rates, but it's a good idea to find out what kinds of jobs students get after graduation. Of course, outcomes can vary widely depending on the school, the student, and their chosen major.

At Gettysburg College, students can choose from Guided Pathways: thematic tracks such as Creativity, Entrepreneurship & Innovation; Global Citizenship & Intercultural Fluency; Justice & Community Change; and Leadership, Teamwork & Collaboration. As Mary Smith, Dean of Admissions, explained to me, "Our goal is to help students connect their personal goals with professional goals, so they leave not just with a degree, but with skills and direction for the future."

REPUTATION ISN'T EVERYTHING

Some schools that used to fly under the radar have stepped into the spotlight with renovated campuses and noteworthy programs. Think about places like Northeastern or Elon, schools once considered regional or second-tier, now drawing competitive applicants from across the country. A college doesn't need to be a household name to be worthy of attention.

One gentle reminder: try not to badmouth a school, even in passing. I've seen it more times than I can count when a parent makes an offhand, dismissive remark, and a few weeks later, their child becomes completely smitten with that very college. Suddenly, what should be a great moment feels a little awkward.

FINDING SCHOOLS THAT FIT: RESOURCES THAT HELP

Good news: you don't have to rely on your hairstylist's sister's opinion to build a college list. These tools make the search process easier, more thoughtful, and a lot more personalized. Here are some personal favorites:

- **Fiske Guide to Colleges:** A well-researched, student-friendly look at 300+ schools, offering honest insights into academic life, campus culture, and vibe.
- **Niche:** A treasure trove of student reviews, rankings, and insights on everything from dorm food to campus parties. Think Yelp, but for colleges.

- **Colleges That Change Lives (CTCL):** Highlights lesser-known but phenomenal liberal arts schools that prioritize individualized learning and rapport with faculty.

SKIP *the* RANKINGS *and* FIND *the* DATA

There's no real "tier list" of colleges, though plenty of parents act like there is. Rankings from *U.S. News & World Report, Niche, The Wall Street Journal,* or *Forbes* can be fun to peek at, but please take them with a giant grain of salt (and maybe a shot of something strong). Most rankings measure things like faculty salaries, endowment size, or "peer reputation," and not whether professors know your kid's name or if the dorm bathrooms are cleaned more than once a semester.

If you really want to understand how competitive a college is, skip the rankings and head over to the Common Data Set (CDS). Every school updates it yearly, and it's loaded with good stuff: average GPAs, test score ranges, admit rates, and which factors (grades, essays, extracurriculars, and more) matter. It's honest, and it gives you a much clearer picture of where your child stands.

Tip: Just Google "[College Name] Common Data Set." It usually pops right up as a PDF on the school's website.

If you're desperate to read the rankings, go ahead. But if you're looking for solid information, the CDS paints a pretty accurate picture of the landscape.

- **BigFuture by College Board:** A great tool to filter schools based on size, location, majors, and other key factors.
- **Naviance (or Scoir):** Many high schools use these platforms to track application data and outcomes. They're great for seeing where students from your child's own school have been admitted and for building balanced lists.
- **YouTube & social media:** Many schools offer day-in-the-life videos and dorm tours on TikTok and Instagram. These can be great tools for getting a real feel of campus life beyond the glitzy marketing and websites.

Encourage your child to explore widely and stay curious. Some of the best-fit schools are the ones they haven't heard of...yet.

Once you've built a college list that feels balanced, and dare we say, exciting, the next step is figuring out how to approach it strategically. This is where things move from dreaming to doing. Who should apply early? Which schools make the most sense for ED1 or ED2? How can a strong major choice and a little planning make all the difference? That's where the "launch" part begins.

EARLY DECISION, EARLY ACTION—WHAT'S THE DIFFERENCE?

You'll hear these terms constantly once application season starts:

- **ED1 (Early Decision 1):** Binding. Apply early (usually November 1) and get a decision in December. If accepted, your child is committed to attend.

- **ED2 (Early Decision 2):** Also binding, but with later deadlines, typically in January. It's often used by students who were deferred or denied in ED1 or by those who needed more time to decide where they could confidently commit. Decisions usually come out in mid-February. If accepted, your child is committed to attend.

- **EA (Early Action):** Non-binding. Apply early, hear back early, but still have time until May 1 to decide.

- **Rolling Admission:** Schools review applications as they're completed and release decisions on a rolling basis. The earlier your child applies, the better their chances. Spaces fill as the season goes on.

- **Regular Decision:** The traditional timeline. Applications are typically due January 1-5, and students receive decisions in March.

THE STRATEGY MEETING: APPLYING SMARTER

Once the list is set, it's time to map out the application plan, just like we do with our students. This is when strategy really counts.

Should your child aim a bit higher with an ED1 choice? A thoughtful reach can be great, but only if there's a realistic shot. If they're eyeing schools like Duke or Penn, make sure the numbers and the narrative align in a convincing way.

Is ED2 worth considering? Maybe. But those pools can be even more competitive than ED1. That's because students deferred or denied from places like Northwestern or Cornell often pivot to schools like WashU, Emory, University of Richmond, or Tufts.

Many liberal arts colleges also admit a big chunk of their class through early decision, and many offer an ED2 option. If your child loves smaller class sizes, tight-knit communities, and that kind of academic vibe, ED2 might be their golden ticket.

A quick note on timing. ED1 deadlines are typically November 1st or 15th with decisions released by mid-December. Students who don't need to compare financial aid packages often take advantage of this route.

If your child is deferred from ED1, the next steps can feel especially tough. Some hang onto that dream school and resist applying anywhere else ED2, hoping lightning strikes in the regular round. We understand, but it's risky. At some schools, the odds are especially slim. The University of Chicago once reported that deferred Early Action applicants had just a **0.5%** chance of eventual admission.[20] We agree that a deferral isn't an absolute no, but it's not a reason to put all your eggs back into the same basket.

With a thoughtful early decision strategy, you could be breathing easier in December instead of panic-snacking your way through bags of Doritos until April. Planning ahead really can bring peace (and fewer orange fingers). A smart strategy doesn't mean playing it safe. It just means giving your kid real choices in the end.

POSITIONING YOURSELF FOR SUCCESS: THE RIGHT MAJOR

Every year, we see students apply for majors that don't reflect their actual experiences, and that disconnect can hurt them in the application review.

One student had her heart set on becoming a doctor but had no research or clinical exposure. What she did have was years of serious dance training, including competitive performances, choreography, and a clear record of commitment and talent. Applying as a dance major, with the option to explore pre-med later, made far more sense. Her application reflected what she had already built.

Another student from a large NYC public high school was part of a Law & Society track, but she didn't have traditional extracurriculars. What stood out? Her job as a grocery store cashier. Less than a mile from home, it exposed her to a world of different cultures, economic backgrounds, and human behavior. She conversed with customers in Spanish and grew curious about the systems shaping her neighborhood. She applied to WashU as a Sociology major, and she got in.

When students apply to different areas, they need to be clear about which major or program they're choosing on the application. For universities with specific schools or departments (like business or engineering), this is especially important.[21] At liberal arts colleges, students often have more flexibility to explore different areas later, but they still need to show a connection between their application and intended path. This

---

20 Ron Lieber, "Tulane and Chicago Are Urging Students to Apply Early. But Why?" *The New York Times*, November 29, 2025. **21 Quick note about universities vs. liberal arts colleges:** A university is typically a larger institution offering both undergraduate and graduate programs. For undergraduates, universities often have specialized schools or departments, such as a School of Engineering, College of Business, or College of Arts and Sciences, allowing students to focus on a specific field of study. A liberal arts college, on the other hand, offers a more flexible undergraduate education across multiple disciplines, encouraging exploration and often providing closer student-professor interaction.

is where students should lead with what they've already done, and colleges typically take notice.

LEVERAGING CREATIVE TALENTS FOR SPECIFIC MAJORS

For students with a strong talent in music, dance, theater, or visual arts, submitting an arts portfolio can be a wonderful way to showcase their abilities even if they're not planning to major in the arts. Many colleges welcome supplemental materials, and while not required, a well-crafted submission can add an important dimension to an application.

I encouraged both of my daughters to put together dance reels. My older daughter teamed up with her ballet teacher to create one but didn't end up submitting it. My younger daughter made hers independently and included it with her early application. One student of ours shared recordings, featuring her saxophone performances. Another, a devoted theater student, included clips from high school musicals, including one unintentionally hilarious moment when a very tall dad accidentally wandered into the center of the shot, proudly beaming at his own child on stage.

These don't need to be professionally produced. In fact, when students create them on their own, they often come across as more authentic. Music and theater portfolios can be as simple as clear video recordings. Art portfolios take a bit more planning, but many high school teachers are happy to help, and there are also summer pre-college programs that walk students through the process.

Most colleges that accept arts supplements use SlideRoom, a platform where students upload materials alongside their application. Each school has its own guidelines, so check their admissions pages for the specifics before getting started.

Anyone can make a list of a dozen colleges. That part's easy. The trick is helping your kid end up somewhere that doesn't make them feel out of step with the college community. It's not about the bumper sticker on your car. It's about the call (or, who are we kidding, the text) a few weeks into the semester that simply says, "I love it here."

That's the moment you've been working toward, and it beats any bumper sticker.

CHAPTER 9

Campus Tours and Car Rides: WHERE THE MAGIC HAPPENS

My dad was my partner-in-crime on college tours. He was the ultimate road trip buddy for a high school junior trying to figure out her future. But then again, he had always been there, showing up for me in every way that mattered. He never missed a school play, band concert, or dance recital. There he was, always sitting in the audience, grinning as if I were center stage at Lincoln Center.

At family gatherings, his jokes had us laughing until we cried. He beamed with pride about my brother, my mom, and me. But what I loved most was his gift for making everyday life feel fun.

Maybe it was the salesman in him. He worked as a national sales manager for a wine and spirits company, and he had a knack for charming anyone, even making the most mundane moments feel special.

Late at night, when I was drowning in homework, he'd appear in my doorway, hand over his heart, feigning a crisis.

"I'm having a Granny Smith attack!"

That was my cue. No matter how much studying I had, he'd whisk me off to

ShopRite, allegedly to satisfy an emergency apple craving, but really, just to give me a break. We'd wander the aisles cracking jokes, and for a few precious minutes, my calculus exam-induced anxiety briefly disappeared.

When it came time to visit colleges, it was no surprise that he turned the process into an adventure. It was another excuse to explore, swap stories, and laugh.

Together, we explored East Coast schools in his Toyota Camry, loading the car with our favorite junk food, and stuffing those unwieldy AAA maps into the glove compartment. The best part? Blasting 8-track tapes on his new car stereo. I credit my life-long appreciation of Neil Diamond and Barbra Streisand to those long hours on the road with my dad.

College tours are supposed to be about finding the right school, but I quickly learned they were just as much about the in-between moments. Many schools made an immediate impression, often for reasons that had nothing to do with academics.

One particularly sweltering June day in New Jersey, our tour group included a dad straight out of *The Official Preppy Handbook*—yellow cable-knit sweater, perfectly worn-in docksiders. A tiny nod from my dad was all it took, and I burst into giggles. We ditched the overly polished campus tour and sweaty sweater-guy to go eat pancakes across the street.

In Boston, we caught a Red Sox-Yankees game because my dad, an expert travel planner, knew that no trip to Boston was complete without a stop at Fenway. (Side note: Red Sox fans are *not* welcoming to Yankees fans. Hot dog remnants were "accidentally" thrown at us the second they spotted our caps.)

More than anything, these trips were about time with my dad. Between the long drives, shared meals, and the occasional splurge on an overpriced sweatshirt when August temperatures suddenly dipped below 50, I learned to trust my instincts and not take the process too seriously.

My dad's stories about my grandparents escaping the pogroms in Russia, or his $35-a-year education at City College of New York, put everything into perspective. While he did the actual driving from campus to campus, he let me take the metaphorical wheel when it came to deciding what felt right. That freedom, coupled with his unconditional support, meant the world.

MAKING THE MOST OF COLLEGE VISITS

Every family has their own approach to conquering college visits, but after years of counseling students and parents, I've picked up a few universal truths that can make these trips productive and fun.

WHEN TO VISIT (AND WHEN TO HOLD OFF)

In a perfect world, visit a college when students are on campus, heading to class, tossing Frisbees on the lawn, and gathering in the dining hall. But real life doesn't always line up with the admissions calendar. If summer is your only window, don't worry. There's still plenty to take in. You can walk the campus and talk to anyone who's around.

One small tip: pay attention to the other families on your tour. The mix of students in the group often mirrors the kind of people who apply and enroll. That quick gut check can tell you practically as much as the tour guide.

BEYOND THE BROCHURES: WHAT LIFE ON CAMPUS IS REALLY ABOUT

A campus tour shows only one slice of life at a school. To get a fuller picture, take a step back and engage in what's happening around you:

- **The students:** Do they seem engaged? Rushed? Friendly? Are they chatting as they walk, or glued to their phones with earbuds in?
- **The energy:** Does the place feel lively and welcoming, or a little flat? Can you picture your child fitting in here?
- **The spaces:** Peek into dorms, study lounges, libraries, and dining halls. Would your kid feel comfortable spending time there?
- **The little things:** Look for blue emergency lights, good lighting, and other safety features. Can they bring a car on campus? For some students, this can be a big deal.

HOW TO GET THE REAL SCOOP ON CAMPUS

After the rehearsed tours and information sessions, encourage your child to ask the questions that really matter. Stopping a few random students is a great start; most will be happy to chat unless they're sprinting to class. If your kid knows someone on campus (or a friend of a friend), they'll get the unfiltered version of campus life. Students are far more honest than any admissions rep when it comes to workload, campus culture, or whether the food is edible.

When Nancy and I visit campuses, we deliberately wander into the student center, cafeteria, or library (not the quiet floor) to chat with students.

Here are some of our go-to questions:

- What do you love most about this school?
- What's one thing you wish you'd known before coming here?
- What do students do on weekends?
- If you could change one thing about this school, what would it be?

- Where else did you apply?
- Why did you ultimately choose this school?

These simple conversation starters usually reveal more than any campus tour or admissions spiel ever could.

Lauren Sefton, Associate Dean of Admission at Rhodes College, takes this a step further. She encourages students to begin college visits with a quick self-reflection: What does an ideal day look like for me? When have I felt most excited to go to school and why? Once a student has that clarity, their campus conversations go much deeper. Lauren suggests asking: "How did you find your community here?" "What does a typical Tuesday look like? A typical Saturday?" "How are you different now than when you first started?" and "What do you wish you'd done differently your first year?" These kinds of conversations get to what daily life on campus feels like.

Don't forget to dig deeper into other important areas, like financial aid, housing options, the career center, study abroad, campus safety, and accommodations for learning differences or disabilities. Ask your child to connect with organizations and clubs they're excited to join. These moments add texture and give a stronger sense of whether a school will be a good fit.

WHAT NOT TO SAY AS A PARENT (BEFORE, DURING, AND AFTER TOURS)

I've seen it happen too many times: well-meaning parents ask questions that make their teenager want to duck behind the nearest tree.

"Are there specific hours when boys are allowed in the girls' dorms?"

"What's the school's policy on beer kegs?"

Watching a teenager pretend not to know his own parent is painful. Save them (and yourself) the agony.

After a tour or info session, it's tempting to share your opinion immediately, but please bite your tongue. Instead of saying, "I really loved the open curriculum here, didn't you?" let your child speak first. Regardless of whether the cafeteria smelled like your kid's middle school gym, or the tour guide had the enthusiasm of a DMV employee, let your child lead the discussion. You can always share your opinions later, but *only* if invited.

A FEW OTHER THINGS NOT TO DO (TRUST US, WE'VE SEEN THEM ALL):

- Don't talk about your own college experience ("When I was here in '89…"). Different era, different process.

- Don't ask, "What are my son's chances with a 3.7?" Admissions officers despise that question, and your kid will likely crouch under his chair.
- Don't corner the admissions rep to discuss your wonderful daughter or your friend who sits on the Board of Trustees.
- Don't ask how the football team is doing, especially when your kid doesn't really care about sports.

Remember this is your child's turn. Let them take center stage as much as possible.

COLLEGE VISITS ARE ABOUT MORE THAN JUST THE TOUR

Having visited over 160 campuses, I'm convinced the dining scene (on and off campus) can make or break your day. A relaxed and yummy meal gives your child a chance to unwind and talk candidly about what they saw, without the pressure of an immediate debrief.

How do we find the best spots to eat? A little research goes a long way. We check the school's website for local favorites, ask students on campus, chat with admissions officers, and text friends who have kids there. Students always know the best late-night eats, and admissions officers often point you to hidden gems.

Some places are too good not to share:

At Purdue, we devoured awesome burgers at Triple XXX (not a strip club!) in West Lafayette, Indiana. We had amazing cocktails and appetizers at The Belvedere Inn in Lancaster, PA, a few blocks from Franklin & Marshall. Surprisingly, Middlebury, Vermont, home to Middlebury College, delivered a seriously good prime rib at Fire & Ice.

When my husband and I took our older daughter to St. Louis, we drove straight from the airport to Sugar Fire Smoke House for arguably the best BBQ in Missouri. My son and I still laugh about how we inhaled the unexpectedly amazing pad Thai at Tuk Tuk Thai in Hanover, New Hampshire.

My all-time favorite food detour came during a visit to relatives in Los Angeles, when I convinced my family to brave an unseasonably freezing day for an afternoon campus tour at the University of California, Santa Barbara. My promise to them? "The tacos in town will be worth it!" We hit not one, not two, but three taco spots, and lost all track of time. We missed the campus tour entirely. But hey, we still rave about those tacos (La Super Rica Taqueria was our favorite).

Beyond food, consider adding local activities to make the trip more memorable.

Visiting schools in Colorado? Pack a pair of hiking boots and explore some local trails. In Austin, TX, don't forget to check out the local music scene. Or head over to

Allens Boots for a mile-long selection of cowboy boots. I almost bought a pair of pink ones until Nancy convinced me that I'd *never* wear them back in NY (I did come home with a cool black pair). When my daughter and I had a flight delay in Atlanta, we turned lemons into Coke with a two-hour tour of the Coca-Cola Factory, complete with tastings of 100 international flavors. It was almost like wine-tasting for my under-age child.

DON'T OVERDO IT

Howard Jones had it right: "Don't try to live your life in one day." College tours can be exhausting. If your kid needs a break, take one. After a marathon of college tours in Pennsylvania, I treated my middle child for a mani-pedi. When my son and I were freezing our toes off after visiting a few campuses in Chicago, we splurged on a huge steak dinner and a carrot cake so good it deserved its own tour stop. Thank you, Gibson's! In Nashville, I carved out time for my youngest to visit a friend from her summer dance camp.

These little breaks matter. They can turn a grueling process into something your family may reminisce about one day.

JOT DOWN YOUR IMPRESSIONS (AND ASK YOUR KID, TOO)

College tours often start to blur together: one historic chapel, one leafy quad, one campus bookstore after another. You might forget what was said about the curriculum, and your kid might be too distracted by the cute student across the room to catch the highlights. Have them jot down quick impressions after each visit. Whether it's a quirky dorm setup, a cool summer research program, an endless supply of warm chocolate chip cookies during finals week, or the goat yoga sessions to relieve stress, those notes will come in extremely handy when it's time to write the "Why Us?" essays.

EXPLORE ACADEMICS, BUT KEEP AN OPEN MIND

Sitting in on a college class might sound like a great way to get a feel for academics, and many colleges offer that option to visiting students. However, it can be a mixed bag. A dynamic professor and an engaged discussion might leave a great impression. But catch the class on a slow day before a major holiday, or one where half the students are glued to their phones? Your kid might walk away feeling underwhelmed. That's why we usually don't recommend it. Instead, encourage your child to check out department info sessions or send a quick note to a professor in their area of interest, but only if they have a specific question. They may not get a reply, but it's still a great way to show interest.

TRUST YOUR GUT (OR YOUR CHILD'S)

If your child takes one look at a campus and flat-out refuses to get out of the car, don't panic or get frustrated, no matter how many miles you've driven or how terrible the traffic was to get there. Sometimes, gut feelings are spot on. However, if you've flown across the country and spent all that time and money, it's probably worth pushing them to spend at least twenty minutes exploring and then offering a strategic bribe. Ice cream usually works wonders.

We've all heard the phrase *trust your gut*. Whether your child's gut is saying "Woo Hoo!" or "Absolutely not," it's worth paying attention. Very often, instinct is spot on. Or it may need some extra time (and maybe a snack) to catch up.

One of our students, Katie, pulled up to what she was sure would be the college of her dreams. But seconds after arriving, she had a feeling this was *not* her place. After driving almost seven hours, her mom wasn't quite ready to turn around, so they compromised: fifteen minutes on the tour, and then decide. By the ten-minute mark, Katie's gut had spoken loud and clear. Walking back to the parking lot, she spotted an ex-boyfriend from high school racing to class, and then, it started to pour. She instantly read the signs, and they dashed back to the car.

But the gut can also surprise you. Another student, Allison, agreed to visit a school on her *"I would never go here"* list, simply to appease her parents. The moment she stepped onto campus and saw fairy-tale-esque buildings lining the quad, she just knew. She turned to her parents and proclaimed, "I think this is it." Good news? It was.

While there's no such thing as a campus covered in puppies and rainbows, if your kid does have an immediate positive reaction to a school, then celebrate it. Make sure, though, to remind them there are plenty of wonderful fish in the sea. Falling too hard for only one school inevitably leads to heartbreak if things don't work out.

CAN'T VISIT IN PERSON? VIRTUAL TOURS STILL COUNT

Virtual tours and online info sessions are great back-ups when in-person visits aren't doable. They give your child a chance to explore campuses, learn about academic programs, meet some current students, and hear directly from admissions reps—all from the comfort of their own couch. Many colleges also track online engagement, so joining a session or registering for a virtual event still counts as demonstrated interest, which is a plus at some schools. A small caveat: not every college's virtual content reflects the full personality of the campus. Some schools have limited videos or older recordings, so don't cross a place off the list just because the online tour felt flat. Think of these as the appetizer before the big road trip. They're an easy, affordable way to get a feel for a school before committing to flights or hours in the car. This might save you a few gray hairs, too.

SOCIAL MEDIA FOR YOUR CHILD (AND FOR YOU) CAN BE HELPFUL

TikTok and Instagram aren't just about dance trends and cute pets; they're surprisingly convenient tools for exploring colleges. With hashtags like #CollegeLife, #CampusTour, and even #DormDecor, your child can get a strong glimpse of daily life. From football games to late-night food runs, social media offers an unfiltered look at daily life, helping them see if a school's vibe, energy, and student community feel like the right fit.

Parents can also use social media wisely. Instagram and YouTube offer plenty of insights into housing, academics, and admissions events. Facebook still has its perks. While your kids are busy scrolling through memes and campus antics, you can zero in on the practical details.

Of course, social media doesn't tell the whole story. Balance those scroll sessions with official college resources to make sure you're getting accurate information. If you catch yourself watching one too many dorm makeover reels or viewing the campus a cappella group for the nineteenth time, don't worry. It happens to the best of us.

BE OPEN TO SURPRISES

Every year, I see students do a complete 180 on their college preferences the moment they step onto a campus.

One student from an all-girls high school in Dallas was certain she wanted a small liberal arts college until she visited the University of Wisconsin. She instantly fell for the big-school energy, the sea of red on the Game Day she attended, and the dangerously good cheese curds at the student union.

Another student, convinced he belonged at a Big Ten school, reluctantly visited Middlebury. He was completely captivated by the world-renowned language programs and the idea of being surrounded by students who spoke five languages daily. Suddenly, a close-knit, intellectual community sounded kind of perfect.

That's why I always encourage families to shake things up. If your child swears that they're meant for a massive state school, take them to a tiny liberal arts college. If they've always pictured themselves in a bustling city, check out a school where the biggest landmark is a cow pasture.

Sometimes, a college that looks perfect on paper feels totally off in person and vice versa. The only way to know is to go.

Teenagers are still figuring it out. Visiting schools helps them do just that. Invite them to explore widely and stay open to surprises along the way.

A SENTIMENTAL NOTE

My dad never got to see my three children and my niece apply to or graduate from college, but I know he would have been bursting with pride. He passed away in 2012, long before the acceptance letters arrived, but his wisdom, humor, and late-night supply of Granny Smith apples stayed with me every step of the way, and they still do.

I like to think he was along for the ride, though, laughing with me at the parents asking awkward questions on tours, indulging in BBQ and baseball games at stadiums we "just happened" to stop at, and nodding in approval when we bailed on a tour in favor of pancakes.

Dad (Pop Pop), this one's for you.

CHAPTER 10

The Game Beyond The Game: ATHLETICS *and* COLLEGE ADMISSIONS

I'll never forget the day a mom sat across from me at the Metro Diner in Scarsdale, sharing a plate of fries, while she looked at me, feeling entirely exasperated: "My son has spent thousands of hours on the baseball field. If that doesn't get him into college, what was the point?"

She wasn't being dramatic. This kid had spent more time in cleats than in regular shoes, juggled three-season sports with schoolwork, and practically lived out of a duffel bag full of sweaty shorts and granola bar crumbs.

Yet when senior year loomed, reality set in. There were no D1 offers, the highly competitive, scholarship-driven recruitment path. There were no guaranteed D3 roster spots, where athletics still play a role, but scholarships rarely exist. And there was no sure path for him as a walk-on, where players try to earn a spot without being formally recruited. That August, while his teammates were deep in pre-season training, he was nursing sore muscles and a growing question mark about whether his years on the field would help him get into college.

For many high school athletes, playing sports feels like a full-time job. Early morning workouts, grueling practices in below-thirty-degree or above-nintety-degree weather (remember that coaches love to build character), weekend tournaments, and endless drills into the evenings fill their schedule. For parents? We know how many weekends, late nights, early mornings, and miles you've clocked as a family to support your child's athletic dreams. Those sacrifices mean something, regardless of what happens in the recruiting process.

For those chasing the dream of playing in college, the recruiting process can feel like online shopping without knowing your size or if the store even has that item in stock. Some athletes get early offers after catching a coach's eye at a showcase or summer camp. Others spend months advocating for themselves, emailing coaches, and sending highlight reels into what may as well be a black hole. Many reach the end of high school realizing that their athletic career might wrap up once college begins.

So how do you, as a parent, help your child make sense of all this? How can you tell if a coach is really interested or just being polite? If your child is a multi-sport athlete who doesn't plan to play in college, is it time to scale back as the high school years move on? Perhaps that time could be better spent exploring other high school experiences that lead to new academic or extracurricular paths.

While Nancy and I don't claim to be athletic recruiting experts (my own athletic career peaked in sixth grade when I placed third at the Menlo Park Elementary School kickball tournament), we've worked with enough families to understand the basics. Our goal is to help students feel confident about their path, even if it doesn't include stadium lights or free Nike gear.

WHEN SHOULD A STUDENT START REACHING OUT TO COACHES?

For D3 athletes, the best time to connect with coaches is by the end of sophomore year or early junior year. Students should take the lead by emailing coaches, sharing stats, attending ID camps (where coaches scout potential recruits), and getting on their radar well before applications are due. By senior year, most coaches already know who they're supporting in the admissions process.

Just keep in mind: D3 coaches don't work in admissions. They can promote you, but they don't make the final call. Even without that authority, early communication gives your student a clearer sense of where they stand.

Understanding the Athletic Recruitment Process: WHAT PARENTS NEED *to* KNOW

Not all athletic recruitment is created equal. If your child is being recruited for D1, the process likely started early, sometimes as early as freshman or sophomore year. These athletes get scouted, attend showcase events, and often commit before their junior year is over. Chances are that if your child is not being wooed by a D1 coach early in their high school career, they most likely will not be recruited by a D1 school.

But this chapter isn't about D1. If your child is a serious athlete who wants to continue playing at the collegiate level but isn't getting those early D1 calls, then self-recruitment for D3 programs is when you and your kid need to roll up your sleeves.

Unlike D1, D3 recruitment requires effort on the student's part. There are no athletic scholarships, but strong athletes still may have an advantage in the admissions process, especially at smaller liberal arts colleges where coaches advocate for their top picks. However, parents should know that even if a coach shows interest, it doesn't mean there's a guaranteed spot or that the coach will give the student a "push" in admissions. We've seen students work through this process successfully, but it requires strategy, perseverance, and luck.

What's the difference between D1, D2, and D3?

- **Division I (D1):** This is the big time. Think nationally ranked teams, jam-packed stadiums, and athletes who often get recruited early and may receive athletic scholarships. It's a serious, year-round commitment.
- **Division II (D2):** Still competitive, but with a bit more balance between academics and athletics. Some scholarship money is available, but not as much as D1.
- **Division III (D3):** No athletic scholarships here. However, these kids are still serious athletes. Coaches often advocate for their top recruits, but decisions are ultimately made in the admissions office.

As Chris Petrucelli, former SMU head coach and now GM of Dallas Trinity FC, explained to me: "I've recruited hundreds of athletes, and the hardest conversations are with families who never understood the level of play where their child fit best. Recruiting is never just about talent (although talent really helps). Coaches look for academic fit, character, and roster needs. My best advice: be honest about ability, keep academics strong, and always have more than one path in mind."

STORIES FROM THE FIELD: WHAT WE'VE SEEN WORK (AND WHAT HASN'T)

Recruitment is more than stats and timelines. It's about real students finding teams where they can belong and breathe. To get a sense of how this all plays out, we're sharing stories of students who found the right fit and a few who learned some hard lessons along the way.

Every sport is different. Timelines, outreach, enthusiasm, and coach engagement can vary, so knowing how things work in your child's specific sport is key.

If your child is a swimmer, congratulations! You've got one of the most straightforward self-recruitment paths. No highlight reels, no complicated skill assessments. It all comes down to times.

For D3 coaches at small liberal arts colleges, it's not just about speed. It's also about the specific events your child swims. Coaches are looking to fill gaps in their roster, so if your child's event times align with their team's needs, the conversation can move quickly. In swimming, fit is as much about the right stroke and distance as it is about raw speed.

We've worked with plenty of swimmers who reached out to D3 coaches, shared their times, and locked in spots without much ado. One landed at Middlebury with a solid but not jaw-dropping time in the 200-freestyle. Another steadily improved her stroke times during junior year, caught the attention of a Franklin & Marshall coach, and was recruited. No theatrics. Just her times and a well-crafted email.

The same principle applies to other timed sports like skiing, track, or rowing, where the numbers prove everything.

Now, let's talk tennis. This one gets tricky.

We worked with a talented player who had been in conversation with the Williams College coach for months. She thought she was a shoo-in. But when she dug in deeper, she realized she was number five on the coach's list, and he had space to promote only three players. When push came to shove, she was left without an offer (a painful but common lesson: if a coach isn't offering a guaranteed spot, your child is in the dreaded "wait-and-see" situation).

No matter how much a coach wants to recruit a player, they only have a limited number of "bullets" with admissions each year. With so many sports and so many coaches advocating for their athletes, those spots are carefully allocated.

Good thing our student had a backup plan. She had also connected early with the coach at Bowdoin, secured a spot before senior year stress set in, and ended up playing happily there. A reminder that in recruitment, clear communication and a solid Plan B can make all the difference.

Baseball recruitment requires an entirely different approach: highlight reels and exposure at showcase events, which are basically summer tournaments specifically designed for scouting talent.

For some students, working with a specialist who understands athletic recruitment can make a huge difference. We worked with one baseball player who, despite not having perfect grades, secured a spot at Williams College after attending key showcase events and working with an athletic recruitment specialist to improve his recruitment strategy. Another player, with strong but not standout stats, landed at Brandeis with the help of his coach's backing.

For baseball families, getting seen is everything. Without the right highlight reel and showcase appearances, even the most talented players might end up without a recruitment offer.

Other sports like football, soccer, lacrosse, and basketball rely heavily on highlight reels, club teams, showcase events, and coach connections. While each sport has its own recruiting quirks, one thing remains the same: the earlier your child understands the process and gets on a coach's radar, the better their chances of finding the right fit.

1. HOW TO TELL IF A COACH IS ACTUALLY INTERESTED

Not all coach communication is created equal. A generic "Dear Athlete" email? Not a great sign. A personal message referencing your child's stats or recent performance? Much better. Here's how to tell if a coach is truly interested:

- Is the email personalized, or does it look like a mass message?
- Is the coach asking for detailed stats and records?
- Has your child been invited to scrimmages, team practices, or campus visits?
- Is the coach communicating with you as parents?
- Has the coach given a verbal commitment or outlined next steps?
- Is the coach arranging a pre-read with admissions to assess the student's chances of being admitted?

I'll repeat this: coaches don't work in admissions. Even if they call your child a top prospect, they don't have the final say. If a coach won't facilitate a pre-read, it's worth questioning their level of interest.

Also, consider who is reaching out. If it's the head coach, that's a great sign. If it's the assistant, your child might be a backup plan. If by September of senior year, the coach still isn't talking to admissions? Then unfortunately, your child is not looking like a top recruit.

2. HOW DOES YOUR CHILD COMPARE TO OTHER RECRUITS?

Just like college admissions, athletic recruiting is competitive. It's helpful to understand where your child stands in the mix. A few questions to consider:

- How do they stack up against other athletes in their position?
- If they're looking at Ivy League schools, does their Academic Index (AI) fall within the typical range for recruits?
- Do they bring something rare or much needed to a team? Are they a swimmer who excels in the 200 butterfly or a standout goalkeeper when the roster is thin?
- Beyond physical skill, do they offer leadership or a unique playing style that makes them stand out?
- Are there open spots on the team in their position, or is the roster already packed?

If your child is aiming for a top academic school, grades and test scores matter as much as athletic ability. Many teams work with "recruiting bands," which are essentially academic brackets. A strong student-athlete can also help a coach gain additional recruits, as they are often easier to admit in the admissions process.

For athletes in "numbers sports" like running or swimming, a quick reality check goes a long way: check recent team times or meet results online. It's often eye-opening. Some students dominate high school meets, but remain outside the competitive range for the colleges they imagine—sometimes only a fraction too slow. This early check helps them decide whether to train into range or plan on joining a club team instead.

Helping your child understand their fit, both athletically and academically, can give them a real advantage and spare a lot of heartache later.

3. THE COLLEGE ITSELF: THE "BROKEN LEG" TEST

Here's something we always encourage families to think about: what if your child got injured during their first year and couldn't play anymore? No more practices, no more competitions. Would they still be happy at that school? If the answer is no, it's worth reconsidering whether that school is the right place. Athletics should be an added bonus to their college experience, not the only reason they're there.

THE REALITY FOR MULTI-SPORT ATHLETES WHO WON'T BE RECRUITED

As parents, it's easy to applaud the dedication and discipline that come with year-round athletics. But if your child isn't planning to play in college or won't be recruited in any of their sports, it's worth considering whether all that time on the field (or on the road, in a plane, or in a hotel room) is the best investment. If recruitment isn't in the cards, ask yourself:

- Is my child missing out on other experiences? Clubs, leadership roles, and internships often take a back seat when sports dominate their schedule.
- Do they still love playing, or are they afraid to quit? Many students continue out of habit and not out of genuine joy.
- Will they regret not exploring other interests? If sports have been their only extracurricular, will they feel lost once high school ends?
- Will they be viewed as a one-trick pony in the application process, dedicated mainly to their sport but unable to contribute at the college level?

Urging your child to take a closer look at how they spend their time can help them create a high school experience that feels meaningful to *them*, not merely to an admissions office. It's also a chance to remind them that it's okay to try new things and drop what no longer fits. No one expects them to have it all figured out at sixteen, but learning to make thoughtful choices about how they spend their time is a valuable life skill.

KEEPING THE BIG PICTURE IN MIND

For some students, sports open doors to college. For others, they're a meaningful part of high school, but not the next step. For a few, they've become an all-consuming commitment that may need a second look.

At the end of the day, sports should add to your child's life, not take over it. The lessons of teamwork and resilience will stick with them far beyond the game. Whether your child's next stop includes a jersey or not, the commitment they've shown is something to celebrate. College will bring new arenas like classrooms, clubs, and internships, where that same drive and focus will shine.

Part Four

Lights, Camera, Application!

CHAPTER 11

CRACKING *the* COLLEGE ESSAY *in* UNDER *an* HOUR

I'm done!" my daughter yelled, racing down the stairs and slamming a few crumpled pages onto my desk with a dramatic thud.

She had been upstairs for exactly forty-one minutes, her reluctant writing session preceded by one of our legendary mother-daughter screaming matches; this one was about when she would finally plant her tush in a chair to start her college essay. It was already the end of August, senior year academics were about to take over, and I was starting to sweat.

After weeks of procrastination, tears, and not-so-subtle threats from me, I resorted to the ultimate bribe: "One draft, honey. Just one, and then we can go shopping for back-to-school clothes."

With a theatrical sigh and a stomp worthy of the Broadway stage, she grabbed her laptop and marched up to her bedroom while I sat at my kitchen desk, distracting myself with Facebook, inhaling pretzels, and counting the minutes.

I'll admit that our battles during the college process weren't among my finest parenting moments. Looking back, I cringe at the hovering, the constant reminders, and the sheer volume of anxiety I projected onto her. I say this with love and regret. In the global rankings of parental nagging, I'd be in the top three. Maybe even a record-holder.

I wish I could have nagged less and listened more. But over years of counseling families, I've learned this: trusting our kids to rise to the occasion is one of the hardest (and greatest) gifts we can give them. They may test every ounce of our patience, but when it comes down to it, they often surprise us.

And boy, did my daughter surprise me that day.

In our family, our middle child is known as the ultimate "ninth-inning gal." She waits until the last possible second to write a paper or study for a final exam, and it was usually accompanied by tantrums and a tsunami of yelling, mostly from me. Yet somehow, she pulls it off.

This time though, she didn't just pull it off. She crushed it. Think bottom-of-the-ninth, bases-loaded, tie-game kind of surprise. Her essay wasn't just a hit; it was a home run. The kind that makes you leap out of your chair, or in my case, cry happy tears into a can of lukewarm Diet Coke.

Her forty-one-minute masterpiece revealed how she overcame her fear of swimming while working as a camp counselor with children battling cancer. Her opening line?

"Superheroes fly, but can they swim?"

She described the moment she stood at the edge of the pool, holding hands with a five-year-old camper who had a brain tumor. Together, they took a deep breath, counted to three, and plunged in. Through vivid, heartwarming details, she captured how the kids she set out to help were the ones who ended up giving her courage.

I immediately called Nancy to read the draft to her. "Yup!" she exclaimed. "Needs some smoothing, but otherwise she's done and it's great. Now go take her shopping."

Yes, it took three or four more drafts to polish it, but the heart of the story was there, beating strong and unedited.

When students tap into something real, the words tend to pour out, raw and unfiltered. Like they've been waiting the whole time.

Uncovering the RIGHT DETAILS

Finding the right story isn't always easy. Over the years, Nancy and I have found that asking the right questions gently brings out the hidden gems that reveal who they are. To reassure you, we're not worried about the Common App prompts at this point. Once we help a student find the right story, choosing a prompt is the easy part.

Here are some of the best questions we use to tease out the gold:

WAS THERE A TIME YOU WERE EMBARRASSED?

One student wrote about working as a lifeguard and heroically jumping into the pool to save a struggling toddler only to realize, as she climbed out to cheers and applause, that her swimsuit strap had come undone, and half her top had slid down. Mortified? Absolutely. But instead of just telling the story, she reflected on how the experience taught her the importance of quick thinking, and equally critical, the value of a well-tied one-piece bathing suit.

Embarrassment is universal, and how we handle it says a lot about who we are. If something makes you cringe? It might be the best essay material.

WHAT'S YOUR FAVORITE BOOK?

A student wrote about *Where the Wild Things Are*—a childhood classic. She would pull out the book as a social icebreaker at her summer internship or after a crushing field hockey loss, proving that humor and simplicity can bring people together in surprising ways.

WHAT'S SOMETHING YOU'RE WEIRDLY GOOD AT?

One student had a "secret shoe system," wearing specific sneakers each day of the week. It was part habit, part superstition, and maybe helped to keep his morning routine simple. But when he accidentally wore the wrong pair on a Wednesday, he realized the world didn't end. That unintentional act gave him the courage to take bigger risks like applying to a competitive science program. Sometimes, real discovery starts with something as simple as a pair of shoes. I can totally relate.

HAVE YOU EVER FAILED? WHAT DID YOU LEARN?

A student once wrote about running for class co-president with her twin brother. She stubbornly dismissed all his campaign ideas, and they lost. That moment taught her to listen, trust, and recognize that even bad ideas (and losing elections) can bring people closer.

WHAT'S YOUR SUPERPOWER?

One student wrote about his talent for seeing beyond the surface. He described his cousin, who has cerebral palsy, and how most people don't notice his sharp wit, kindness, or the way he warms up people in every room. Tired of the assumptions and the inequities he saw in healthcare and education, he headed to Capitol Hill to press for change. His superpower? Seeing what others miss, speaking up, and encouraging others to do the same.

I've read almost every essay-writing book out there, and they're packed with tips and step-by-step guides. But it was my own kid's messy, last-minute writing session that taught me what literally moves the needle. The best essays don't come from perfect outlines or impressive achievements. They come from students who tune into who they are and say something honest. Something you wouldn't find anywhere else in their application. Authenticity above all.

WHAT'S MY STORY? EVERYONE HAS ONE

One of the most common concerns I hear from students is, "I don't have a story!" They're convinced they don't have anything interesting to say, and that their lives are too ordinary, too uneventful. They fear they have nothing that screams "college essay material."

The reality? Everyone has a story. Even your straight-A, never-missed-a-homework-assignment rule-follower child, who swears nothing remotely interesting has ever happened to them. Yup, even them.

The trick isn't having some grand, life-altering moment that you can spin into an essay; it's asking the right questions to uncover the meaningful details that need to come out of hiding. Every student has an experience that shaped them, an event that changed their perspective, a moment that challenged them in a way that left an imprint.

It just takes a little digging.

HOW TO FIND YOUR STORY

When students sit down to write their college essays, they often think they need to showcase their biggest accomplishments or sound as impressive as possible. But admissions officers aren't hiring CEOs or awarding the next Pulitzer Prize. They're looking for *real* people with quirks, flaws, awkwardness, and heart.

Some of the most memorable essays we've read weren't about gene editing for cancer, or scaling Everest, though, yes, we've had students do both. One of the best? It was about working in a smoothie shop.

Jamie, a self-described "average" student, wanted to prove to her parents that she was responsible. She went out and got a job at a local smoothie shop.

It was a disaster.

She hated the smell of bananas, and her manager and co-workers constantly barked orders at her:

"Jamie, restock the cups! Jamie, blend faster!"

She dreaded every shift, but quitting wasn't an option. She was determined to prove herself. Eventually, her best friend convinced her to try working in retail instead. At the mall, Jamie discovered she had a knack for managing customers, especially frazzled moms shopping with their picky daughters.

Her essay wasn't really about smoothies or retail. It was about resilience, having the courage to pivot when things didn't go as planned, and finding her strengths in unexpected places (even behind the juice bar).

Your child doesn't need to be a perfect writer or have some jaw-dropping story to craft a great college essay. The good stuff happens when it's personal and unmistakably theirs.

SHOWING VULNERABILITY IS BETTER THAN BRAGGING

Let me fill you in on a secret: admissions officers aren't moved by personal statements about awards and trophies. They prefer stories of vulnerability over victories.

One student wrote about impulsively dyeing her hair one night. What seemed like a styling regret became the first step toward bigger leaps: performing original songs for her classmates and discovering strengths she didn't know she had. Her essay wasn't about a change in hair color. It was about courage.

Or take the student who wrote about "singlehandedly" launching a nonprofit to support female writers from underserved communities. Impressive? Definitely. But we gently encouraged her to include a few of the inevitable roadblocks. When she opened up about her early missteps and the moments where she nearly gave up, the essay became far more human.

We always remind our students and their parents that no meaningful achievement happens without some stumbles. Admissions officers can spot an over-polished, too-good-to-be-true story from miles away.

When students are willing to share even their smallest moments of doubt or failure, that's when their essays hit home.

ALWAYS START WITH A BANG

Admissions officers are buried in essays, skimming through thousands of them while running on lukewarm coffee and very little sleep. If the first sentence doesn't catch their attention, they may mentally check out and start thinking about their next meal or their next nap.

Some of the best college essays I've seen begin with a single, surprising sentence that practically begs the reader to keep going. Here are a few real examples from students we've worked with, shared with permission and lightly revised to protect privacy:

- "BANG!" (Yes, that was the entire first line. The student was obsessed with the Big Bang and volunteered at a planetarium.)
- "There I stood, peering at the dead body on the cold metal table." (Not a crime scene, but a veterinary office. This student's essay explored compassion and grief.)
- "A half-eaten tuna salad sandwich. A brand new Lululemon shirt with tags still attached. A bra." (Found while sorting a lost-and-found bin at a summer job. The essay explored privilege and perspective. Months later, when we once asked an admissions officer to share the year's most memorable essays, he mentioned this one. We smiled and told him the student was ours.)

The best openings drop us right into the middle of something. Skip the "I've always loved…" or "One day I hope to…" Instead, start with a moment. Make it bold. Make it intriguing. Make the reader want to keep going.

KIND OF CRAZY

SOMETIMES *the* SMALLEST STORIES *are the* MOST MEMORABLE

I was reminded of this when I spoke with Elyan Paz, Assistant Vice President and Dean of Admissions at Macalester College. She shared one of her favorite student essays, which focused on an unexpectedly tender question: who would mow the lawn after he left for college? The student worried about his parents, what his absence would mean for them, and how this small chore symbolized something much bigger in their lives. It was heartfelt and entirely unique. Elyan still remembered it years later because it showed the student's depth of character, all without ever boasting about his accomplishments.

That's the magic we're craving. A college essay doesn't have to be dramatic to be unforgettable. It has to be real. If it matters to your child, it will probably matter to the reader.

THE "SO WHAT?" TEST

Ever read your kid's essay and thought, "Okay…but so what?" That's exactly what we're trying to avoid. A great essay makes an admissions officer pause, or maybe smile, and walk away thinking, "I really get this kid."

Take a story about standing up to a bully. What kindled their courage? How did it change their perspective? If an essay doesn't make the reader think, *"Wow, I really understand this student now,"* it's time to go further beneath the surface.

THE AI TEMPTATION: SHOULD YOUR TEEN USE IT?

With so many essays on their plate, it's no shock some students desperately turn to AI for help. As a seventeen-year-old studying for AP Biology, writing a paper about *The Great Gatsby*, cramming for a calc quiz, and needing more than four hours of sleep, who wouldn't be tempted? The idea of typing in a prompt and getting a polished essay in seconds could be the perfect panacea. But beware. AI cannot write a great college essay.

Admissions officers aren't looking for an essay that sounds like it was generated by a chatbot. They want to hear the student's real voice: how they think, why they fear certain things, what excites them, and how they view the world.

Here's a big heads-up: as AI becomes more commonplace, so does the ability to recognize it. We've spoken to plenty of admissions readers who say they can now spot AI-generated essays easily, thanks to the telltale sentence structure, vocabulary, and tone that doesn't quite sound human. Nancy and I can usually tell, too, especially when there's a big gap between a student's casual writing (like emails, idea drafts, or activity descriptions) and the polished, slightly robotic prose of a first essay draft. It's like watching someone suddenly go from texting in emojis to reciting Shakespeare. Something doesn't add up.

Now there's research to back that up. A recent *Inside Higher Ed* article reported on a Cornell study showing that AI-written college essays stick out like sore thumbs. After comparing tens of thousands of human essays with ones written by ChatGPT, researchers found the difference was clear. The AI versions were impersonal and predictable. When they tried to make the essays more "personal," they piled on identity buzzwords that no real teenager would ever write. One author, Rene Kizilcec, states that using AI to edit might help struggling writers, but relying on it to write will only result in something that "just does not sound like any real applicant."[22]

AI isn't all bad. When used responsibly, it can act like a built-in editor. It can clean up grammar and polish writing. But it can offer ridiculous suggestions like "my path toward academic excellence has been fueled by an unrelenting pursuit of optimization." Eeew. It can also spit out information that's flat-out wrong.

Despite those pitfalls, students are turning to it. According to a national survey

---

22 Johanna Alonso, "Admissions Essays Written with AI Are Easily Identified, Study Finds," *Inside Higher Ed*, October 6, 2025.

reported by *The Chronicle of Higher Education*, about 50% of students have used AI to brainstorm college essays, and 20% have used it to generate full drafts.[23] That doesn't mean they're cheating; it means they're overwhelmed and looking for anything that might ease the pressure.

But no matter how tempting it is, I will repeat myself: AI cannot tell a personal, compelling, human story. Only your kid can do that. As Ellen O'Connell Whittet noted in *The Chronicle of Higher Education*, AI can imitate the outline of a personal essay but can't supply the beating heart or the deeper understanding that comes from writing it yourself.[24]

The best essays aren't filled with fancy words you'd hear in the final round of a spelling bee or in the valedictorian's graduation speech. The best ones feel like an honest conversation with someone you'd be excited to meet. If your teen is stuck, remind them that essay writing is about being real. No AI required.

MAKING SURE THE TOPIC WORKS

Great prompts set the stage, but the chosen topic makes all the difference. The strongest essays reveal a student's ideas or character. Some ideas resonate naturally, while others fall into the overused category. Before your teen settles on an essay topic, it's worth asking: Has this been done a thousand times? If so, is there a way they can give it a fresh twist?

KEEP IT SIMPLE

Encourage your child to forget about the Common App prompts for a second. Seriously, no one's keeping track. Admissions officers are trying to figure out who your child is and what matters to them. Instead of overthinking the prompt, they should pour their energy into telling a story that's undeniably theirs. A strong essay often ends up answering multiple prompts without even trying. Like a great conversation, it covers a bit of everything.

"POINT IN TIME" STORIES ARE OFTEN EASIEST TO TELL

Encourage your child to zoom in on one moment that reveals something meaningful about who they are. No one can possibly write an autobiography crammed into 650 words. Think of the essay as a snapshot, not a documentary. One story, one scene, one insight can go a long way.

23 Beth McMurtrie, "How Are Students Really Using A.I.?" *The Chronicle of Higher Education*, July 17, 2025, https://www.chronicle.com/article/how-are-students-really-using-ai. **24** Ellen O'Connell Whittet, "Students Are Using ChatGPT to Write Their Personal Essays. Now What?" *The Chronicle of Higher Education*, August 11, 2025, https://www.chronicle.com/article/students-are-using-chatgpt-to-write-their-personal-essays-now

TOPICS *that* MIGHT *be* OVERDONE

While there's no such thing as a "bad" topic, deeply personal experiences like loss or unexpected challenges can create powerful essays when told with insight. Here are a few topics that admissions officers often see, but may not always find compelling:

THE SPORTS INJURY ESSAY Torn ACLs, concussions, the missed championship, or the hard-earned victory. "I worked harder, I got better, I overcame." Sure, it's a great personal triumph, but thousands of students tell this *exact* same story. If sports are a huge part of your child's life, the essay should reveal more layers on what sports have taught them beyond perseverance. After being cut from the football team, one student picked up a camera and launched a media team that transformed his high school's spirit. His story wasn't about loss. It was about reinventing himself and staying connected to what he loved.

THE PET ESSAY I'm sure your dog is adorable. But unless Teddy has secretly been coaching your child in leadership skills or inspiring deep existential thoughts, an essay about a beloved pet can be sweet but often doesn't reveal much about your child. One student took a different angle. He wrote beautifully about his longing to have a pet after working one summer at a vet clinic. After comforting an owner who lost their cat, he learned about empathy and the beautiful bonds between humans and pets.

THE DEATH ESSAY Losing a loved one is incredibly painful, and many students naturally want to write about it. The challenge? Grief is universal, but an essay that centers only on the loss itself can feel more like a eulogy than a personal statement. If your child wants to write about this, encourage them to delve into how the experience shaped them moving forward. One student, after losing his mother to leukemia, became fascinated by cancer research and driven to pursue medicine.

THE LEARNING DIFFERENCES ESSAY Overcoming ADHD, dyslexia, or executive functioning challenges is a big deal, but colleges are not interested in reading a diagnostic report. If this is a defining part of your child's journey, it's often better addressed in the "Additional Information" section of their application, rather than the main essay (keep it concise and to the point).

THE SERVICE TRIP TO BUILD SCHOOLS IN A DEVELOPING COUNTRY If an essay focuses more on what your child *did* than how the experience changed them, it can feel generic or unintentionally privileged. Make the story about what they learned, not about mixing cement. One student who helped build wells in Africa came home to Massachusetts and noticed water-access issues in her own town. She researched local contamination and partnered with community groups to help address it.

One student wrote about a long flight with her dad and how she learned the art of compromise by watching his favorite documentaries on their shared iPad. In telling that story, she wove in everything from the history of the Grand Canyon to the evolution of men's hairstyles, showing that a cross-country flight and a documentary can reveal a lot about a person.

Another student wrote about the awkwardness he felt during a power outage at summer camp. With only one flashlight to share among twelve kids, everyone was on edge. One new camper, who was quieter, ended up sitting alone. The student admitted he was unsure what to do in the moment, but he failed to speak up. Later, he reflected on how much that silence stayed with him and how he's made a promise to be more inclusive moving forward.

MAKE SURE IT PASSES THE WEDDING TOAST TEST

If you've ever sat through a wedding toast, a Bar or Bat Mitzvah speech, or a retirement dinner tribute, you know the difference between a speech that captivates the room and one that makes guests start plotting their escape to the bar.

The best toasts don't rattle off generic compliments like "Sarah is kind, hardworking, and loves her family." That could apply to half the guests in the room. What makes a toast memorable is a story like the time Sarah tried to cook a romantic anniversary dinner and nearly burned down the kitchen.

A college essay works the same way. "She pulls all-nighters before exams, volunteers on weekends, and aspires to make the world a better place" sounds like it could describe any overachieving high schooler. It needs to tell a story that only your child could tell. Like at a wedding, no one remembers the clichés. They remember the lines that make them belly laugh or reach for a tissue.

PROOFREAD, PROOFREAD, PROOFREAD

I'm known in my house as the Grammar Police. My three kids still laugh about how they used to proofread their letters before mailing them from sleepaway camp. Not because I told them to, but because they were terrified of how I'd react to a misplaced modifier. Nothing's perfect, of course, but the grammar and spelling in your child's college essay should be as close to perfect as humanly possible. Admissions officers aren't expecting the next Toni Morrison, but they prefer students who can express their thoughts clearly. Sloppy writing signifies not caring enough to proofread, and that's just not a good look.

Here are some foolproof ways I've gently urged my students (and my own kids) to catch mistakes and tighten things up:

1.   **Have them read it out loud.** They might roll their eyes, but it helps catch awkward phrasing and sneaky typos.
2.   **Tell them to take a break.** Stepping away for a few hours (or a day) and coming back with fresh eyes makes a world of difference.
3.   **Get a second opinion.** A teacher, friend, or counselor can spot mistakes that you and your child overlooked.

Quick reassurance: one tiny typo won't wreck their chances. We heard from a colleague about a student who once submitted an essay about her summer research on the brain in a cognitive science lab. She wrote, "I loved being in a lab where scientists are dedicated to figuring out how the Brian works." Despite multiple proofreaders at home and at school, no one caught it.

Despite this typo, did she still get in early decision to Brown? Yes. Now, would she have done so with multiple mistakes? That's a different story... Remind your kid to polish that essay and maybe give autocorrect a second chance.

PARENTS: KEEP OUT!

Admissions officers can smell a fifty-year-old parent's language from a mile away. One year, a mom hijacked her son's essay and wrote, "I had found my carbon copy at the robotics competition." This kid would never have used or understood that ancient reference to an outmoded technology. It was painfully obvious who had taken over. Parents, please step away from the keyboard and be a cheerleader, not a ghostwriter. Offer support and some good snacks, and then let your child's voice speak for itself.

Krista Evans, Dean of Admissions at Lafayette College, echoed this when we spoke. "We can always tell when an essay doesn't sound like a teenager. Sometimes a parent's involvement is obvious. Other times, it's clear a student leaned too heavily on a chatbot. But the essays that stay with us are the ones that feel genuine, where the student's real voice comes through. That's what makes me want to keep reading."

If your child can turn in an essay that sounds like only they could have written it, they've accomplished the most important part.

Another important piece? Teacher recommendations, which give colleges a window into how your child shows up at school...

CHAPTER 12

The Secret Sauce BEHIND STANDOUT TEACHER RECS

"Who's your favorite teacher this year?"

I used to spring this question on my three kids a few weeks into every school year, usually over dinner or during a car ride. They'd light up as they told stories about the teacher who made them excited to come to class. One year it was the chemistry teacher who cracked jokes and cursed during labs. Another year, it was the U.S. History teacher who challenged them to describe the Battle of 1812 through their own Hamilton-style rap. Sometimes, it was just the teacher who "got" them—the one who noticed when they were having an off day and pulled them aside to check in after class.

Along with tales of the "best of the best" were always the stories of the duds. My kids complained about the teacher who could put an entire room to sleep with her monotone voice. They laughed about the one on the verge of retirement who skipped teaching history past 1929. These stories offered a delicious mix of gratitude, giggles, and groans that gave me a window into their school day.

Even now that my kids are grown, I still love asking them to reminisce about their favorite teachers. It's become a cherished family ritual, with the same names coming up again and again, almost like characters in a well-loved book. There's the inspirational fifth-grade teacher at the local elementary school who believed that eleven-year-olds were fully capable of changing the world and assigned them community projects to prove it. Or their compassionate fourth-grade teacher from their elementary school in San Mateo, California, who magically made fractions unforgettable by using real pizza slices. Denominators never tasted so good. They chuckle about the middle school English teacher who ruled her classroom with an iron fist, but taught grammar so well that the rules stuck for life. We will always revere the devoted high school science teacher who also coached the Speech & Debate team, treating his students like capable young adults whose voices mattered. He cared so deeply that he'd practically clear a path through airport crowds to ensure his team boarded first on their way to tournaments. I can still picture him clutching his clipboard and announcing to flight attendants, "We have no time for overhead bin drama!"

What made these teachers stand out wasn't their teaching styles or quirks: it was their heart. They made their students feel like they mattered. They didn't hand out easy grades or coddle anyone. They didn't need to. They left their mark by making my kids feel seen and capable, long after the tests and report cards were forgotten.

I can't resist chiming in with tales of my own most unforgettable teachers because, let's face it, we only remember the *truly* terrific or the *truly* terrible. My kids have heard about Mr. DeNicola,[25] my fearless high school band teacher who pushed us to practice and believe we were one performance away from Carnegie Hall, even if we were playing "Eye of the Tiger" for the 99th time before the spring concert. And Mr. O., my ruthless ninth grade geometry teacher whose bathroom policy was so strict that one unlucky classmate, who wasn't allowed to leave, ended up vomiting onto the kid in the row in front of him. Geometry really is a battlefield! Miss K., my fifth-grade teacher, never left her chair—*ever*—when she taught us. She'd roll herself from one end of the chalkboard to the other like a Formula One driver, somehow managing to scribble everything from math equations to rules on developing a paragraph. My childhood friend Deborah and I even made up a parody (with simple choreography) to "Greased Lightning" about that infamous chair.

---

25 Mr. DeNicola was the most dedicated band teacher at John P. Stevens High School, a true legend in our community. To this day, I still play the piano and often think about the love and discipline he instilled in all his students. When he retired in the spring of 2022, nearly 500 students and faculty gathered in Edison, NJ, to celebrate his incredible legacy at a retirement dinner. It was a gathering that spoke volumes about how much he meant to his students.

These stories, whether they're about my kids' teachers or mine, have a way of reminding my family and me what education is really about. It's not about the perfect syllabus or the trendiest teaching methods. It's about the relationships that stick. The best teachers, whether they're using pizza for fractions or rolling across a classroom to teach, leave an impact long after we've forgotten the themes from King Lear's tragedies or the purpose of the quadratic formula.

Not surprisingly, the most compelling recommendation letters come from those stand-out teachers who truly know the student. A great rec doesn't regurgitate a student's academic record; it paints a real picture of a student's curiosity and growth in a classroom.

SHOT OF SANITY

The "secret sauce" isn't about picking the most impressive teacher on paper—it's about choosing the one who has really seen your child learn.

The AP Bio teacher might write a technically strong letter, but if the English teacher witnessed your kid wrestle with ideas and take feedback to the next level, that voice will be more powerful every time. Colleges can tell when a teacher is writing from the heart, not from a template.

WHY DOES THIS MATTER SO MUCH?

In the admissions process, the teacher recommendation often provides what numbers can't: tone, texture, and context. Grades and test scores show achievement, but teacher letters show engagement—how a student learns, leads, listens, and responds to challenge.

As Victor Thomas, Director of Admissions at Washington University in St. Louis, told me, "In selective admissions, a teacher's recommendation can reveal what grades and test scores can't: how a student thinks, engages, and perseveres. When a teacher captures a student's curiosity, humor, or quiet determination in the classroom, an application comes alive. Sometimes, that kind of insight becomes an influential factor in making a final decision."

Let's not overlook the beauty of character either. Perhaps there's a teacher who observed your child stepping in to help an overwhelmed classmate without ever being asked, and now the student is a "go-to" tutor for several kids. These are the glimpses that define a student, and the very ones the teachers write about in their letter.

The RIGHT TIME *to* ASK *for* THESE GLOWING ENDORSEMENTS

Junior year is prime time for students to be building these relationships. Eleventh-grade teachers are usually the best bet, since junior year is the most heavily scrutinized. But exceptions exist: that tenth-grade teacher who's also the soccer coach and really understands your kid? Gold mine. That B in a tough class where the teacher saw real growth might outshine a rec letter from a teacher in a class where the student got an easy A. Everyone loves an underdog.

Whether a student is breezing through a subject or grinding it out one quiz at a time, a teacher's recommendation is an opportunity to highlight their curiosity, resilience, determination, and how they treat people around them. Teachers notice when a student cares not just about the grade, but about the learning and the class community.

It's hard to ignore a student who willingly asks for extra practice problems or gets ridiculously excited about the French Revolution (even if they're secretly in it for the guillotine drama). Developing a good rapport with teachers is always a win, even if they don't end up writing a recommendation letter.

WHO SHOULD STUDENTS ASK?

Ideally, students should think about asking one teacher in the humanities realm (English, history, or foreign language), and one in STEM (math or science). If your child is destined to spend their days debating philosophy and pondering existential truths, they still need to balance that commitment with a solid demonstration of problem-solving grit in physics or trigonometry. Remember that Aristotle had to deal with numbers at some point! The same holds true for aspiring Nobel Prize-winning phys-icists. It's equally important to showcase an appreciation for literature or language. Balance is key.

Please don't panic if your child's strongest connections are with two teachers from the same area. What matters most is that the recommendations are thoughtful and speak to who your child is in the classroom.

One other important note: if your child is applying to an arts program, don't for-get their art, drama, or music teacher. No one knows their creative fire better than the person who's seen them lose themselves in a canvas or bring down the house with a solo. This letter should complement the required core teacher recommendations, not replace them.

HOW SHOULD YOUR CHILD APPROACH TEACHERS FOR A RECOMMENDATION?

Asking a teacher for a recommendation can feel intimidating for students, but it's a meaningful milestone and far less nerve-wracking than a promposal. It's a chance for your child to reflect on the adults who've seen them struggle and grow.

That's why I always encourage students to make the initial ask in person. A quick, respectful face-to-face conversation of, "Would you be willing to write a letter of recom-mendation for me?" goes a long way. It shows maturity, and it allows your child to gauge the teacher's body language and response.

Does the teacher seem genuinely enthusiastic? Fantastic. That energy often leads to a strong, heartfelt letter. But if the teacher hesitates or offers a vague, "Sure, I guess," it's okay for your child to say, "I really appreciate it, but I want to make sure this is the right fit. Would it be better for me to ask someone else?" Most teachers appreciate the chance to bow out, and your child can move on to someone who can speak more fully to their strengths. If a teacher declines, it's rarely personal. Sometimes they're stretched too thin. Popular teachers, especially at large high schools fill up quickly. Ask early.

Once a teacher agrees, your child should send a thoughtful follow-up email. It's the perfect chance to thank them again and share anything that will make their job eas-ier, like a resume, activities list, or a few sentences about why they chose this teacher. Maybe they want to mention what they learned during that brutal group project in Spanish class or how this teacher inspired their love of French literature. Many teachers also have their own questionnaire for students to complete.

Teachers are everyday rockstars, and it's important to remember that they are busy people, often juggling multiple recommendation requests on top of their regular responsibilities. Between grading papers, revising lesson plans, and coaching volleyball, they tackle these requests alongside everything else, *without* extra pay in an already underpaid profession. Invite your child to be organized and respectful. A polite follow-up a few weeks before the deadline (along with a note of appreciation) isn't just a practical reminder; it's a way to say thanks and ensure everything stays on track. While gentle reminders are also helpful, hounding teachers is not. They do this every year. Even if they come in by the skin of their teeth, the letters get done. The kids may sweat it out a bit, but the teachers always pull through.

WHAT ABOUT OPTIONAL LETTERS?

Sometimes, it makes sense to include a third letter from a coach, clergy member, research mentor, music or dance teacher, or someone who can speak meaningfully about your child's talent or character. But use this option sparingly. Colleges are not looking to wade through extra letters unless these recommendations offer something genuinely new and valuable. If this person knows your child well and can highlight something that wouldn't otherwise come through in the application, it might be worth including. Keep in mind that policies differ. Some colleges allow additional recommendations and others do not, so please check each school's guidelines before submitting anything extra.

Most students and parents never see these letters, and that's by design. When students sign the FERPA waiver on the Common App, they're agreeing not to access their recommendations later. FERPA (the Family Educational Rights and Privacy Act) protects student records and waiving that right assures colleges that the teacher's letter is candid and confidential. Admissions officers tend to value these letters more when they know the student hasn't read them.

The most impactful letters come from teachers who see the student as more than just a grade. When that happens, the recommendation becomes more than a letter; it becomes a portrait of a young person ready to take on the world. Those become the stories admissions officers never forget. If your child is lucky, the teacher writing their letter is the one who made fractions, Shakespeare, or the French Revolution unexpectedly fun. That's something no checklist can measure.

CHAPTER 13

Unplanned And Unforgettable: EMBRACING *what* YOU *didn't* SEE COMING

Parents often ask Nancy and me, "How can we make our kid stand out?"

Our answer: "You don't *make* it happen. You *let* it happen." While this can be hard to hear for families who want to map out their child's success and help facilitate their path, the truth is that sometimes the best approach is to let kids fall into something life-changing by complete accident. If there's one thing I've learned, it's that some of the most defining moments in life usually aren't the ones we script. They're the ones that sneak up on us.

That was me in the spring of 1985, when I was standing on a stage as the newly elected Girls State Governor of New Jersey. I didn't plan for it, I didn't expect it, and I certainly didn't think it would become my golden ticket to college admissions.

In June of my junior year, I was selected along with one other girl from J.P. Stevens High School to join 550 promising young leaders from across the state of New Jersey at Rider College (now Rider University). Girls State, run by the American Legion, promised a week-long crash course in local and state government—elections, campaigns, debates, the whole nine yards. Politics semi-intrigued me. I'd spent a year as

Student Council Vice President, though my biggest contribution was selling branded school supplies out of the Woodrow Wilson Junior High School student store.

I often daydreamed about becoming a lawyer, not out of some noble love of justice, but because I had a solid history of winning arguments against my older brother about where our family went to dinner: Friendly's (my choice) or Burger King (his). Model UN was interesting too, though let's be real; giving dramatic speeches was way more fun than debating foreign policy. To be honest, I thought Girls State would look good on my college applications and maybe—just maybe—be interesting.

At first, it wasn't. It was the first week of summer break, and I stood in a room full of sugary sweet girls, earnestly and endlessly chatting about their hours spent volunteering for their local hospital or church. I felt ridiculously out of place. That first night, I snuck out after "lights out," and called my mom from the dorm's pay phone.

"Mom! Please rescue me," I begged.

In her loving but no-nonsense Bronx accent, she firmly advised, "Beth! Give it twenty-four hours and call me tomorrow."

As usual, Mom was right.

HOW I ACCIDENTALLY BECAME GOVERNOR

Soon, I realized that politics wasn't just about law-making, budgets, and delivering long speeches. The gist of it was talking to people (something I loved), understanding their needs, and figuring out ways to make things better—a lesson I wish today's politicians could absorb. Within twenty-four hours, I was intrigued. By midweek, I was all in. I went after every minor position I could get my hands on, from dog catcher to city councilor. Soon, I set my sights on the top spot: Girls State Governor.

To win, I'd need a platform, and that's where Professor Purple was born. My party, the Nationalists, was red; the opposing Federalists were blue. I declared myself a symbol of compromise, blending red and blue into purple (still my favorite color). High school teachers and civic leaders volunteering as facilitators led debates and guided us through the workings of state government as we crafted policies and delivered speeches like semi-pros. My platform had three P's (Performance, Progress, and, well...I can't remember the third one since it's been so many decades). Apparently, it was a hit.

I spent nights having candid conversations with candidates from all sides, diving into debates, and researching until 4 a.m. in the Rider College library, tackling issues like Superfund sites and sanitation (this was New Jersey, after all). At the end of the week, Governor Thomas Kean arrived by helicopter to swear me in after I'd been elected as Girls State Governor. The moment was surreal.

When Governor Kean walked down the aisle in the auditorium toward me up on the stage (me, in my long Gunne Sax dress with perfectly feathered hair), I was so overwhelmed that I did what my parents had always instructed me to do when greeting someone: I hugged him.

You can imagine his surprise. The crowd burst into laughter, and I went on to give a speech about civic duty and finding ways to make a difference. My parents were in the audience, undoubtedly relieved and proud that I'd miraculously made it through the week. They even brought a Hebrew Bible for the swearing-in, adding an extra layer of meaning to the ceremony.

WHAT DOES "STANDING OUT" REALLY MEAN?

Winning the title of Governor wasn't about the prestige; it was about the process.

That week gave me more than a great story for my college applications. Sure, it gave me a fun title to own for a year, but more importantly, it taught me the value of channeling a little *chutzpah*,[26] and saying "yes" to the unknown. Girls State taught me that some of the best experiences come when we let go of the plan, push past doubt, and allow ourselves to be surprised. It's a lesson that I've carried into my work as a college counselor.

SHOT OF SANITY

Funny thing about life—the moments that stay with us usually aren't the ones we plan. Not because they were part of a grand plan, but because they weren't. They slip in through a conversation that runs long or a project that's plain fun to keep going.

EVERYONE'S KID IS EXCEPTIONAL IN THEIR OWN WAY

For most students, standing out doesn't mean winning national awards. It's about paying attention to those moments when something grabs their interest, even if it doesn't fit with who they think they're supposed to be.

There was a boy who *swore* he was going to be a doctor until he spent many eve-

---

26 *Chutzpah* is Yiddish for audacity, nerve, or guts with a dash of flair. Think boldness with heart—the kind that makes your grandma proud.

nings skipping bio homework to chat with his grandfather about New York City in the 1940's. He didn't mean to veer off course, but listening to those stories was more fascinating than delving into mitochondria. What began as a few conversations with his grandfather turned into digitizing old photos and piecing together an oral history project about the Lower East Side of Manhattan. He's majoring in history now, something his freshman-year self never would have predicted.

Or the teen who, stuck at home during quarantine, offered to grocery shop for an elderly neighbor who could no longer drive. What started as a kind gesture turned into regular visits and a friendship that bridged decades. He didn't set out to build intergenerational bonds; he just followed what felt right. That neighborly act grew into an interest in how communities work, and today he's studying sociology.

That's exactly what colleges love: students who follow where their hearts lead, even if it's not where they originally meant to go. Plus, these stories, like the students behind them, feel completely real and 100% human.

KIND OF CRAZY

The "STANDOUT" FACTOR *(Minus the Stress)*

If your kid is gunning for one of those ultra-selective, single-digit acceptance rate schools, then yes, standing out might take something a little extra. These schools aren't simply looking for strong students; they're drawn to stories that are unquestionably rare. Like the teen who spoke at City Hall about clean water and ended up being invited to join the local city council, while still in high school. Or the student who volunteered at a local planetarium, created bilingual astronomy shows for neighborhood kids, then joined a summer research program where he helped track the orbit of an asteroid.

These stories don't happen every day, and they're certainly not the norm. But they're what can happen when an interest takes off and becomes something more.

That's the part that parents need to hear more often: those schools are the exception, not the norm. Most colleges aren't expecting the next Malala Yousafzai or Lin-Manuel Miranda. They want students who have dug into their interests and built something real and personal. And that is truly more than enough. Dayenu.[27]

---

27 *Dayenu is a Hebrew word that means "it would have been enough." It's the refrain of a cherished Passover song that celebrates gratitude for each step of the Israelites' journey from slavery to freedom.*

THE TAKEAWAY

What should parents do?

Help your child notice what excites them even when it doesn't match the "plan." Standing out doesn't require superpowers; it requires self-awareness. Sometimes, what lights them up at fourteen might look entirely different at seventeen. That's more than okay. It's normal. The greatest thing you can do is cheer them on as they follow the thread, whether it leads to performing in a school musical for the first time or mentoring younger students in something they love. The right college isn't looking for perfect kids. They're looking for real ones. The kind who are inquisitive and gutsy enough to be themselves.

We once worked with a family whose daughter, Amy, had been laser-focused on science since middle school. She'd spent two summers in a lab pipetting and charting and doing all the things future researchers are "supposed" to do. Everyone assumed Amy would write her ticket to a top program in chemistry. Then, junior year hit, and she managed to land the lead in *Mamma Mia!* Suddenly, she wasn't only measuring molecules. She was belting out "Dancing Queen" like a seasoned Broadway actress. For once, Amy was having a blast. Her application became a brilliant blend of sharp analysis and creativity: equal parts periodic table and jazz hands. Admissions officers ate it up.

Colleges aren't looking for superheroes. They're looking for students who seize opportunities and dive in. As I learned at Girls State, some of the best adventures and the best versions of ourselves, emerge when we're brave enough to go along with it.

If you're still wondering how to help your kid stand out, here's the secret: you don't. They already do. Nancy and I have worked with hundreds of students over the years, and every single one has something that makes them remarkable. Our job as adults is to give them the freedom to follow it, even when it looks nothing like the plan we imagined. Along the way, let them remind you, again and again, just how exceptional they already are.

CHAPTER 14

HOW *to* PAY *for* COLLEGE WITHOUT LOSING *a* KIDNEY

A dad once proudly declared that he'd sell a kidney to pay for his daughter's dream school. He was joking (well, mostly). Another mom and dad swore they'd work three jobs and eat nothing but ramen for the rest of their lives if their daughter got into Yale. (She got in. I sincerely hope they occasionally splurge on other meals.) Then there was the student who started baking cookies in her dorm kitchen and selling them during study breaks to fund her textbooks and her addiction to bubble tea.

While we strongly advise against organ donation, an all-carb diet, or running a dorm-room bakery without a permit, we do believe that with some savvy strategies, and a little patience, you can make college more affordable without resorting to desperate measures.

We also recognize that not everyone is starting from the same financial place.

Some families can afford to write the tuition check without blinking. However, this book is for every parent trying to make thoughtful, informed decisions about an increasingly expensive process. Maybe your kid is looking at schools that offer need-based aid. Maybe you have friends or family members deep in the financial aid throes trying to figure out what's what. Maybe, like me, you love a good deal and treat finding tuition discounts the same way you'd hunt for a once-a-year Bloomingdale's sale, even if you are there for the window shopping.

Even if you don't qualify for need-based aid, why overpay for college if you don't have to? Financial aid and merit scholarships aren't only for families on tight budgets; they're for anyone looking to make college more affordable. Whether you have a school counselor, a private advisor, or nothing more than a highlighter and a hopeful attitude, you deserve to understand your options.

If you're reading this chapter, you've probably figured out that four years of college tuition today can rival the price of a house. But instead of getting hardwood floors and an eat-in kitchen, you end up with a thin twin XL mattress, a used desk, and a communal bathroom that always seems to be out of toilet paper.

Dorm accommodations notwithstanding, there are real ways to bring the cost down. So wherever you are in this process, I hope this chapter will make it a little less overwhelming.

QUICK DISCLAIMER

WE ARE NOT FINANCIAL AID EXPERTS

Nancy and I are not certified financial planners or aid officers. Trust me—that's better; this stuff often feels like you need a Ph.D. just to decipher it. We don't claim to have all the answers, but after working with hundreds of families over the years, we have a sense of which questions keep parents up at night.

FINANCIAL AID 101: WHAT IT IS (AND ISN'T)

Let's start with the big one: the **FAFSA.**

The FAFSA—short for *Free Application for Federal Student Aid*—is the form that unlocks practically everything: grants, work-study, low-interest loans, and sometimes even scholarships. You fill it out once a year for each kid you have in college. If you skip it, you could be leaving thousands on the table.

Filling out this form used to be as painful as assembling IKEA furniture without instructions (or maybe even *with* instructions). However, in 2024, the FAFSA got a major makeover, cutting down the number of questions and simplifying the process by allowing you to directly input numbers from your tax return with the push of a button. Hallelujah.

Before you dive in, please gather your tax returns, savings info, and a healthy dose of patience. Have more than one kid in college? Congrats! You get to do it again. Every year. The good news? It gets easier after the first round, and having multiple students in college at the same time can increase your eligibility for aid.

Once submitted, you'll receive a number called the **Student Aid Index (SAI)** (formerly the **EFC** or Expected Family Contribution). This SAI indicates how much the government thinks you can contribute to college. The lower the SAI number, the more aid your student *may* receive.

Try not to get too excited by that number. Every college interprets it differently, and many use their own formulas (and their own version of reality) to determine what they'll really offer. Some meet full need. Others shrug and wish you luck.

Also, many parents take one look at this number and assume they must have filled out something wrong. You make what feels like a solid income, and the formula still says that you can afford far more than seems humanly possible. With what? A hidden trust fund no one told you about? What about the mortgage and groceries? Oh, and your other kids? None of that gets factored in the way it should. I promise you're not crazy.

AND THEN THERE'S THE CSS PROFILE (COLLEGE SCHOLARSHIP SERVICE PROFILE)

While the FAFSA covers federal and some institutional aid by evaluating your income and assets, the CSS Profile goes deeper. This form asks about home equity, business assets, and other goodies. Honestly, if it could ask for your height, weight, and Amazon password, it probably would. Most private colleges use the CSS Profile to determine how much additional aid to offer from their own institutional funds. A handful of public universities have added it in recent years as well. For example, the University of Michigan and the University of Virginia now require it. The CSS may feel invasive, but it gives schools a fuller picture of your financial situation, whether you like it or not.

That brings us to the next big question:

What will college cost, for real?

Let me introduce you to your new best friend: the **Net Price Calculator**, or NPC.

It's not perfect, but it's the best tool we've got for estimating what a college might actually cost *you*—after grants, scholarships, and need-based aid are applied. While facing the realities of tuition is definitely not the fun part of the college process, it's smart to run the numbers **before** your kid falls in love with a school's unlimited post-dinner Chipwiches.

We recommend starting with the official government Net Price Calculator (NPC) (studentaid.gov/aid-estimator), which tends to be more reliable than many third-party sites. Think of it as your college tuition fortune teller: it won't give you exact numbers, but it'll estimate what your out-of-pocket costs might look like.

Please remember that it's an estimate, not a binding contract. Each school has its own way of crunching numbers, and the final offer can look dramatically different from what the calculator predicts.

Another great option is the College Board's tool at bigfuture.collegeboard.org, which links to over 160 school-specific calculators. It's especially handy if your kid is casting a wide net, and many are. Many schools also offer their own NPCs on their websites.

LET'S TALK SPECIFICS

Understanding financial aid is like trying to decode an argument between your teenagers in the family group chat. It may be important, but there are way too many messages and even more acronyms to follow.

There are three primary types of aid: federal, state, and institutional.

1. **Federal aid** includes grants (which don't need to be paid back), loans (subsidized or unsubsidized), and work-study programs (students must earn these amounts while working on campus). While federal aid is based on a standard formula, the actual aid offered to the same student can vary between schools due to differences in funding and distribution policies. In the 2024–25 academic year, undergraduate students received an average of $5,260 in federal grant aid.[28] However, individual awards can vary widely based on factors like financial need, cost of attendance, and enrollment status.

   One important thing to note: While most federal aid and Pell Grants are guaranteed to eligible students who submit the FAFSA on time, some schools and states have their own funding that may be limited. Submitting the FAFSA by your institution's deadline ensures that students are considered for *all possible aid*, including school-based grants and work-study programs. No need for alarm. Just don't wait until the night before it's due when you're bound to be immersed in snack wrappers and rising blood pressure. Earlier is better.

---

28 College Board. "Trends in Student Aid 2024," The College Board. https://research.collegeboard.org/trends/student-aid

2. **State aid** varies significantly depending on where you live. Some states are incredibly generous, offering grants that make public universities much more affordable. Others provide little to no aid, leaving students to fend for themselves (sorry, New Hampshire). In New York, students can apply for the Tuition Assistance Program (TAP), which awarded an estimated $698 million to about 255,000 students in the 2023-24 academic year.[29] This program helps many students cover tuition at in-state public and private colleges. Not all states offer substantial aid, and some don't offer any aid at all. Many prioritize their own residents, while others allow out-of-state students to apply for certain scholarships or tuition reciprocity programs. Sometimes, attending a college just across the border can be significantly cheaper than staying in-state. One last tip: Some states have deadlines that are much earlier than federal financial aid deadlines, so try not to wait until the last minute to apply.

3. **Institutional aid** comes directly from colleges and can be as unpredictable as a pop quiz in AP French. It often includes both need-based grants and merit scholarships; it's basically any money the school awards from its own funds to help reduce a family's cost. One college might offer a generous grant, while another provides little to no aid, leaving families to cover the full cost. Because of this variation, it's smart to compare financial and merit aid offers carefully before making a final decision. Tools like the College-Data "Compare Awards" can help families evaluate different packages and spot the best fit.

Let's break down federal aid even further:

1. **Grants (Money you don't need to pay back)**
    Grants are awarded based on financial need—not grades, extracurriculars, or competitive sports. Many colleges and states offer them based on FAFSA data. If your family qualifies, take them. They're free money, and you don't have to pay them back (woo-hoo!).

    Among the most common federal grants are the Pell Grant and the Federal Supplemental Educational Opportunity Grant (FSEOG). The Pell Grant is the largest need-based federal grant, awarded to students with significant

---

29 New York State Higher Education Services Corporation, *2023-24 Annual Report*, (Albany: HESC, 2024), 4, https://www.hesc.ny.gov/about/news-releases/new-york-state-higher-education-services-corporation-announces-release-its-2023.

financial need. The FSEOG provides additional aid for students with the greatest financial need, but funds are limited and awarded by individual colleges that participate in the program, about 3,700 nationwide.

2.   **Work-Study (Campus jobs for books, living expenses, and maybe late-night pizza)**

Work-study is a federally funded program that allows students to earn money through part-time jobs on campus. Their paycheck goes directly to them, helping cover personal expenses like books, food, and late-night Uber-Eats treats. Unlike grants, money from work-study isn't automatic. Students must apply for a job and work to earn their money.

In addition to federal work-study, many colleges also offer their own institutionally funded work-study programs. These provide similar opportunities for students who may not qualify for federal work-study but still want an on-campus job (that pays more) to help with expenses. Students are responsible for keeping track of their earnings so they don't exceed the amount they were awarded through work-study. If this happens, they may have to stop working or transition to a non-work-study position.

While there isn't a federal cap on weekly hours, schools often set their own limits to ensure students maintain a healthy balance between work and academics. For instance, Stevens Institute of Technology caps student work-study hours at twenty per week.[30]

A handful of the best work-study gigs we're familiar with include:
- **Library Assistant:** Getting paid to whisper "Shush!" to other students while possibly getting some studying done.
- **Gym Attendant:** Watching other people work out while sitting comfortably behind the check-in desk (great for fitness buffs).
- **Tour Guide:** Boasting about the school like it's the next best thing to Disney World (awesome for extroverts).
- **Dining Hall Staff:** Replenishing salad bars and serving food or tidying up dining halls (maybe not so great for neat freaks).

---

30 Stevens Institute of Technology. "Federal Work Study Information." Accessed February 2025. https://www.stevens.edu/page-right-nav/federal-work-study-information.aid

3.   **Federal Student Loans—a helpful tool but with limits**

Federal student loans make college possible for millions of students, but understanding the borrowing limits is important. The current maximum amount in 2025 that a dependent undergraduate can borrow over four years is $27,000—starting at $5,500 for the first year and increasing slightly each consecutive year. This is generally considered a reasonable amount to help make college affordable.

Here's a breakdown of the main types of loans:

- **Subsidized Loans (The best-case scenario):** The government covers the interest while your child is in school and for six months after graduation. Think of this as a temporary free lunch. However, these are need-based, so not everyone qualifies.

- **Unsubsidized Loans (The proceed with caution loans):** Interest starts accruing the second the loan is disbursed. Consider this your teenager's laundry pile that grows the second you turn away. The smart move? Pay off the interest while they're in school if you can, so it doesn't pile onto their balance later. Both subsidized and unsubsidized loans still tend to have lower interest rates than private loans.

- **Parent PLUS Loans (The "are you sure about this?" option):** These are federal loans taken out by parents to cover whatever tuition remains after aid. Approval depends on credit history, though the standards aren't as strict as obtaining a mortgage. Apparently, it's easier to borrow for college than to buy a home.

Under the new One Big Beautiful Bill Act (OBBBA), Parent PLUS loans will now be capped. Most of the legislation focuses on limiting graduate borrowing, but this specific cap applies to undergraduate Parent PLUS loans, too.

LOAN REPAYMENT OPTIONS

If you're going to take out loans, it's important to have a payback plan. Federal loans still offer income-driven repayment (IDR) options that set payments based on income and family size. Public Service Loan Forgiveness (PSLF) can erase remaining balances for borrowers who spend ten years working in public service and making steady payments. In other words, if your child becomes a teacher or social worker, they may not be vacationing in Fiji every winter, but at least they can follow their passion without being buried in debt.

Rules are evolving. In late 2025, the Education Department clarified PSLF rules to make it clearer which employers qualify and which don't.

Separately, Congress and the Department of Education are phasing in new repayment rules starting in 2026. A new **Repayment Assistance Plan** (RAP) will eventually replace most current income-driven options for future borrowers, while those with existing loans can keep their current plans.

Bottom line: payments still depend on income, and public-service workers may qualify for forgiveness. Please keep an eye on rule changes before committing to a plan.[31]

WHO ACTUALLY GETS AID? IT'S NOT JUST WHO YOU THINK

Before you freak out over a school's sticker price, take a breath and check out the school's Net Price Calculator (NPC). Many families rule out a $75K-per-year school, only to later realize their actual cost could be far lower and sometimes even competitive with their in-state public university. It's like spotting an item you thought was out of reach, only to find out it's on sale after all.

We've witnessed it firsthand. One of our pro bono students through YPIE (Yonkers Partners in Education) received such a generous financial aid package from Manhattan College that it covered almost everything. It was an incredible outcome for a student who wanted to stay close to his single mom, a mere fifteen minutes away. Another pro bono student, whose parents both worked double shifts as nurses, earned a tremendous package from Smith College that made her first-choice school possible. It's stories like those that remind me financial aid isn't only about forms and formulas. It can make college possible and may change everything for a family.

Some of the best deals in college admissions are like understudies. They're easily overlooked, but ready to "wow" you the moment they get a chance to perform. Many families are stunned when they discover their student qualifies for substantial merit aid. We've also seen plenty of students with solid but imperfect transcripts, including some B's, maybe even a C or two, receive generous scholarships from both public and private universities. If your child is open to going a little farther from home, there are real opportunities out there. Many out-of-state public schools and lesser-known private colleges offer attractive incentives to recruit students who bring something distinctive like geographic diversity or a special talent. Some of these awards are based purely on academic merit, while others go to students who may not qualify for traditional need-based aid but are still a strong match for the school's enrollment goals.

---

31 U.S. Department of Education, "U.S. Department of Education Announces Final Rule on Public Service Loan Forgiveness to Protect American Taxpayers," news release, October 31, 2025; Federal Student Aid, "Repayment Plans" and "Income-Driven Repayment Plans," and Federal Register, Public Inspection: Final Rule—Public Service Loan Forgiveness, Doc. No. 2025-19729.

While policies vary by school and can change from year to year, there are a few tools that make it easier to research merit scholarships by college. Try the CollegeData "Compare Awards" feature or the federal StudentAid.gov scholarship search. Both let you explore how schools typically award merit aid and compare the kinds of scholarships students receive.

Here are a handful of examples:

- **The University of Arizona** hands out hefty Arizona Tuition Awards to many out-of-state students. Ideal if your kid craves sunshine 24/7.
- **The University of Missouri** actively recruits top students with substantial merit-based scholarships, aiming to make tuition more affordable for out-of-state students.
- **The University of Kentucky** offers big scholarships (delicious fried chicken is likely an extra bonus).
- **The University of Kansas** provides significant scholarships to attract high-achieving students from across the country, reducing the financial burden for non-residents.
- **The University of Maine** allows out-of-state students from partner states to pay the equivalent of Maine's in-state tuition through its Flagship Match program, making it a cost-effective choice.
- **The University of Vermont** gives generous merit aid (and easy access to Ben & Jerry's).
- **Oregon State and the University of Washington** are also known for strong merit aid for out-of-state applicants.

PRIVATE VS. PUBLIC: WHICH ACTUALLY COSTS LESS?

Thanks to hefty endowments, private schools often have more money to throw at students in the form of merit and need-based aid. That can bring the actual cost down to a number that seems shockingly reasonable, or at least less terrifying. On the flip side, some out-of-state public universities can be just as pricey, especially when there's little or no merit aid available. In fact, a $75K-per-year private school might end up costing $30K after aid, making it cheaper than a $40K public option.

Some private colleges are more generous than you might expect. Schools like Amherst, Bowdoin, and Rice routinely pledge to meet 100% of demonstrated need for admitted students, often without requiring loans. You can check whether a college makes this promise on its financial aid website or on trusted resources like CollegeData.

Others, like Tulane, the University of Southern California, and Emory, offer substantial merit-scholarship packages that can ease the tuition burden in a big way for many applicants.

Do YOU NEED *to* APPLY *for* FINANCIAL AID *to* GET MERIT AID?

This is one of those murky areas in college admissions.

Most schools do not require the FAFSA or CSS Profile to award merit scholarships. Every year, we see students receive tens of thousands of dollars in merit aid without ever filling out a financial aid form. Still, it's always smart to double-check each school's policy.

WHAT'S THE TRADEOFF?

- If you apply for financial aid and don't qualify, a need-aware school may flag your student as "not full pay." This typically only affects students who are right on the edge of admission. Strong applicants are still admitted, regardless of need (For context: need-aware schools may consider finances in admissions; need-blind ones don't). You can usually find this information on a college's admissions or financial aid webpage or in national listings like the U.S. News list of need-blind colleges.

- If you skip the financial aid forms entirely, you may miss out on certain scholarships at the handful of schools that require them to award merit aid.

Here's the skinny: colleges aren't out to build the least expensive class; they're aiming to build the strongest one. High-achieving students often receive merit aid, whether they apply for financial assistance or not. But in borderline cases at need-aware schools, full-pay status can occasionally give students a slight edge.

What should you do? Do you skip the paperwork to protect admissions chances? Or do you submit the forms in hopes of snagging merit money?

It's a bit like choosing between a direct flight and one with a layover. One might be smoother, but the other could save you a bundle.

There's no one-size-fits-all approach. It really depends on your family's financial priorities, your child's academic profile, and the colleges on their list.

Harvard University recently announced that starting in the 2025–26 academic year, it will eliminate tuition fees for students from families earning up to $200,000 annually.[32] For families earning under $100,000, the university will also cover housing, food, and health services.

Similarly, Stanford University offers free tuition for families earning under $125,000, with most families earning under $150,000 paying significantly reduced tuition. Stanford also has a no-loan policy, meaning financial aid packages do not include loans. Finally, a break from the dreaded student debt.

Don't let the sticker price scare you off. One student we worked with got into his in-state public university for $32K per year but was offered a scholarship at a private college that brought his cost down to $27K. Same degree, lower price, happy kid, ecstatic parents.

WHEN YOU NEED TO ASK FOR MORE HELP

Your first financial aid offer isn't always the final word. Colleges understand that life can throw unexpected challenges your way. Job losses, medical bills, or other major financial changes can absolutely justify asking for more help. We've seen plenty of families go through this, and yes, it's possible to appeal and succeed. Here's how:

1. **Reach out to the Financial Aid Office early.**
   Don't wait until your child's tuition bill shows up. Most schools have firm deadlines for appeals, and financial aid officers aren't mind-readers. The earlier you contact them, the more options you'll have.

2. **Write a short but clear letter explaining your situation.**
   If you've experienced a job loss, attach a termination letter or proof of unemployment benefits. If medical expenses are the issue, share relevant documents. Keep the tone respectful and honest. Colleges don't want to read about emotion or drama. They want a factual update on your family's circumstances.

3. **Ask about additional aid.**
   Some schools have emergency funds or limited discretionary aid that isn't widely advertised. You may not know what's available unless you ask, "Is there any additional help available based on our current situation?"

4. **Be realistic, but don't be afraid to follow up.**
   Appeals aren't guaranteed, but some families do receive thousands of dollars in additional aid simply by advocating for themselves. Follow up politely if you haven't heard back, but understand that every school's resources are different.

---

32 "Harvard to Eliminate Tuition for Families Earning Up to $200,000," The New York Times, March 17, 2025, https://www.nytimes.com/2025/03/17/us/politics/harvard-free-tuition.html.

5. **Use competing offers to your advantage.**
   If your child has a better financial aid offer from another school, you can (respectfully) share that information when you appeal. It doesn't guarantee a match, but many colleges will reconsider an award if it means enrolling a strong candidate.

OTHER THINGS TO WATCH OUT FOR

Not all financial aid packages are as generous or reliable as they first appear. Some colleges front-load aid, offering large grants and scholarships for freshman year, only to reduce them later. This "bait and switch" tactic can leave families facing much higher tuition bills than anticipated.

Unlike merit aid, which is typically renewable for four years as long as students maintain the required GPA (see below), need-based aid can fluctuate yearly. While some schools, like Princeton, guarantee to meet full financial need every year, others, like Cal State Polytechnic, may pull back support without much warning. It's worth asking schools how they handle aid beyond freshman year. Do they meet 100% of demonstrated need all four years? Or does that commitment drop after year one?

Merit aid can also come with strings attached. Many scholarships require students to maintain a minimum GPA. If your child's grades dip, their funding can, too. Make sure your student understands those requirements early to avoid icky surprises down the line.

Even with a solid financial aid package, hidden costs can sneak up fast. Flights home for holidays? Pricey. A meal plan upgrade when your kid realizes they hate cafeteria food? Extra. Greek life dues, mandatory health insurance, lab fees for science classes? Yes, more money.

Go in with eyes wide open. Families who ask the right questions early on and build in a little cushion are far more likely to avoid financial stress later. One more thing to check: some colleges require families to submit the FAFSA and the CSS Profile in freshman year if they want to be eligible for aid in future years. Policies vary but missing that first-year deadline can close the door later, even if your financial situation changes.

WHERE TO GET HELP

Feeling underwater? Here are some solid resources that may help you find the right path through the financial aid labyrinth:

- SCHOLARSHIP SEARCH ENGINES Websites like Fastweb, Cappex, and Going Merry can help identify scholarships, some of which you'd never think to Google.
- NICHE SCHOLARSHIPS FOR SPECIFIC GROUPS There are tons of scholarships for students based on their background, interests, and even weird

talents. (There even used to be a scholarship for left-handed students.[33] Who knew?) First-generation students, underrepresented minorities, and women in STEM have access to millions of dollars in specific scholarships. So do students who create prom dresses out of duct tape.[34]

- **FINANCIAL AID CONSULTANTS** If your financial situation is complicated by divorce, self-employment, sudden job loss, medical issues, or other complicating circumstances, a specialist may be able to help you strategize and maximize aid. One of our favorite experts in this field is Jeff Levy of Big J Educational Consulting in LA. He's no-nonsense, incredibly knowledgeable, and has helped countless families make sense of these issues.

- **COLLEGES' FINANCIAL AID OFFICES** Don't overlook these. You'd be surprised how helpful they can be, especially when appealing an aid package or finding hidden grants you didn't know existed.

COLLEGE IS EXPENSIVE, BUT THERE'S HOPE

No one likes paying full price for anything, even if retail therapy counts as cardio in your home. That's why it's worth asking questions, appealing aid decisions, applying wisely, and considering whether applying at all might hurt your child's chances of admission.

Whether you're stretching every cent or comfortably covering tuition, there's money out there. You just need to know how and where to look.

Before you start worrying about carrying a crushing amount of debt or consider selling a major organ, call the financial aid office first. College is expensive, but persistence pays off. Literally.

Financial aid policies can change faster than a teenager's mood, especially when budgets tighten or the Department of Education's priorities shift. What's true this year might be outdated by next. So instead of hyperventilating (or popping champagne), check the latest info. Staying informed and treating the process with the same determination you bring to any worthwhile challenge can go a long way.

---

33 The Frederick and Mary F. Beckley Scholarship was awarded to left-handed students attending **Juniata College** in Pennsylvania. Typical award amount ranged from $1,000 to $1,500 per year. **34** Duck® Brand, "Stuck at Prom Scholarship Contest," https://www.duckbrand.com/stuck-at-prom.

Part Five

Beyond the Checklist: Emotions and Everything Else

CHAPTER 15

MENTAL HEALTH MATTERS
(For Students And Parents)

When I was in high school, no one talked about mental health. Stress? That wasn't even a word people used. Anxiety? It wasn't something you *had*; it was something you *got over*. Therapy? That was seen as something for people in real crisis—not for teenagers who were overwhelmed or struggling inside.

Looking back, I can see how many of us were just trying to keep our heads above water. If you were overwhelmed, you just pushed through. If you felt anxious sometimes (or even all the time), you probably didn't even have the vocabulary to describe it. We just thought we were bad at coping, when really, we just didn't know how to ask for help.

When I think back to those years, I remember the confusion I felt around my own body—feelings I didn't yet know how to name.

The best I could do was playfully label myself a "serial snack stealer."

My mom was always on my case, reminding me like a broken record, that I "just needed to lose ten pounds." She even dragged me to Weight Watchers in tenth grade. Picture this: me, a teenager, getting weighed in front of a room full of adults, their eyes filled with pity, while I stood there, completely mortified. I wish I could go back and hug that girl.

The meetings didn't motivate me. They backfired. Instead of sticking to the program, I raided cereal boxes at the breakfast table for the raisins. I snuck Wheat Thins and Mint Milanos into a secret stash under my bed. Even the chocolate bars meant to fundraise for my marching band trip to Ocean City, Maryland mysteriously disappeared.

Late at night, after finishing my homework, I'd quietly reach under my bed for my hidden treasures. That was when the house was silent; no one was there to scold or sigh at me about my weight.

"You'd be so perfect if you would lose ten pounds," my mom would chide, often in front of my dad and brother.

"Yeah! Basketball face!" my older brother chimed in, thrilled to have the opportunity to torment me in the way only a sibling can.

The truth is that I wasn't even big. Not really. But in my family, being thinner wasn't about health: it was about worth.

It also didn't help that the culture around us reinforced these ideals.

Dieting was practically a national pastime. Every glossy magazine at the checkout line screamed some version of *"Lose 10 Pounds in 10 Days!"* There were before-and-after photos, miracle diets, and perfect-looking women smiling over bowls of lettuce. Sigh. It was relentless, and we didn't have permission to question it. Even my beloved ballet teacher, Miss L., who adored her students and kept us entertained, would give my tush a light tap at the barre and say with a smile, "Time to lose the baby fat, Beth!" I didn't laugh. I just stood there, feeling embarrassed, and awkwardly absorbing the message that something about me needed fixing.

Years later, as a mom, those old messages came roaring back. I've thought about them while raising my own two daughters, and the truth is, I haven't always gotten it right. I've said things I wish I could take back. I've worried too much about things that didn't matter, and not enough about the things that did. It's hard to unlearn what was ingrained in me for so long. Helping them navigate body image and confidence around food in a world that still prizes thinness hasn't been easy. But every day, I do my best to show them love, to listen (not always perfectly), and to keep going, even as I'm still learning. I've learned to repair what I can and try to be better going forward, all while figuring it out in real time.

Still, some things linger longer than we expect.

Sadly, that shame and secrecy from my childhood packed up and went to college with me. There, it morphed into something more serious. I didn't realize it at the time, but what I was dealing with wasn't just self-consciousness or bad habits. It turned out to be an eating disorder. And like so many students, I hid it well.

Yet, as difficult as it was, I found a way out. I saw a therapist for months and slowly started the process of healing. It wasn't easy, but with time, I learned to lean on the support of my parents. Ironically, it was my big brother, the same one who had taunted me in high school, who reminded me of my worth. "Lou," he said, using the nickname he had given me back in elementary school. "You're strong enough and smart enough to change this." His belief in me gave me the confidence to trust that I could overcome it, and eventually, I did.

After years of working with hundreds of students, I've learned that when we ignore the emotional lives of our kids, those feelings don't disappear. They merely get buried. Kids are pushing through, staying polished on the outside, while falling apart underneath.

At our 35th college reunion, I had the chance to catch up with Bruce Y. Lee, MD, MBA, a professor of public health and behavioral science at CUNY. When I asked what he's seeing among students today, he told me: "Parents and students are operating in a system that constantly reinforces performance over well-being. When students feel they're only as valuable as their accomplishments, anxiety and burnout aren't surprising. They're inevitable. What we need is a cultural reset that prioritizes mental health not as optional, but essential."

Bruce isn't alone in seeing this.

When I spoke with Denise Pope, Ph.D., senior lecturer at Stanford University and co-founder of Challenge Success, she shared what she sees in students nationwide: "High-achieving teens are overwhelmed by stress, overload, and chronic sleep deprivation in the pursuit of grades and college admissions. In our surveys of more than 300,000 students, the top stressors remain the same every year—schoolwork, grades, and college pressure—and only about one-third of teens feel they have healthy coping strategies to manage it." She and her colleagues spent a year reviewing research on long-term outcomes of selective colleges, which they published in their report *A Fit Over Rankings*.[35]

This is exactly why I debated putting this chapter early on in this book. I joke about the madness of the college admissions process, and yes, parents really are *Crazy for College*. However, there's a cost if we take it too far. Beneath the humor, there's too much at stake.

As college admissions season ramps up, the tension rises. And it's not only the kids who feel it. We do, too.

---

35 Denise Pope et al., *A Fit Over Rankings* (Stanford, CA: Challenge Success, Stanford Graduate School of Education, 2018), https://challengesuccess.org/research/a-fit-over-rankings/

If we don't manage our own stress and keep things in perspective, we may overlook what's happening beneath the surface in our children. The impact, unfortunately, can run deeper than we think.

Nancy and I see it almost everywhere.

At our local high school, one student started an Eating Disorder Awareness Club. Maybe she hoped it would look good on a college app, but mostly, it stemmed from seeing so many of her friends struggling.

She's not alone. Mental health awareness clubs are popping up in high schools across the country.

One expert, Jennie Kramer, LCSW-R, a therapist based in Scarsdale who specializes in eating disorders, explained it this way: "We've seen a staggering increase in disordered eating among students, particularly between the ages of twelve and twenty-two. As academic pressure and social expectations intensify, kids are turning to food, or away from it, as ways to cope. Diet culture only makes it worse. Early detection is essential, but so is steering the conversation toward what really matters in life."

That kind of momentum is a wake-up call.

WHAT WE ARE SEEING NATIONWIDE

Nancy and I belong to several national networks for independent educational consultants. These are groups that span public and private schools, big cities and small towns, high-pressure environments, and more laid-back communities. No matter where a student lives or what kind of school they attend, we're hearing a consistent theme: mental health challenges are real, and they aren't always visible.

For some families, the struggles go beyond stress or burnout that can be managed by a local therapist. This is where therapeutic educational consultants come in. If you've never heard of them, that's probably a good thing. These professionals specialize in helping families when a child's anxiety, depression, school avoidance, or other issues require more specialized support. They guide parents toward therapeutic boarding schools, wilderness programs, or short-term residential treatment options designed to help students reclaim their health.

The demand for this kind of help has grown significantly. According to the Independent Educational Consultants Association (IECA), roughly one in five educational consultants now specializes in therapeutic placements. That's not meant to cause alarm. It's merely a reflection of how many families are confronting challenges that were once rarely discussed. But even the kids who seem "fine" are carrying more than they let on.

SOME REAL-LIFE STORIES:

- A mom called us, frantic. Her daughter's therapist had just recommended a residential treatment program for an eating disorder. "How is she supposed to finish junior year?" the mom asked. "And how am *I* supposed to handle this?"
- A dad confided in us about his son, once a social, high-achieving student, who had completely shut down. He refused to go to school. He barely left his room. His parents were at a loss. With steady support from therapists, school counselors, and an educational consultant, they eventually found a high school environment where he felt safe and where he slowly regained confidence. Today? He's back on track and attends college four hours from his home.
- Another dad asked if his daughter could skip SAT prep altogether. It wasn't that she didn't want to; it was that she couldn't. Her anxiety was so debilitating that adding one more thing to her plate felt impossible.
- These stories aren't outliers. They are happening everywhere. In every community. In families just like ours.[36]

SHOT OF SANITY

> *While we're so hyper-focused on our kids' well-being, we need to pause and ask ourselves: how are we holding up as parents?*

The pressure, the expectations, the constant second-guessing are real. Are we doing enough? Are we doing too much? It's exhausting. We see it in our communities and in our own homes. We've created a culture where even the strongest among us can feel like we're falling short. If you're reading this and thinking, "Am I doing this right?" then you're already doing better than you think.

So, parents, please pay attention.

To your kids.

To yourselves.

To the messages we're sending and the expectations we're setting.

---

[36] **Note:** There's no hotline or magic program for this, but families can start local. Talk to your child's school counseling department, pediatrician, or a trusted therapist in your community. They can connect you with the right kind of support. If things ever feel unsafe, call or text 988, the Suicide and Crisis Lifeline, for immediate help.

SOBERING STATISTICS *and the* PRESSURE COOKER OUR KIDS ARE IN

If you're wondering just how widespread these mental health issues are, the numbers reveal a sobering story. If what follows feels overwhelming, you're not failing. You're paying attention. More than a third of high school students reported experiencing poor mental health during the pandemic[37], and nearly half of students ages eleven to eighteen said they were hesitant to reach out for help.[38]

Kids are weighed down for all kinds of reasons. Nearly half of U.S. teens aged thirteen to seventeen have experienced some form of online harassment, with older teen girls especially vulnerable.[39] One student told us in between sobs: "I used to love going home because it felt like a break from school. Now? Snapchat and Instagram bullies follow me into my own bedroom." Imagine your child being unable to escape the voices that tear them down, even behind a closed door.

The fear doesn't stop there. More than half of high school students worry about a school shooting.[40] Remember fire drills when we were growing up? Now, kids practice hiding from an active shooter. Lockdowns and bomb threats have become routine.

It's not just students who carry that fear. Parents do, too. Many of us have gotten *that* text: the one saying their school is in lockdown because there's a reported threat or an active shooter nearby. Your stomach drops. The world goes silent. You're stuck refreshing the news, checking group chats, calling and texting your child every thirty seconds to make sure they're okay. This is simply the background noise of growing up *and* parenting in today's world.

All of this exists alongside the crushing pressure to perform.

More than half of teens feel like they need to be exceptional in everything they do: 53% say they feel pressure to "be impressive through their achievements," contributing to stress and burnout.[41]

Ask any high school junior if they feel like their entire future rides on every test and every extracurricular, and you'll see why.

---

37 Centers for Disease Control and Prevention, "Mental Health, Suicidality, and Connectedness Among High School Students During the COVID-19 Pandemic—Adolescent Behaviors and Experiences Survey, United States, January–June 2021," *Morbidity and Mortality Weekly Report* 71, no. 3 (2022): 16-21, https://www.cdc.gov/mmwr/volumes/71/su/su7103a3.htm **38** "Four in 10 Schoolkids Struggle to Discuss Mental Health—As They Battle Mood Swings and Sleep Issues." *The Sun*, August 28, 2024.

Mental health isn't just another box to check on the college application process. It's the foundation for everything that comes next.

When I spoke with Art Markman, a psychologist and professor at the University of Texas at Austin, he reminded me: "One of the hardest things for parents and kids alike to remember is that mental health is health. No matter how stressful the college admissions process becomes, it's important to develop good habits for living, because the stress won't magically disappear after an acceptance. There is always something next. Parents and students need to make time for things they enjoy that aren't tied to achievement. Spend time with friends and family. Take a moment alone. Read for pleasure. Unplug. Enjoy the journey."

That's why we often tell every family: let your kids still be kids.

If your kid wants to spend one last summer at sleepaway camp before senior year, let them. If they'd rather skip that high-pressure AP class and take something that doesn't make them dread third period, support that. If they want to miss an ACT prep session to celebrate a friend's birthday, say yes. If they open-up and tell you they're struggling, the best thing you can do is listen and remind them they're not alone.

MENTAL HEALTH IN COLLEGE

When students don't get the emotional support they need in high school, these problems don't evaporate when they get into college. If anything, they often get worse.

Consider these statistics:

- 76% of college students experienced moderate to serious psychological distress in 2023.[42] In other words, three out of four students caught in some level of distress. That's not just "I have a big test tomorrow" stress. That's the kind of distress that makes it hard to sleep or even get out of bed.

- Suicidal thoughts among college students have increased by 40% in the last decade, with 14% of students reporting serious thoughts of suicide in 2022–2023.[43] Let that sink in: One in seven. This isn't an overreaction. Someone your child knows, or maybe even someone you know, has been in that dark place. This isn't rare.

- According to the Centers for Disease Control and Prevention, more than 49,000 people in the United States died by suicide in 2023. That's about one

39 Pew Research Center, *Teens and Cyberbullying 2022*, December 15, 2022, https://www.pewresearch.org/internet/2022/12/15/teens-and-cyberbullying-2022/. 40 Kerri M. Raissian et al., "Adolescents' Fear of School Gun Violence in the United States," *Journal of Adolescent Health* 72, no. 4 (2022): 421-428, https://pmc.ncbi.nlm.nih.gov/articles/PMC11875268/. 41 Common Sense Media, "The new burnout generation," Vox, October 17, 2024. 42 American College Health Association, "National College Health Assessment: Undergraduate Student Reference Group Executive Summary Spring 2023," American College Health Association, 2023. 43 American Council on Education, *Key Mental Health in Higher Education Stats*, 2024.

every eleven minutes.[44]

- Over half (51%) of students reported feeling lonely in the spring of 2023.[45] Even when they're surrounded by people, many students still feel utterly alone. In a world of 24/7 group chats, FaceTime, and TikTok, loneliness is through the roof. Why? Because when they're already hurting, scrolling through everyone else's highlight reel can make it feel even worse. Plenty of the kids they see in real life are hiding their battles, too.

HOW DO THEY COPE?

With this much strain, students need a way to let off steam. But if they haven't developed healthy coping mechanisms, they may turn to more destructive ones.

Nearly 30% of these college students aged eighteen to twenty-five engaged in binge drinking. This is defined as consuming five or more drinks on one occasion for males and four or more for females.

Illicit drug use is highest among young adults aged eighteen to twenty-five, with nearly 40% using in the past year.[46]

For some students, substance use isn't about partying or having fun. It's a way to numb the pressure. When expectations feel unbearable, some check out. Others self-medicate. Either way, it's a sign that something deeper is going on.

WHY IS THIS HAPPENING?

1. **The Pressure Cooker Is on Full Blast**
    It used to be, "Get good grades, join a club, and you'll be fine." Now? Kids feel pressure to earn perfect grades and launch a nonprofit to prove they're "successful" enough for the colleges they think they're supposed to aim for. Sometimes those schools aren't even the right fit.

2. **The Pandemic Did a Number on Them**
    This generation missed critical social years. Their high school or college experience started on Zoom. Their "classroom" was their childhood bedroom. Their "social life" was a group chat titled *Is This Ever Gonna End?* Remember that in many ways, they're still catching up.

3. **Social Media: Everyone Else Is Thriving (Except You)**
    Remember when you had to actually talk to someone to discover they were

44 "Suicide Data and Statistics," Centers for Disease Control and Prevention, last reviewed September 2024, accessed October 13, 2025, https://www.cdc.gov/suicide/facts/data.html 45 Ibid. 46 Substance Abuse and Mental Health Services Administration, *Highlights for the 2023 National Survey on Drug Use and Health* (Rockville, MD: U.S. Department of Health and Human Services, 2023), https://www.samhsa.gov/data/sites/default/files/NSDUH%202023%20Annual%20Release/2023-nsduh-main-highlights.pdf

having more fun than you? Now, all it takes is one scroll through Instagram. Kaboom. Your college kid is convinced they're the only one eating a chicken stir fry in the dining hall alone while everyone else is at some idyllic sunset bonfire with their twenty-seven new BFFs.

SHOT OF SANITY

The mental health crisis among students is real, and the pressure they're under isn't going away anytime soon. But if we keep the conversations going and reveal a little vulnerability ourselves, we can help improve the culture even more.

THE GOOD NEWS? THEY'RE STARTING TO TALK ABOUT IT

This generation is getting better at recognizing when they need help. Most aren't waiting until they hit rock bottom.

We often get emails like this one:

"Hey, can we reschedule our college essay brainstorm session? I have therapy at that time."

That was it. No awkwardness. No whispering the word "therapy" like it's a secret. This student might as well have been telling me she had soccer practice or a dentist appointment. Kids are starting to normalize mental healthcare in a way older generations never did. I *love* that.

They're more open with each other about anxiety, ADHD, OCD, eating disorders, and depression. They talk about what they're going through. They share what's helping. They're even kinder to each other about their struggles. Sure, the stigma isn't completely gone, but they're light-years ahead of where we were at their age.

Even colleges are starting to rethink how they offer support. A growing number of campuses are placing embedded counselors directly in dorms and academic buildings so students can find help without having to go very far. The model has reduced stigma and increased access to care, with some schools reporting fewer crisis calls and greater student engagement.[47]

47 Christina Caron, "The Therapist Next Door: College Students Are Meeting with 'Embedded' Counselors in Dorms and Academic Buildings, with Promising Results," *New York Times*, October 8, 2025, https://www.nytimes.com/2025/10/08/well/mind/college-embedded-counselors.html

Let's remind our kids (and ourselves) that success isn't about where they get in. It's about being okay, maybe even better, when they get there. We can't control every burden our kids face, but we can be the place where they can exhale.

A GENTLE REMINDER

Here's what I keep coming back to: mental health isn't a side issue in the college process. It's woven into everything: how students show up, how they cope, how they grow.

Check in with your kids. Don't just discuss their grades or their applications but ask about them and how they're doing. Ask twice if you need to.

While you're at it, check in with yourself, too. This whole ride filled with parenting, high school, and college admissions is a lot. You don't have to be a perfect parent. You just need to be a present one. No trophy, no test score, no grade, no early decision letter is worth your kid losing sleep or themselves.

If all else fails?

Take a deep breath, cancel the AP Bio tutor, and order in Chinese food.

What they'll remember is that you were there when the going got tough, and that they weren't alone.

CHAPTER 16

SAYING THANK YOU MATTERS
More Than You Think

Growing up, thank-you notes weren't just encouraged in my house—they were mandatory. My mom treated them like the eleventh commandment. Birthday gifts, Chanukah presents, you name it. She'd stand in my doorway, arms crossed like a drill sergeant, and order, "Sit down and write a note!"

After my Bat Mitzvah, I spent hours hunched at my white desk in my Laura Ashley-inspired bedroom, writing on my turquoise and lavender personalized BETH stationery, expressing thanks for every single gift I received. I thanked Aunt Florence for her $18 check. Nearly every friend and relative gave checks or U.S. savings bonds (remember those?) in multiples of eighteen, a symbol of chai, or life, in Judaism. I thanked Uncle Herbie for the unique three-foot hanging clock adorned with birds, because obviously that's exactly what every thirteen-year-old girl hopes to unwrap on her big day.

That habit of expressing gratitude followed me straight into adulthood.

When my husband and I got married in September 1996, during my second year of business school at Northwestern, we snuck away for a two-day "mini-moon" to Kohler, Wisconsin (yes, *that* Kohler, the one famous for bathtub fixtures and fancy faucets). While Jeff was busy testing every faucet in our hotel room like a kid in a candy store, I spent four straight hours writing thank-you notes for everything from the fine china we had registered for at Bloomingdale's, to the hideous vase we never removed from the box.

My mom, a kindergarten teacher for decades, cherished the crayon-scribbled notes from her five-year-old students. But it was the heartfelt messages from parents that made her day. She understood something that took me years to appreciate: gratitude goes beyond good manners; it's about humanity.

Years later, I found myself giving the same lecture to my own kids. This time, it was about showing appreciation to the teachers, counselors, and anyone else who helped them through the college process.

KIND OF CRAZY

The POWER *of* SAYING THANK YOU *in* COLLEGE ADMISSIONS

Want to improve your child's chances in the college admissions process? Teach them to say thank you and mean it.

From teachers to tutors, receptionists, and interviewers, being grateful isn't only polite: it's powerful. Your child's college journey isn't a solo act; it takes a village. Acknowledging that village can make a world of difference.

As parents, we can model and reinforce the importance of saying thank you. I've seen firsthand that students who take a moment to show appreciation stand out. Helping your kid understand that gratitude shows respect and leaves a lasting impression is a life skill that will serve them well long after the college process is over.

SO MANY WAYS TO SAY THANK YOU

Over the years, Nancy and I have received hundreds of thank-you notes from students. Some are handwritten, some are typed, some are sprinkled with emojis. I still keep a crumpled handwritten note tucked in the back of my desk drawer from a student who thanked us for believing in him and helping him apply as a transfer junior to his dream program. Other kids have sent quick texts and tear-jerking emails. I vividly remember getting a "thank you" phone call from a student in London who stayed up past midnight to find out she'd been accepted to her Early Decision school.

Parents have sent us flowers, chocolates, charcuterie boards, and spa certificates. But it's the notes from our students that mean the most. Those small gestures land big (though I won't complain about the spa certificates).

When my son started high school at Scarsdale, I went to an assembly where one of the counseling deans firmly stated, "Don't forget to thank the teachers who write your kid's recommendation letters. And remember to be kind to the receptionists in the counseling office. They're the ones who have the power to make or break your transcript request!" he chuckled.

I thought, *Mom would love this guy!*

In a recent *Chronicle of Higher Education* article, professors at the University of Florida and the Citadel shared creative ways to encourage students to express thankfulness toward their instructors. They say it's a simple way to teach students that showing appreciation can open doors and make relationships stronger not only in college, but in life. Learning to say "thank you" is more than a gesture; it's a skill that carries weight.[48]

I'm clearly not alone in waving the thank-you banner. Glenn Kramon, a longtime *New York Times* editor and now a lecturer at Stanford Business School, wrote an op-ed urging people to resurrect the lost art of thank-you notes. He calls them "the simplest investment with the highest return."[49] A short note may help you land a job, revive a friendship, or show respect in a world that often forgets to do so. If Pulitzer-winning editors and business professors are pushing gratitude, maybe my mom and I are not the only ones who think it never goes out of style.

THE FIRST THING TO DO AFTER AN ACCEPTANCE? SAY THANK YOU.

It reminds me of one of the happiest, most chaotic days in our house: December 2016, the moment my first child's college acceptance came through.

There were happy tears, hugs, and the kind of screaming usually reserved for winning big at a blackjack table in Vegas. My mom, fully aware that we were all anxiously waiting for this college decision, made a surprise entrance, armed with enormous red balloons she just happened to have in her car. But smack in the middle of the celebratory madness, I channeled my inner thank-you sergeant and called for a time-out.

"Stop!" I declared, turning to my son. "Before we even think about going out for dessert, you need to send quick texts to everyone who helped you get here. Just a short note to share the news and thank them again."

---

48 Beckie Supiano, "Teaching: Thanking Instructors," *The Chronicle of Higher Education*, October 31, 2024, https://www.chronicle.com/newsletter/teaching/2024-10-31. 49 Glenn Kramon, "Why You Should Send Thank-You Notes, Even Years Later," *The New York Times*, August 22, 2025, https://www.nytimes.com/2025/08/22/opinion/thank-you-notes-gratitude.html

So, my son stationed himself at the kitchen island, phone in hand, and fired off messages to his village: the SAT tutor, the physics teacher and the Spanish teacher who wrote his letters of recommendation, and his high school counseling dean. Each one got a thank-you text announcing his big news along with a healthy side of thanks.

Timing is everything. A note sent within a week feels warm and genuine. One that arrives months later? It feels like an afterthought, or worse, like your kid suddenly rediscovered an old to-do list. Ideally, thank-you notes should be sent *before* hearing back from colleges. That way, it's about acknowledging effort, not just celebrating an outcome (although, honestly, teachers love hearing when a student gets in).

IT TAKES A SQUAD: TEACH YOUR KIDS TO ACKNOWLEDGE EVERYONE

My two daughters' dance teachers went above and beyond. My older daughter practically lived in ballet slippers from age three through college, and my youngest manages to keep her love of hip hop alive while juggling college classes. These dance teachers deserved more than a quick thank-you text; they put in countless hours, shaping not only dancers, but disciplined and resilient young adults. Watching them pour so much into their students reminded me how many people work behind the scenes to help raise our kids.

Getting into college isn't about GPA and test scores. It's also about recognizing the entire squad behind these kids: the teachers and school counselors who stay late to write glowing recommendations, the coaches who push them when they'd rather collapse on the field, the school counseling staff who make sure transcripts don't disappear into a black hole, and, ahem, if you're lucky enough to have one, the private college advisor who keeps them on track.

Reaching the finish line takes a whole platoon, and they each deserve a little appreciation.

Kindness doesn't stop at the school walls. There are a few others who also deserve a thank-you. Like those college admissions officers who make the rounds to high schools, answering the same questions about test-optional policies and dorm life. They've driven or flown miles, conducted countless presentations, and given their "Why Our School" speech so many times they could recite it in their sleep. Encourage your child to send a quick thank-you email; a small gesture means a lot.

There's also the alumni or student interviewer who took time out of their evening or lunch break to chat with your child on Zoom, even if the conversation was mostly about their favorite book or an embarrassing middle school moment. The interview may have only lasted twenty minutes, and your kid may have spent half of it nervously fiddling with their earbuds, but guess what? A simple, "Thanks for chatting with me. I hope you have a great rest of your week!" email can go a long way. Whether it's emailed or handwritten matters far less than the fact that it's sent.

LAST, BUT CERTAINLY NOT LEAST...

Remind your kids to thank **you**—the parents, the siblings, their family, the whole behind-the-scenes crew. After every dance performance, my daughters know the first people they should hug are me and my husband. After all, we're the ones (okay, mostly me) who've schlepped them to rehearsals, hunted down last-minute costume accessories, and rallied family and friends to come cheer them on.

The same goes for the college application process. You're the ones who've stood by them through late-night meltdowns and proofread essays to the point where you can probably recite them by heart. When the moment comes, they should hug you first.

Kids may not always realize it, but you're a crucial part of their support system, and it's more than okay to teach them that gratitude begins at home.

In this topsy-turvy world, a little kindness goes a long way. A thank-you email or a quick text can brighten someone's day and maybe make them a little more willing to help out the next time you need something. Or at the very least, it probably stops them from rolling their eyes the next time your name pops up in their inbox.

A NOTE FROM ME

Working with students and families over these past fourteen admissions cycles has been one of the great privileges of my life. It still amazes me how much trust it takes to let someone into your kid's hopes, fears, dreams, and late-night chaos. I don't take that lightly. The thank-you notes mean more than people realize, but the real joy is watching these kids grow up and step into the world a little more confident than when they started. I'm grateful for every family who lets me tag along for the ride.

CHAPTER 17

JUST TALK:
The Best Things Start With HELLO

By now, you're practically old friends with Nancy, my partner at Acceptance Ahead and the person who has been alongside me in so many of the stories I've shared. What you don't know yet is how we met. Like so many of the best things in life, it didn't start with a business plan. It started with an unexpected conversation I never saw coming...

It turns out, our story is just one of many. A quick interaction in a coffee shop, at the end of a Pilates class, or during a college tour can lead somewhere completely unexpected. We've seen it happen again and again, with students, parents, and yes, with ourselves.

Take one of our students who was waiting in line at DeCicco's (our local supermarket), when she overheard a mother and daughter chatting about their spring break college visits. She joined in, mentioning she was putting together a dance portfolio. The mom laughed, "That's funny! I'm a professional videographer. I'd be happy to help you with a reel." Two weeks later, our student had a polished video. She absolutely did not need a professional one (the homemade reels can be equally strong or better), but this was a lucky break that helped her feel confident hitting "submit." Proof that in-person grocery shopping still beats Instacart.

We tend to think of networking as formal and strategic. But most of the time, it's about being present and willing to talk to the person standing next to you. Even when you're not in the mood. Especially when you're not in the mood.

I didn't know it at the time, but one of the most important conversations of my life would be waiting for me at a nail salon.

A PEDICURE AND A PLOT TWIST

I wasn't on a mission. I wasn't networking. I was just trying to survive a quiet holiday weekend with my kids and maybe squeeze in a little self-care. But that's the thing about these twists; your calendar means nothing to them. They sneak up on you, sometimes with a pedicure.

It was a quiet holiday weekend in Scarsdale. The streets were empty, and I was still in a fog of grief after losing my father a few weeks earlier. On a whim, I took my daughters to Elegance Nails for a little escape.

As we walked in, a woman from my book club spotted me. "Beth! You must meet Nancy," she said, shepherding me toward the back like I was meeting a celebrity. "She's the lawyer I told you about. The one who just helped her daughter through the college process. You're both obsessed with admissions!"

I wasn't exactly in the mood to chat, but you can't really hide in a nail salon. After settling my girls at the manicure stations, I made my way to the pedicure chairs.

Nancy and I started talking, and it felt easy, like bumping into an old friend you didn't know you had. I told her how much I loved working with students on essays and interviews, and how I'd been toying with the idea of starting something but had no idea where to begin.

Until that moment.

We swapped emails and promised to meet again. As I left the salon with my daughters, I felt something I hadn't in a while: a twinge of excitement.

A few days later, we met for lunch at the Metro Diner (she's from Long Island, and I'm from New Jersey; our diner loyalty runs deep). I showed up with scrappy ideas. Nancy came armed with a notebook full of educational workshops, names of graphic artists, and a real to-do list. Three hours, two omelets, a side of fries, and a dozen cups of coffee later, we waltzed out of that diner with a purpose, a partnership, and a plan. I had a strong hunch we were destined to become co-conspirators and lifelong friends. And I was right.

Just like that, Acceptance Ahead was born.

WHERE IT ALL BEGINS

Every so often, one of us shakes our head and says, "Can you believe this all started with one random conversation in a nail salon?"

That's the thing about conversations. You never know which ones will stick or even redirect your path.

This doesn't only apply to us.

Ask any of our students.

One student, Teagan, ended up in a supply closet (!) with a Hamilton College admissions rep during a high school lockdown drill at her private school in Northern California. With thirty unplanned minutes to kill, they talked about everything from books to food to favorite classes. When the drill ended, the rep smiled and said, "No need to schedule an interview. I already know you." The student applied and now calls Hamilton home.

Serendipity strikes more often than you think. In a café, one student, Sam, studying architecture at the University of Virginia struck up a conversation with a stranger at the next table who was chatting about building designs. That *stranger* turned out to be a partner at a top architecture firm in D.C., and several weeks later, reviewed Sam's portfolio. No networking strategy, no LinkedIn cold message. Just an overheard comment and a bold hello.

While touring a college down south, a student, Kevin, and his mom asked someone for directions to the admissions office. The person offered to walk them there and casually chatted along the way. Turns out, he was the university president. The school went from looking like a castle on a postcard to somewhere this student could imagine pulling all-nighters. With real humans.

Then there was Janine, already a college student who hadn't picked a major until she struck up a conversation with her roommate's older sister, who was visiting for the weekend. The sister worked in environmental policy and casually described her unexpected path from biology to law. That one conversation stuck with Janine, and after a few dives into course catalogs, she landed on environmental studies with a plan to minor in public policy.

My friend's son Max once sat next to the owner of an NHL franchise on a cross-country flight. They started chatting about sports, and by the time they landed, he'd been invited to a game. That conversation eventually led to his first job out of college: doing statistical research for the same team, thanks to the owner's introduction. Score one for good old-fashioned luck.

One mom I worked with started chatting in the locker room after Pilates with the woman next to her. Turns out, she worked in public health and later helped the mom's daughter find a mentor for a summer science research project in genetics.

TALKING TO YOURSELF IS ALSO GOOD

Sometimes it's not who you're talking to. It's what you hear yourself say out loud.

I'll never forget our student, Michelle, who had just wrapped up an investment banking internship and asked me to help her prepare for interviews for the following summer. When I asked what part she liked most, she said, "Making the slides." Not the deal flow. Not the finance. The slides.

She lit up as she talked about fonts and color schemes, how she loved making things look clean and beautiful. We spent the next twenty minutes deep in conversation about design, and within a year, she had changed her major to graphic design and landed a creative role at an online magazine.

That move didn't come from a career coach or a personality test. It came from hearing herself discuss what really lit her up.

I saw something similar with my own daughter. She spent the summer after freshman year of college in Taiwan studying language and culture, fully immersed in linguistics. One afternoon, after fracturing her finger, she waited at a crowded hospital, trying to navigate treatment. Amid the waiting room bustle, she noticed a woman struggling to communicate with the staff. No one was available to translate.

She stepped in. Switching between Mandarin and English, she helped bridge the gap as calmly and as clearly as possible. Later that night, she recounted the experience to her friends, and the conversation took a turn. "You know you'd make the perfect doctor, right?" one asked. "You're great under pressure. When something matters, you focus like nobody else."

She laughed, but a new idea took root. A few days later, she FaceTimed me. "Guess what, Mom? I'm seriously thinking about switching to pre-med!" I nodded as if this were perfectly ordinary news, while in my head I was picturing her in a clean white coat explaining diagnoses I couldn't pronounce. She's now taking the classes and loving every minute.

All of this came from paying attention to how she felt in that moment and listening when the people who knew her best held up a mirror.

Then there was the "car" kid, Theo, who was obsessed with cars. He'd wash his parents' car, the neighbor's car, and anyone who would let him wash theirs. He couldn't stop talking about engines and detailing products. Eventually, that same neighbor introduced him to her mechanic, and Theo snagged a summer job at the garage. From there, he started his own car washing and detailing business. There was no career workshop here —only soapy water, initiative, and a neighbor who said, "I know who you should talk to."

Sometimes, the conversation starts with a cupcake. One student brought homemade cupcakes to her hairstylist's salon to celebrate a birthday. She offered them to other clients, mentioning she had spent the summer testing out new flavors on her very willing younger brothers. Another client, mid-blowout, took a bite, looked up, and asked, "Who made these?" When my student raised her hand bashfully, the woman smiled: "I own a bakery down the street. Ever think about doing this professionally?"

She invited my student to intern at the bakery before college. All because of a cupcake and a conversation.

You don't always know which conversations will change you. A compliment from a stranger, a casual suggestion from a friend, or your own voice stepping up and saying something out loud. Any of these openings can shake things up.

KIND OF CRAZY

The BEST THINGS START *With* CONVERSATION

If your head's buried in your phone, you'll miss the moments that open doors. The overheard chat in the coffee line. The offhand comment that hits like a caffeine jolt you didn't know you needed. College and life often grow out of those tiny, unexpected encounters.

And it doesn't stop at admissions. As my friend Lisa Tretler, Founder of *My Gradvantage* and a career coach to young adults, likes to remind students: "The absolute best way to unearth hidden career opportunities is by engaging in live conversations with people you share a common interest with. This could be a family friend, a school alum, or even a fellow sports fan. Adults are naturally inclined to share their wisdom and help young individuals succeed. I'm seeing more students secure internships and jobs today through these personal connections than through any job board."

Students often believe they need perfect resumes and a master plan to get ahead. But often, it's the spontaneous conversations that lead to mentors, internships, research opportunities, and eventually, first jobs.

Look up. Say something. Anything. You never know what might come from a random hello. Go ahead and start the conversation.

Worst case, you walk away with a good story.

Best case? You walk into something that changes your future, maybe with a cupcake in one hand and fresh polish on the other.

YOU DID READY

You've made it this far. Now let's make sure every box is checked and those "submit" buttons actually behave. Here's a final checklist before you hit submit:

1. COMMON APP (OR OTHER APPLICATION PLATFORM) IS SPOTLESS.

No typos, no half-finished sections, no red check marks, and no mysterious activity labeled "miscellaneous."

2. SNACKS ARE ON STANDBY

Application season requires fuel. Keep a bag of pretzels or something chocolate nearby at all times.

3. YOUR ESSAY SOUNDS LIKE YOU

Not your mom, not your teacher, or anyone who uses the word plethora.

4. YOUR SUPPLEMENTS ACTUALLY ANSWER THE QUESTION

Make sure they're school-specific and highlight your fit.

5. YOU'VE CONFIRMED DEADLINES, PORTALS, AND PASSWORDS

You know which schools are EA, ED, ED2, Rolling, or Regular, and you've triple-checked that you marked the correct box.

IT! YOU'RE
TO APPLY

6. YOUR RECOMMENDERS AND COUNSELOR ARE ALL SET

They've submitted (or promised to), and you've thanked them. A quick note, in-person hug, or latte doesn't hurt.

7. YOUR TEST SCORES ARE IN

You've picked them correctly, sent them in, and they're showing up where they're supposed to be.

8. FINANCIAL AID FORMS ARE SUBMITTED—OR AT LEAST UNDER CONTROL

FAFSA, CSS Profile, scholarship applications. Make sure nothing's still sitting on your desk.

9. YOU HIT "SAVE" (OR EVEN PRINTED THE PDF) BEFORE "SUBMIT"

The Common App will let you view the full PDF anytime, even after you submit. You won't be able to make changes once it's in. A printed copy for your files is always a good thing to have.

10. YOU TAKE A MOMENT TO CELEBRATE

No matter what happens next, you've done something big.

Part Six

After You Hit Submit

CHAPTER 18

SURVIVING *The* WAIT *Without* LOSING YOUR MIND

Tom Petty put it best: "The waiting is the hardest part."

When I went through labor and childbirth three times, physical agony took over my entire body, which I thankfully only now vaguely remember. What I *do* remember clearly, however, is feeling blindsided that none of the women in my life who had already gone through childbirth warned me how intense the pain would be. Maybe they didn't want to scare me? Maybe it was some kind of unspoken rite of passage? Or maybe it's because the second they hand you that baby, the agony leading up to that moment gets swallowed by the joy of what comes next.

Well, at least for most people.

Jeff, my otherwise wonderful husband, managed to make my second childbirth memorable, but for all the wrong reasons. During the birth of our second child, I was in the delivery room, breathing through my final contractions, sweating and swearing, while Jeff was outside in the hallway asking for a few more minutes to finish a conference call.

Yes, a conference call.

When the labor nurse finally stormed out to retrieve him, he casually strolled back into the room barely in time to witness the birth. To this day, despite all the jokes, laughter, and the fact that our child turned out more than fine, Jeff knows he will never, ever live that moment down.

Waiting for college decisions can feel a lot like childbirth. No one really prepares you for how excruciating it is to sit in limbo, refreshing your email and praying for news. It's not about which school comes through first. The relief comes with that first "yes."

Before my three children had even applied to college, I remember Nancy admitting one afternoon in my office, "After my oldest daughter hit submit, I would lay awake at night, staring at the ceiling and worrying about rejection letters."

I didn't fully grasp it at the time. My kids were still a few years away from applying, but I felt grateful that she let me in on the agony of waiting. When it was finally my turn, her words came rushing back. As usual, Nancy was 100% right.

It's not easy to wait for a decision. After my oldest applied to college, I too was up at 4 a.m., mindlessly scrolling through Facebook or re-reading *Eligible* by Curtis Sittenfeld. When that failed, I turned to meditating, counting to 500, and drinking an endless supply of herbal tea. I tried doing push-ups before bed to tire me out, but nothing did the trick (and yes, I made it to thirty! I had super buff arms that year).

I needed a better approach. That's when I turned to seasoned parents, the wise counselors at Scarsdale High School, and a few psychology experts. By blending their advice with a few of my own trial-and-error strategies, I made it through the waiting period with a little less pain (okay, maybe not as bad as childbirth, but close). Over the years, this collection of insights has continued to evolve, shaped by experience and the never-ending changes on the admissions scene.

SURVIVAL STRATEGIES FOR THE WAITING PERIOD

Once your child hits submit, try not to dwell on it. You may be tempted to obsess, second-guessing where your kid applied, who wrote their letters of recommendation, and the SAT score you thought was great...until a mom on Facebook posted about her daughter's 1590 (please don't be the parent who posts that!). You might be tempted to delve into statistics from your child's high school and beyond. You might even call your own mom to discuss every possible scenario, including whether the metaphor in your kid's Common App essay was *too* dramatic.

DON'T DO IT

Hitting refresh on the admissions portal won't make decisions come any faster, just like pressing an elevator button repeatedly doesn't make it arrive any quicker.

While we're at it, do yourself a favor: resist the urge to re-read the PDF version of your kid's submitted application. No good can come of this. Despite the fifteen proofreads before submission, you *will* find some infinitesimally small typo like a missing comma or an extra space. Beware the doom spiral.

SHOT OF SANITY

> ***Here's the reality check: 99.9% of the time, that tiny imperfection will have zero impact on how the application is reviewed. Admissions officers are not sitting in a dark room, magnifying glass in hand, deducting points for an accidentally misplaced "its."***

Relax, breathe, step away from the computer. Instead, focus on these suggestions:

START A GRATITUDE JAR Every time you feel the urge to panic, jot down something you're thankful for like your community (remember to thank your best friend for listening to all this college talk on repeat), or the fact that your days of researching hotels and restaurants in the Northeast are almost over. When the stress spikes, revisit the jar for a pep talk.

HAVE A LITTLE FAITH If you pray, go ahead and say one before bed, at church or temple, or to yourself on a morning walk. Light a candle. Repeat a blessing. Just take a moment to send your hopes somewhere bigger than yourself. If prayer's not your thing, then pause, breathe, and trust that something good is still unfolding.

When speaking with my friend in Nashville, Rev Farrell Mason,[50] she reminded me that waiting is its own kind of faith.

"Faith isn't about knowing exactly how things will turn out," she said. "It's about staying open while you wait. It's trusting that something good is still working beneath the surface, even when you can't see it yet."

I love that. Because even when it feels like your child's inbox is eerily quiet and the portal hasn't budged, something is happening. It just might not be visible yet.

When the waiting feels endless (and it will), channel Nancy's best piece of advice: "This too shall pass." Somehow, it always does.

---

50 Rev. Farrell Mason is the author of SOULFULL, creator of the *Bread and Honey* blog, and host of the *Soulfull 7 Conversations* podcast.

STAY AS BUSY AS HUMANLY POSSIBLE Reorganize your closet, drag a friend to hot yoga, and give yourself permission to binge-watch every season of *Bridgerton*. Let distraction become your new best friend. Encourage your child to do the same. School plays, sports practices, going out to dinner, a part-time job—literally anything that doesn't involve refreshing their email inbox seventeen times a day.

LIMIT COLLEGE TALK Share application details only with a trusted circle: parents, siblings, therapists, and hairstylists (Special thanks to Michelle, who patiently listened to me rant through all three "waiting" periods while she fixed my gray roots).

At family gatherings, establish some ground rules: "No college talk at the table" should rank right up there with "no politics," "no religion," and "no discussing Uncle Barry's third wife." If Aunt Carol inevitably asks your child, "So, where did you apply? What are your chances?", you, as the parent, have two choices:

1. Tell her to be quiet (tempting, but maybe not worth the family drama).
2. Smile, sip your wine, and redirect: "Carol, we're not talking about college today. But I heard you're heading to Florida this winter. Tell us everything."

This is self-preservation. For both you and your kid. Stand up for them, and politely steer the conversation to something equally riveting, like the sanitation laws in New Jersey. Honestly, anything else would be better.

WHAT TO DO DURING THE ACTUAL WEEK THAT DECISIONS ARE EXPECTED:

On the day that my oldest child received his early decision news, I scheduled an in-person traffic court meeting to contest a speeding ticket. Dragging my mom along for moral support, I figured the distraction might help pass the time. It sort of worked, until I got flustered when they called my name, failed to ask for a lower fine, and stupidly paid the ticket anyway. So much for my righteous attempts.

HOW TO STAY SANE: SOME TOOLS

Waiting is hard and the week college decisions are due can feel especially brutal. There's actual science behind why it's so excruciating: psychologists say that uncertainty itself triggers stress. It's human nature to crave answers and fast. When I spoke with Emily Stern, Ph.D., a clinical psychologist, she explained it this way:

"Waiting for college decisions can feel unsettling for students and parents who've spent years focused on goals and deadlines. Once the applications are submitted, the process shifts into a phase with no tasks to complete and very little control—

and that uncertainty is normal. Our job isn't to eliminate it, but to keep living full, meaningful lives alongside the discomfort. Gently refocus on what you can control each day, and commit to small, purposeful, joyful actions. This shift moves families away from draining worry and toward a healthier, more balanced mindset during the waiting phase."

A FEW EXTRA TOOLS CAN HELP:

1. **FOCUS ON WHAT YOU CAN CONTROL.** Make a to-do list of things unrelated to the news you're waiting for. Accomplishing even small tasks, like cleaning out your fridge, reorganizing your desk drawers, or unsubscribing, for once and for all, from all those emails you swore you'd deal with, can give you a tiny bit of accomplishment when everything else feels up in the air.

2. **PRACTICE MINDFULNESS OR RELAXATION TECHNIQUES.** Activities like yoga or meditation can reduce stress and help you stay in the moment instead of spiraling into worst-case scenarios. You can also pretend to be "chill" in front of your child, even if you're freaking out inside.

3. **TALK ABOUT YOUR FEELINGS.** It's fine to share your anxiety with a trusted friend or family member, but try to avoid turning every conversation into a stress-fest about college. Nobody wants to hear "what if" scenarios on repeat, and your friends will appreciate the break if you've recently been bombarding them. Remember how much you hated hearing about your sister-in-law's kitchen renovation on repeat? Don't be that person.

4. **REMIND YOURSELF AND YOUR CHILD OF OTHER POSITIVE OUTCOMES.** They will bloom wherever they're planted. You've helped them through uncertainty before, and a little perspective can go a long way. After all, you've survived raising a child, from politely clapping through elementary school band concerts that sounded like dying geese to gripping the passenger seat during their first driving lesson.

Fun fact: One of my own kids failed their first road test and came home to me manically popping the balloons I had prematurely arranged for a celebration.

BEFORE THE CURTAIN RISES

At some point, all the distractions and "no college talk" rules can't hide the fact that decision day is creeping in. The whole mood in our house was...jittery. I probably called Hilary, my trusted friend in California, at least thirty times that week. My mom wasn't spared either. She was on speed dial, listening to the same updates on a loop like I was trapped in my own admissions-themed Groundhog Day.

I became convinced that everyone around me (my neighbors, the mail person, the guy at the gas station, and the cashier at our local supermarket, DeCicco's) could tell I was waiting for something big. It's like the hush right as the curtain before a wonderful production goes up. But whatever the next act brings, the show *must* go on.

All that's left is to be ready to cheer from the front row or offer comfort in the wings if the scene doesn't go as hoped. The wait might be nerve-wracking, but the real drama begins when that portal opens.

CHAPTER 19

Decisions, Decisions: NOW WHAT?

It's finally here. Decision Day. The college's verdict is coming, and it's the moment you and your child have both been waiting for—and dreading—for months. By now, your house has probably reached peak craziness. The dog seems to know something's up. Phones are charged, laptops are open, snacks are within arm's reach, and the clock is ticking toward that fateful release time.

At exactly 2:00 a.m. in Athens, Greece, one of our students sat up in bed, eyes still adjusting to the glow of his laptop screen. He had set multiple alarms in case one failed him in that crucial moment. His college fate (which at seventeen feels like *actual fate*, as if the universe is watching) was about to be revealed through a series of portals from institutions scattered mostly across the Northeastern United States.

Fingers clicking at record speed, he refreshed. Clicked again. And then?

A mix of joy and utter disbelief. He had gotten in. To multiple schools.

Like any good Gen Z student, he filmed himself in real-time, half-asleep, hair-disheveled, wildly exhilarated. After all, who else was awake to celebrate with him? In the video, you can hear him praying fervently for each decision in a mixture of Greek and English, as if summoning the mythological admissions gods.

"Come on, Dartmouth, come on, Dartmouth!"

What was astonishing was *him*. The way he handled each rejection or waitlist with such aplomb. When he got into a school, he tossed his arms in the air like he had just scored a game-winning goal and shrieked "Yes!" But when rejection arrived, he simply nodded, shrugged, and moved on. No wailing, no cursing the universe. It was incredible to watch, especially since he sent the video to me and Nancy with nothing but gratefulness.

Meanwhile, on the opposite end of the globe, in a high school classroom in Northern California, another student of ours was experiencing decision day in an entirely different way. She sat at her desk, phone hidden under the table, refreshing her portal every thirty seconds and waiting. Her AP Literature class discussion blurred into background noise. Was it out yet? Had anyone posted an update? And then, finally...the notification about results came to her email. She needed to find a private spot to check.

Heart thumping, she raised her hand, muttered something about needing the bathroom, and bolted.

Inside a cramped single stall, she locked the door, took an enormous breath, and pulled out her phone.

This was it.

When she saw the decision? Sobbing (the good kind). Screaming. Alone.

Both of these students later shared their "big reveal" moments with us—videos, messages, tears, all of it. Watching their reactions reminded us exactly why we do what we do.

Whether it's 2 a.m. in Greece, or 2 p.m. in a high school bathroom stall in California, the truth is the same: this process is a whirlwind of hope, heart, nerves, and probably, some indigestion. No matter where or how your child opens that portal, they feel it all at once, and you will undoubtedly, too.

I remember the agonizing wait for WashU to announce when early decisions would be released for my oldest daughter. The school was maddeningly noncommittal about giving an exact time, which was pure torture (mostly for me, not her). When the email with the precise time finally came through, Jeff and I squeezed onto her bed, practically holding our breath as she shakily logged in. Then? A huge grin.

My oldest was away at college, and my youngest was deep in rehearsal at the dance studio, but seconds later, the shrieking over FaceTime made up for their absence. Almost immediately, my daughter's friends began pouring into our kitchen, hugging, celebrating, and making themselves completely at home. Within minutes, Jeff and I were sprinting out to pick up four pizzas, fully aware they'd disappear before we even found the paper plates. I must confess that Jeff and I were absolutely *kvelling*.[51]

---

51 *Kvelling* is Yiddish for bursting with pride, and it's usually accompanied by excessive bragging to anyone within earshot.

THE BIG MOMENT: HOW FAMILIES REACT ON DECISION DAY

For parents, it's an emotional roller coaster. We ride the highs, the lows, the hopes, the uncertainty, all while pretending to be calm (when we are decidedly not calm). Whether pacing the kitchen, hovering on their bed, or scrolling aimlessly through our phones, we feel everything.

HAVE A GAME PLAN FOR DECISION DAY(S)

Some parents want to be in the room when their child checks results; others prefer to give them space. The key is to ask *before* the moment, "Would you like me there when you check, or would you rather have a little space?" Some will want a hug no matter the outcome while others need time to process alone (so try not to hover).

Most colleges give students a heads-up about when decisions will be released, usually weeks in advance, though sometimes only a few days. A few announce only a general timeframe, and others send a last-minute email or text minutes before portals open, which can instantly make everyone's Apple Watch think they're halfway through an advanced Soul Cycle class.

Whatever their answer, respect it. If you have more than one child, remember that they're different people. What feels right for one may not be what the other needs. Your presence (or perfectly timed absence) is one of the best ways to show your support.

On the day your child is supposed to hear back from schools, don't ask them every five minutes if a decision has been posted. They will check when they're ready. Constantly badgering them with, "Did you hear yet?" will only add to the stress. Instead, distract yourself...anything to keep from staring at them like they're the countdown clock on New Year's Eve.

REAL-LIFE DECISION DAY SCENES WE'VE SEEN

- **The Super Bowl Crowd:** Some families gather around the computer like it's the Super Bowl, ready to scream for joy or provide emergency emotional support.
- **The Filmmakers:** Others record the whole thing, hoping for a joyous moment, but they'll instantly delete the footage if it's a rejection, deferral, or waitlist.
- **The Door-Slammers:** Many students insist on opening their portal alone, while their parents are pacing outside as if they're waiting for a surgeon to deliver life-or-death news. One student, Daniel, banished his family to the basement while he marched up to his room to check. They waited for the signal to come back upstairs (thankfully, to screams of elation).
- **The Letter Writers:** Some parents, knowing how high emotions run, even

write their child a note ahead of time to read before opening their decision: *Dear Justin, You are still amazing. You are still worthy. A college decision does not define you.* It sounds dramatic, but it's a reminder that their kid's worth was never up for debate.

- **The Nonchalant Crowd:** Some families don't make a big deal out of this. At all. My daughter's friend Emma's parents—both doctors—worked late nights at the hospital and didn't even know the decision date. Emma gathered her friends around the kitchen counter, opened her email, and squealed when the inbox announced: "Congratulations on your acceptance to Wesleyan!" Some parents find out days later, almost in passing: "Oh, you got into college? Cool. How was school?" For them, college decisions are one small moment in their child's much bigger life.

- **The Secret Keepers:** A family friend in Texas didn't tell a soul when their son Peter got into Princeton in mid-December, Early Action. They wanted the big reveal only after he'd made his final decision. Proof that not every acceptance needs to be Instagrammed immediately.

REAL PARENT REACTIONS: TEXTS, TEARS, AND TOTAL SHOCK

As college advisors, we've received plenty of messages in the moments after decisions come in. A few favorites:

- *"SHE GOT IN!!!!!!!!!"*—sent with approximately thirty-seven exclamation points.
- *"He's sobbing. I'M SOBBING. We are thrilled! I can't believe it."*
- *"WE GOT A YES! THANK YOU THANK YOU THANK YOU!"* (Side note: these moments still give me goose bumps.)

Then, of course, there are the other texts:

- *"Deferred. We're stunned."*
- *"Rejected. She's trying to hold it together, but she is devastated."*
- *"Why did we even waste our time with this school? I'm FURIOUS."*

One of my favorite moments? A dad called me, screaming and sobbing in the best possible way, when his daughter got into Hamilton. I was (yet again) standing in the frozen food aisle at Trader Joe's, somewhere between the pizzas and the pastas. I am now convinced all major life events happen in that aisle.

For parents of twins, the emotional whiplash reaches a whole other stratosphere. One child gets into their first-choice school and is over the moon. Another hears "deferred" or "waitlisted," and suddenly your heart is both bursting and breaking at the same time. Do you pop champagne? Cry in the bathroom? Handle both at once?

Right when you think you've seen it all, there are shockers, too.

One student had been deferred from Cornell, and when it was time to hear from USC Early Action, her mom braced herself for more disappointment. But instead, an acceptance! Her text?

"IT'S LIKE SHE JUST WON THE LOTTERY!"

HANDLING A REJECTION, DEFERRAL, OR WAITLIST

Not every decision will be the one your child hoped for, and that's tough. Please know that this isn't the end of the road; it's only a detour. Here's how to approach the next steps based on the outcome.

IF THEY'RE REJECTED

A rejection hurts, no matter how much you tried to prepare them for it. Give your child space to process. This is a loss. Grief (even if temporary) is normal. Avoid the urge to immediately launch into a pep talk. Instead, try these tips:

- **Listen before fixing.** Sometimes, they need to vent. Let them feel what they're feeling.
- **Validate their disappointment.** A simple "I know this really hurts. You worked so hard, and I'm so proud of you," goes a long way.
- **Ease into next steps.** Once they've had time to process, help them refocus on their other great options. If this was an ED rejection, is there an ED2 school they liked almost as much? If not, redirect their attention to their favorite Regular Decision schools.

I've said this before, but it's worth repeating. We've seen so many students heartbroken over a rejection, only to end up at another school they grew to love. Truly love. Often, they can't even imagine having gone anywhere else.

IF THEY'RE DEFERRED

A deferral puts them in emotional limbo. They're still in the running, but without the certainty they wanted. If your child is still excited about the school, here are a few meaningful next steps they can take:

- **Send a well-crafted Letter of Continued Interest (LOCI).** This should express enthusiasm, update the school on any new achievements, and reaffirm why they'd love to attend.
- **Keep up their grades.** Mid-year reports matter and slipping grades could hurt

their chances. Remind them to keep the momentum going.

- **Stay realistic about all outcomes.** Some years bring little movement in the spring, but there's no way to predict whether it'll be a generous year or a quiet one. Use this as a moment to focus on utilizing an ED2 choice or other great schools on their list.

IF THEY'RE WAITLISTED

Waitlists can be brutal. It's like being told, "we like you, but not *quite* enough." The decision simply dangles there, like a lone matzoh ball, floating in a pot of soup. Unfortunately, at many highly selective schools, the odds of getting off the waitlist are slimmer than finding a parking spot at Costco on a Saturday afternoon. Yet those odds can vary in surprising ways from year to year. Pandemic deferrals, FAFSA delays, and changes in international student enrollment may all cause unexpected movement. While it's smart to temper expectations, it's also okay to hold out a little hope.

If your child wants to stay on the list, here's what they can do:

- **Accept the waitlist spot quickly.** Follow any instructions from the school.
- **Send a Letter of Continued Interest (LOCI).** Like with deferrals, a short, enthusiastic update can help.
- **Fully commit to another school by the May 1st deadline.** Waitlists are unpredictable, so it's important to make a big deal out of each acceptance. It's fine to put a deposit at a school you love while remaining on a waitlist, as long as this works for you financially.

We've seen it countless times—students who don't get into their top choice end up somewhere else and fall completely in love.

REFRAMING THE OUTCOME

The right school isn't always the one your child had at the top of their list. That first-choice college is merely *one* choice; it may not even end up being the *best* choice. If they don't get in, let them have time to process and grieve (because yes, it's really a grieving process), and then gently help them refocus on all the good possibilities still ahead.

Also, decide ahead of time how you'll celebrate or regroup. If it's good news, maybe it becomes a spontaneous pizza night or a giant sigh of relief that this part of the process is finally behind you. If the outcome is disappointing, prepare to offer support, slowly and gently. Resist the urge to problem-solve in the first five minutes. Often, the best thing you can do is be present, offer a hug (or tissues), and give them space to feel what they're feeling.

HAVE A PLAN B AND MAKE IT A GOOD ONE

When I drive through Scarsdale, I sometimes go out of my way to pass the Greenville Church on Ardsley Road. Their marquee, updated regularly by Reverend Edward Schreur, always seems to feature the right message at the right time. My favorite: "If Plan A doesn't work out, there are 25 other letters in the alphabet." Honestly, I can't think of a better piece of advice for this stage of your student's journey.

Whether they're shouting or recalibrating, Plan B isn't about settling. It's about finding the next best fit and moving ahead confidently. If the news isn't what they hoped for, acknowledge all the work and energy that went into the process. Take them out for their favorite meal or do something that reminds them how proud you are. Not because of an acceptance letter, but because of everything it took to get here. That's the moment to feel a little *nachas*,[52] the happy, proud feeling that says, "No matter what, we raised a good one."

SIBLING REACTIONS: SUPPORT AND KNOWING WHEN TO "ZIP IT"

Let's start with younger siblings. They may not say much, but they're soaking it all in. Even if they're years away from applying, they feel the weight of what's happening. Try not to make them feel like they're up next in the hot seat. Give them room to be kids a little longer.

OLDER SIBLINGS NEED TO LET NEWLY ACCEPTED STUDENTS HAVE THEIR MOMENT

Big brothers and sisters usually have the best of intentions, but they can jump right into advice mode, acting as if they've been promoted to College Admissions Expert:

- "You should start working on your roommate questionnaire."

---

52 *Nachas is a Yiddish word for pride or joy, especially the deep kind parents feel when their kids make them proud.*

- "That's ridiculous that you were deferred. There are way better schools on your list."
- "I knew you aimed too high..."

We've seen this movie. They've been through this before, and they think they're helping. But maybe...give it a minute. Let their younger sibling breathe before bombarding them with unsolicited guidance. Here are some of the kindest things an older sibling can say:

- "I'm proud of you."
- "It's their loss. Stupid school."
- And my favorite: "I love you no matter what."

Social Media Madness: WHAT NOT TO DO

Those screaming acceptance videos on Instagram and Facebook? I get it. Your kid worked hard, and you're both thrilled. It's a huge moment, and you want to celebrate. But before you hit "post," take a breath. Please remember that another parent is sitting beside their devastated child, trying to offer consolation while scrolling past someone else's happiest day.

Another trend I don't love? Those high school "Class of 20XX" Instagram pages where students share baby pictures alongside their future college and intended major. It's a sweet idea on the surface, but for kids who didn't get into their top choices or haven't figured everything out yet, it can feel like salt in the wound. Watching those posts stack up is hard.

Your family's good news is certainly worth celebrating. But maybe not at full volume. A little sensitivity can go a long way.

HOW TO BEHAVE AT SCHOOL THE NEXT DAY

Let's talk etiquette.

If your kid got into their dream school, that's awesome. But remind them that showing up the next day decked out in head-to-toe college merch and announcing their acceptance to anyone within a fifty-foot radius might not be the nicest move. It's like spending all Monday raving about an amazing Saturday night party when half the class wasn't invited. Yikes.

Some schools handle this well. At Edgemont Junior/Senior High School (Nancy's kids' alma mater), students weren't allowed to wear college gear until a designated day well after May 1st when colleges typically ask for a commitment. Maybe all high schools should consider this approach.

Why not set a specific College Day after decisions are made? Seniors could proudly wear their sweatshirts together, turning it into a shared celebration rather than an isolating experience. This way, no one feels left out, and the whole class acknowledges the milestone together.

Even if their school doesn't have a policy like this, encourage your kid to be mindful. Some classmates are still waiting. Others got news they weren't hoping for. They can absolutely rejoice but tell them to be thoughtful about it. People always remember the kind kids. The ones who instinctively find the right words to say. The ones who check in on a friend who's having a hard week.

If your kid doesn't know what to say, suggest something simple: "Hey, I know today is hard, but I promise you'll end up somewhere great."

It doesn't take a marching band or a head-to-toe outfit in school colors to show excitement. A little kindness goes a long way, and those moments stay with us the longest.

ADDING JOY FOR OTHERS (EVEN WHEN YOU'RE STILL WAITING OR DISAPPOINTED)

College decisions come in waves, and it's natural to be caught up in your own kid's results. At the same time, one of the best things you can do is celebrate someone else's success, even when your own kid's future feels uncertain.

I remember this well from when my oldest child was still waiting for his early decision results. It was mid-December, and I was at a middle school chorus concert for my youngest, sitting with my friends Tracey and Erika. As we chatted in the auditorium, we suddenly got word that Erika's son had just been accepted to his top-choice college. In that moment, nothing else mattered. We screamed, we hugged, and we were beyond thrilled for our friend's son.

The pride, the crazy excitement, the hard work behind every acceptance all matter.

Someone else's dream school may not be yours, but that moment of happiness is universal.

When it comes down to it, we all want people cheering for our kids. So, let's be the kind of people who cheer for theirs.

MAKING THE ULTIMATE DECISION

If your student didn't apply ED or has multiple acceptances, now comes the fun part: choosing where to go. While parents can weigh in, remember that this is your kid's decision. Many schools offer an Accepted Students' Day, which is basically a giant lovefest designed to woo undecided students. Visiting a college with an acceptance in hand feels totally different from a regular campus tour. Persuade your kid to go. Let them take it all in: the energy, the students, the food, the vibe. Often, it comes down to something intangible. The campus that just feels right. A conversation with someone from a remote part of the world. Maybe even the school colors. Or the dining hall with the best late-night munchies.

Your child has already thought about geography, size, and weather when building their list (*see Chapter 8*). But now it's real. What once looked exciting online can feel totally different when they're standing on campus. It's worth revisiting many of those same questions, along with a few new ones, by asking: Where will I feel happiest and thrive for the next four years?

Beyond the little things, here are some key factors worth weighing (and re-weighing):

- **Financial Aid:** This can be a game changer. If your child is waiting on financial aid or scholarship offers, make sure they understand the real costs before getting emotionally attached to a school. Loans may seem abstract at eighteen, but they're very real at thirty. If they need help comparing packages (which often come in confusing formats), they should check with their school counselor. Make sure they know which parts are grants and which are loans.

- **Geography:** Do they want to be close to home? Far away? Near a city? With easy airport access? Kids often envision attending college in a different part of the country, but do they really understand what that will feel like? What the travel back and forth will entail? How will it feel to be far from family? Let's also not forget time zones: if they need to vent about classes or a squabble with friends, it might be 2 a.m. back home. Those are questions worth considering.

- **Weather:** Do they thrive in sunshine, or crave slushy winters?

- **Greek Life & Social Scene:** Is a strong sports culture a must? Do they want a big rah-rah school, or something more laid-back? Would they enjoy the camaraderie of a fraternity or sorority, or do they prefer a more informally organized social scene?

- **Academic Requirements:** Check the curriculum and general ed requirements. No kid wants to be blindsided by a mandatory foreign language class or lab science. Ouch.

- **Semester Structure**: Semester, trimester, or quarter? Do they prefer longer terms or faster-paced ones? Differences in calendars also affect breaks, which matters if friends or siblings are on a different schedule.
- **Cultural Fit**: Can they see themselves walking across the quad? Sitting in those classrooms? Do the students seem like people they can relate to? Go to a party with? Sob about a breakup on the dorm floor at 3 a.m. with?

When the dust settles, the best choice is the one where your kid feels like they can breathe and fully be themselves—horrible days, messy rooms, imperfect roommates, and all. They really do land where they're meant to be. And if not? They transfer...

CHAPTER 20

WHEN YOUR DREAM SCHOOL... ISN'T: *Truths About Transferring*

Every fall, we hear from a handful of families feeling that same sense of panic. The euphoria that surrounded move-in day starts to fade, and the reality of college life sets in. We also hear from plenty of students who love where they've ended up. They've found their people and their late-night pizza spot, but not everyone adjusts at the same pace. For many, the first semester feels more like a crash landing into adulthood.

TEXT FROM A FORMER STUDENT:

"Hey, Beth & Nancy. I don't think this is the right school for me. I don't feel like I've found my place, and it's already November. The classes are fine. I just don't feel like I'm having a great time. It feels clique-y and small."

EMAIL FROM A PARENT:

"Beth, I don't know what to do about Benji. He calls me every single day on the verge of tears. He hasn't found friends. He's unsure about his classes. Is this normal? Did he make the right decision?"

No one really prepares students or their parents for the whirlwind that is the first semester of college. It's basically *Adulting 101*. Suddenly, they're responsible for things like separating their laundry, making their own bed, and (gasp!) taking out the trash (hopefully, they've mastered this by now). They might juggle shifts at the cafeteria or the library on top of their coursework. While no one's going to stop them from binge-watching *Love Island* all night to avoid studying for a mid-term, no one's going to wake them up for that 8:00 a.m. Mandarin class either.

On top of these everyday inconveniences, there's the stress of making new friends, adjusting to college-level academics, managing the time between classes, and figuring out who they are without the comfort of their high school safety net. It's no wonder so many students feel completely unmoored.

Thanks to the illusion of social media, your child might call home, upset that *everyone else* is thriving. Their high school friends at USC, Wisconsin, or Vanderbilt seem to have it all. They're posting pictures of football games, rooftop parties, and omelet stations that could rival the brunch buffet at the Ritz Carlton. However, what they don't see are the kids who choose not to share the nights they spend alone in their dorm room, just wanting a hug from a familiar face (or their goldendoodle).

Some students push through, suffering the awkward small talk and lonely weekends until, slowly but surely, campus starts to feel like home. Others? They hop on a train and ring their parents' doorbell at midnight. My friend's daughter, only two weekends into college, decided she'd had enough of dorm life, enough of missing her boyfriend, and enough of Philly. Without a word to her parents, she packed a bag, took the train back to her hometown just north of NYC, and rang the doorbell. When her groggy, confused mom opened the door, she blurted out, "I just needed to come home."

Was she the only kid who felt that way? Certainly not. She was just desperate enough to act on it.

The first few months of college are disorienting for almost everyone, not only your kid.

Before you start Googling transfer deadlines alongside them, ask them to pause. The first few months are weird and hard and lonely...until they aren't.

COLLEGE LIFE NOW VS. THEN

Here's something to reflect on: adjusting to college today is a whole different experience than when we went.

Back in the day, dorm room doors were always open. Kids lingered in dining halls for hours just talking, and one communal TV in the lounge meant everyone watched *Friends* or *Seinfeld* together. Making plans? You knocked on someone's door or scribbled a note on their whiteboard. Remember those?

Fast forward to today, and things look different. Walk into most dining halls and you'll see tables filled with students on their phones, earbuds in, eating alone. Socializing isn't as organic as it used to be. One dad told me about visiting his daughter at Johns

Hopkins for freshman parent weekend. He walked into the cafeteria and saw table after table of students sitting alone, scrolling. "It broke my heart a little," he confessed. Phones have become an appendage. Making friends takes more effort, and that's why so many kids feel like something is off those first few months.

It also doesn't start when they arrive on campus. Social media connects students the moment they're accepted; group chats and Instagram threads pop up within hours. Some kids feel like they've already found a crowd long before move-in day, while others worry about being left out. For some, that creates a false sense of belonging. For others, it deepens feelings of isolation. Either way, it can make those early weeks harder to navigate.

College life has changed and so have the challenges that come with it. But the fact that this transition is harder, doesn't mean it won't get better. It usually takes time.

Still, what if a student gives it time and things don't fall into place? Occasionally, it becomes evident that the school they once imagined as the perfect match isn't the right environment after all.

SOME COMMON REASONS FOR TRANSFERRING

SIZE SHOCK: BIG AND SMALL

Some students crave a small, tight-knit community, until they realize it's a little *too* tight-knit. One student left Lafayette College (picturesque campus, solid academics) because after one semester, she felt like she had already exhausted many of the social opportunities. She transferred to the University of Michigan, where she was ecstatic about constantly meeting new people. The packed football stadiums and the sheer number of clubs were exactly what she'd been missing.

Meanwhile, another student transferred from the University of Michigan to Middlebury College after realizing he hated feeling like a tadpole in a massive sea of 50,000 students. "I was tired of feeling anonymous," he confessed to us. "At Middlebury, I genuinely know my professors, and people say 'hi' to me when I walk across campus."

A NEW ACADEMIC INTEREST

Once in a while, a student stumbles into a class that completely changes their path, and suddenly, their school doesn't quite have what they need.

One student at the University of Virginia fell head over heels for art history, only to realize that Charlottesville isn't exactly a mecca of world-class museums. She transferred to Boston University, where she could dive into the vibrant art scene.

Another student started at a small regional college, worked hard, transferred to NYU, and then discovered a calling she never expected: she wanted to become a cantor.

That realization led her to apply to the Jewish Theological Seminary and Columbia's joint program during junior year. She got in. *Mazel tov!*[53]

Interests evolve. Sometimes, a school that once seemed like the perfect fit just isn't, and that's okay.

THE GREEK LIFE SITUATION

Then there are students who get to college, rush their first-choice sorority or fraternity...and don't get in. For some, this is just a bump in the road. For others, especially at schools where Greek life dominates the culture, it can be isolating enough to make them want to leave.

We once got a panicked call from a mom whose daughter hadn't received a bid from the same sorority she'd joined decades earlier at Cornell. The mom was devastated. She was convinced her daughter's college career (and maybe her life) were over. Meanwhile, her daughter was holding it together far better than she was.

Another mom reached out after her son's rough start at Indiana University. He'd spent the first few months *schmoozing*[54] with guys at different frats, convinced he'd fit in somewhere. But after making it through a few rounds of rush, he was cut from every house. Suddenly, the campus that had seemed welcoming felt lonely. He called home, embarrassed and ready to transfer.

Parents are often blindsided by how severely this part of college culture can affect their kids. At some schools, Greek life isn't a choice among many; it defines the social scene. When students don't get the bid they hoped for or decide not to rush at all, they can feel alienated before college life has even taken off.

Most students bounce back faster than their parents. They eventually find their people. But some don't, and that's reason enough to step back and ask whether the fit is right. For many, transferring to a school where Greek life doesn't dominate makes all the difference.

A DESIRE FOR DIVERSE PERSPECTIVES

Last year, Nancy and I worked with a wonderful young woman who felt stuck at a small Catholic school in Southern California. Coming from an all-girls' Catholic high school, she assumed a similar environment would feel familiar. But once she got there, she quickly craved a broader range of perspectives.

One literature class flipped everything on its head. She was introduced to authors and ideas she'd never encountered before, and it opened her eyes to the kind of academic

---

53 *Mazel tov* is a Hebrew and Yiddish phrase that means "congratulations" or "good fortune." It's often used to celebrate milestones, from weddings to big achievements like getting into an incredible academic program. 54 *Schmoozing* is a Yiddish word that means to chat or socialize in a friendly, easygoing way.

community she wanted. She realized she was craving a more diverse and dynamic intellectual environment. She transferred to Barnard and never looked back.

ACADEMICALLY, THEY'VE OUTGROWN THEIR SCHOOL

Some students may not have been great high school students but hit their stride in college.

One student landed at a small, regional, largely commuter school in Florida, but after earning a 4.0, she transferred to Emory University, where she felt pushed and inspired by her classmates and professors. It's common for kids to transfer to more selective academic fits after proving themselves.

THE STUDENTS WHO ALMOST TRANSFERRED BUT END UP STAYING

Every year, Nancy and I work with at least one student who fills out every transfer application, writes all the essays, gets accepted to multiple schools...and then decides to stay put. Why? Time spent in a new place is everything.

The first semester of college is tough for almost everyone, but by spring, things tend to gel. Students find their people and their groove. Classes feel more manageable, friendships start to cement, and suddenly, transferring doesn't feel so urgent anymore.

One student who almost left Georgetown expressed it best: "By the time I got a few transfer acceptances, I had finally started feeling at home. It turns out what I needed was more time."

That idea of feeling at home isn't just emotional; it's measurable. According to research reported by *Inside Higher Ed*, even small increases in a student's sense of belonging are linked to higher graduation rates, with each one-point rise on a belonging scale associated with better four- and six-year completion outcomes.[55]

If your child is miserable in September, don't assume they'll feel the same way in May. Encourage them to be patient. Join new clubs, especially ones that they've never even thought of trying. Meet their professors during office hours. Push past their comfort zone. They might surprise themselves.

KNOWING WHEN IT'S TIME TO START THE TRANSFER PROCESS

If by winter they're still Googling transfer deadlines during their 9 a.m. lecture, that might be a sign it's time to explore other options. That's perfectly fine. Sometimes, just filling out transfer applications takes the pressure off. We often tell parents that once

55 Joshua Bay, "Belonging in College Isn't Just Nice — It Can Boost Graduation Rates," *Inside Higher Ed*, January 6, 2026, https://www.insidehighered.com/news/student-success/retention/2026/01/06/belonging-college-isnt-just-nice-it-can-boost-graduation-rates.

students have submitted their applications, their stress levels drop, and many find themselves settling in more comfortably during the second semester.

If, by the end of spring, they're still unhappy and receive transfer acceptances, they have the choice to leave.

A thoughtful conversation, however, should come before any transfer talk. A few essential questions can help clarify whether this is merely a rough patch or a sign that something more serious isn't working:

1. **Are the challenges short-term or long-term?**

   Feeling lonely or overwhelmed during the first semester is common. But if they're miserable with their academic program, feel completely unstimulated, or discover their "perfect" school doesn't even offer their intended major, that's worth a closer look.

2. **Have they made a real effort to settle in?**

   Have they joined clubs, met with professors, or tried to meet people outside of their dorm or the dining hall salad bar? Or are they mostly tethered to their room, scrolling through Instagram, and convinced that everyone else is having the time of their life?

3. **Do they know what they're actually looking for?**

   Are they hoping to transfer because they've found a better fit, or are they desperate to leave? Transferring should be about moving *toward* something, not just running away from a tough situation. If all they can say is, "I just don't like it here," it might be worth staying a little longer to sort it out.

Here's how we like to frame it:

You wouldn't keep wearing a pair of shoes that give you blisters just because they were majorly on sale. No matter how good they looked in the store, at some point, you have to admit they're not the right fit.

SHOT OF SANITY

Often, a school that seemed ideal on paper turns out to be wrong in person. That doesn't mean your child made a bad decision. It just means they learned something important about what they need.

Before committing to a new school, encourage your child to look closely at how it supports transfer students both socially and academically. Some colleges offer robust orientation programs, dedicated advising, and transfer-friendly housing, while others expect students to fend for themselves. A little research here can make a big difference in how easily they adjust. Many transfer students say it was the best decision they ever made, not because their first college was awful, but because their new school felt more like home.

KIND OF CRAZY

TRANSFERRING *Isn't* FAILING: *It's* GROWING

I've moved across the country five times: from New York to Los Angeles, to Chicago, to New York, to San Francisco, and back again to New York. Each move was about love, school, career opportunities, or doing what was best for my family. Each time, I learned the layout of new supermarket aisles (my favorite is Mollie Stone's in Burlingame, CA), met new friends, and became a master of packing and unpacking boxes—although I still have no idea where to shove the kitchen utensils.

College isn't any different.

Your child is figuring out where they belong, and that often takes a few tries.

Transferring isn't about quitting. It's about recognizing what isn't working and having the courage to make a change. For the students who go through the transfer process, get accepted elsewhere, and then choose to stay? That's growth, too.

A REAL-LIFE STORY

For years, Olivia was convinced she would go to Wake Forest. It wasn't just her dream; it was *the* dream. Her parents met there, her older brother went there, and she grew up in a house filled with Wake Forest sweatshirts and game-day flags. She applied Early Decision and called us screaming when she got in. This was it. Her place. Her future.

UNTIL SHE GOT THERE.

Within three weeks, she realized something wasn't clicking. The Greek-heavy culture, which she had once yearned for, now felt exclusive and exhausting. The psychology department, which had seemed nurturing when she visited, suddenly felt restrictive and small.

By October, she was secretly checking application deadlines. By December, she had called Nancy and me for advice. Unsure but determined, she started drafting a few transfer essays. By April, she had a new acceptance letter from New York University, and for the first time all year, she exhaled. Today? She's thriving, and she'll be the first to tell you she made the right move.

IS TRANSFERRING A BIG DEAL?

Not as big as you think.

Most parents assume that transferring is rare and something students only do if they are on the verge of failing or unhappy beyond repair. This is simply not true.

According to the National Student Clearinghouse Research Center, 13.2% of all continuing and returning undergraduates in fall 2024 were transfer students, and that number is rising.[56]

A WORD OF CAUTION:

While transferring is common based on the statistics, getting accepted *to* transfer isn't as easy as it used to be. Years ago, a student with solid first-semester grades had plenty of transfer options. Now, transfer applications are more competitive, and if you apply as a freshman, colleges will review your high school transcript, test scores, and everything else. A transfer is far from guaranteed, so your child should not rely on it as an escape plan.

Colleges are paying attention to this shift, too. In 2025, Northwestern University announced a binding Early Decision application track for transfer students, following a similar move by the University of Chicago. This reflects a broader shift: transfer applicants are no longer an afterthought, but a group that colleges are actively courting.[57]

A binding Early Decision option gives students a way to demonstrate real commitment and gives colleges more certainty in shaping their incoming classes. The result? Earlier deadlines, clearer expectations, and a transfer process that looks more like first-year admissions than it did even a few years ago.

Whether they stay, transfer, or take the long scenic route to finding their place, they'll get to where they're meant to be. And so will you.

---

56 National Student Clearinghouse Research Center, *Transfer and Progress: Fall 2024 Report*, https://nscresearchcenter. org/transfer-and-progress. **57** Megan Liu, "Northwestern Adds Early Decision Application Track for Transfers Following the University of Chicago," *The Daily Northwestern*, October 24, 2025, https://dailynorthwestern.com/2025/10/24/campus/ northwestern-adds-early-decision-application-track-for-transfers-following-the-university-of-chicago/

CHAPTER 21

From GETTING IN *To* GETTING READY

One night, smack in the middle of tenth grade, my daughter flopped dramatically onto the family room couch and groaned, "I hate that everyone at school is already thinking about college. Can't we just enjoy high school while we're in it?"

I can still picture her that night. She was curled into the couch, self-aware, and one of those rare teens who genuinely liked high school. She wasn't in a rush to leave it behind. I think about that moment often, especially now that I've watched so many seniors navigate that strange stretch after senior year ends but before college begins—when the grades are in, the prom photos are posted, and the college sweatshirts have been ordered. Everything is technically decided, yet somehow, it doesn't feel quite real.

Maybe that's why I keep returning to her wish to slow down and simply enjoy the moment we're in.

Bruce Feiler, in *Life Is in the Transitions*, writes that "transitions are a vital period of becoming." They're not just the awkward bridge between chapters: they *are* the story. We often treat transitions like a pause between real events, something to endure or rush through. In truth, they're the moments when growth takes root. The changes may be subtle or even a little chaotic, but they mark the beginning of something new.

Watching my own kids move through that post-high school, pre-college phase, I can tell you that it's a weird, emotional time. It's astoundingly important and probably not talked about enough.

In our house, the summers before college came with their considerable share of emotional whiplash. I've sent three kids off to college, and each of them, at some point, started acting a bit...*off*. They'd come home hours later than they said they would or snap at me about what I made for dinner ("Seriously? Turkey tacos *again*?"). They generally behaved like home was the last place they wanted to be. At the time, I felt irrelevant and irritated. I muttered, (okay, shouted) things like, "Who *are* you, and what have you done with my child?"

Then one morning, during our daily phone call, my friend Hilary asked, "Are they soiling the nest? You know, it's a real thing!" I laughed because it sounded like something she'd totally make up, but nope, it's legit. Psychologists use it to describe how teens, often without realizing it, start creating distance before they leave home. Adolescence already brings its share of obnoxious behavior, but this stage takes it up a notch. They get prickly, pick fights, or suddenly find your very existence offensive. It's not about being rude; it's their way of loosening the grip emotionally, so the imminent goodbye doesn't hit quite so hard. For them *and* for us.[58]

Once I understood what was happening, it made more sense. My three kids weren't turning into ungrateful monsters (well, maybe temporarily). They were doing the awkward work of separating and reaching for their future independence all while hoping I'd fold their laundry one last time. It's weird for all of us, as if we're fumbling through a dress rehearsal for a play that none of us totally understands.

That stretch of time, between "You got in!" and "We need to be there at 8 a.m. on move-in day," can feel like being stuck on the tarmac waiting for takeoff. However, it's a turning point. The spotlight moves from getting in to getting *ready*.

For some students, that means hunting for a roommate (if their college doesn't assign one), scrolling through their future college's Class of 20XX Instagram page, and planning dorm room decor down to the color-coded storage bins that may or may not fit under the bed. For others, it means freaking out about how to manage money or make a single decision without consulting you every five minutes.

For parents? Sometimes it means obsessing about shower caddies and mattress toppers. When my oldest was getting ready to leave, I fell hard down that rabbit hole. He couldn't have cared less, but I was convinced his future depended on the right com-

---

58 Lisa Damour, "My College-Bound Kid Is Soiling the Nest. Help!" *Dr. Lisa Damour*, https://drlisadamour.com/resource/my-college-bound-kid-is-soiling-the-nest-help.

forter and sheets. We spent over two hours at Bed, Bath & Beyond (back when it was still a physical store, blaring with fluorescent lights and designed to convince you to buy three times more than you need). My middle child came along, partly thanks to her great eye for design, and partly because she makes her brother laugh even when he's nervous. She was the comic relief that day, especially when she plopped herself in the shopping cart and rode it up the escalator, despite the giant sign that read "Carts only, no people." But the real hero of that night was a no-nonsense salesperson named Sean, who helped us focus on the essentials and directed us away from the most expensive gear. To this day, we laugh about that trip and fondly remember Sean.

As AnnMarie and Anne, the creators of *Simply2Moms*, a platform that helps families navigate everything from parenting to dorm decor, told me: "Making a dorm room cozy doesn't mean it has to look like something from a magazine. It's more about finding ways to make their new space comfortable and functional; someplace that feels like a home away from home. Getting our students' dorms ready was our way to help prepare ourselves to let go, too."[59]

SHOT OF SANITY

This time is a gift. It's a window to turn the page from college admissions to college readiness. Your child doesn't need to stress just yet about which classes to register for, though it doesn't hurt to encourage them to sift through the course catalog. What makes the biggest difference? Learning how to take care of themselves.

They need to understand that they may live with someone who may be neater or messier than they are (think color-coded sock drawer...or wet towels that become science experiments on the floor). They need to know how to make their way around a campus health center. They need to learn how to ask for help and how to be their own advocate.

59 Jessica Grose, "College-Dorm Influencers Decorating Momfluencer," *New York Times*, August 20, 2025, https://www.nytimes.com/2025/08/20/style/college-dorm-influencers.html. See also AnnMarie and Anne, "About Us," *Simply2Moms*, https://simply2moms.com/about/

At some point, they need to figure out how to leave home without looking back every five minutes.

ROOMMATES: THE ULTIMATE BLIND DATE

If your student's college doesn't assign a roommate, then prepare yourself. The roommate search is like a bizarre mix of online dating, detective work, and mutual stalking via Instagram.

Some students dive in, messaging potential matches with phrases like, "Hey! Are you a neat freak?" Others overanalyze Spotify playlists and social media posts as if they're decoding classified CIA files.

There's no perfect formula, but here's our advice: encourage your child to look for someone who seems compatible, not a clone. They don't need to find a new best friend. They need someone they can co-exist with comfortable in a shared 12'x15' space. Someone who's trustworthy and won't FaceTime their mom at full volume every night. Yes, we've heard about those.

If their school doesn't allow roommate selection but assigns someone at random? That's often better. Some of the best college friendships start between two students who are nothing alike: different backgrounds, different political views, different corners of the country, and maybe wildly different sleep schedules. All it takes is mutual respect and the wisdom to steer clear of the dining hall scrambled eggs.

MONEY TALKS

Before your child leaves for college, make sure you've had the talk. No, not *that* one. The *money* talk.

Too many students arrive on campus with no idea how much things cost or how one too many poke bowls can drain a bank account.

Here's our advice about what to go over the summer before college starts:

- Who's paying for what? Tuition, books, plane tickets, laundry, late-night Uber-Eats delivery?
- Is there a budget or allowance, and how will it be managed?
- What happens if they overspend?
- Do they have a bank account? A debit card? A credit card (and do they know it's not free money)?
- Who's connected to their Venmo account, and do they realize it isn't a bottomless pit of free money?

It might feel awkward, but teaching your child how to manage money now is one of the greatest forms of independence you can give them.

OTHER STUFF WE FORGET TO TEACH

LAUNDRY Yes, your child should know how to do it. And yes, they *will* turn everything pink at least once before they figure it out. Many colleges offer laundry services, and if your student takes advantage of that, then great. No judgment. But learning how to separate the lights from the darks (and what *not* to put in the dryer) is one of those small-but-mighty life skills.

PRESCRIPTIONS Make sure your student knows how to refill their medications and where the campus health center is. Print a copy of their insurance card (maybe print two) and ask them to save a photo on their phone. One of those will likely go missing.

APPOINTMENTS Have them practice making their own doctor's appointment or even just a haircut. It sounds basic, but for kids raised on texts and DMs, calling an actual grown-up can feel like performing without their clothes on if they've never done it before.

The summer before college is the ideal time to walk through these basic skills without making it feel like a boring course in Driver's Ed. Talk through a few things and let them practice on their own. That way, they can stumble while they have a safety net (aka you), and you can guide them without jumping in to fix it.

Remind them (and yourselves) that adulthood doesn't arrive all at once. It slowly creeps in with Tide pods and the realization that no one is automatically restocking their supply of Advil.

LEGAL FORMS Consider whether it makes sense to fill out documents like a healthcare proxy, HIPAA release, or power of attorney before your student leaves for college. These forms give you the ability to step in during a medical or legal emergency, but what's appropriate can vary by family and by state. It's probably worth consulting a local attorney to see what makes sense for your family.

FOOD, FUN, AND EVERYTHING IN BETWEEN

Your student will learn quickly that dining hall vegetables are often unidentifiable and that midnight pizza is its own food group. It's worth reminding them that skipping meals for iced lattes isn't self-care.

Have the talk about alcohol. And sex. It doesn't have to be a big, awkward talk, but an honest conversation about consent and respect. Make sure they understand what sexual assault is, what it isn't, and that help exists on every campus. Remind them that a real friend steps in when someone's had too much or looks uncomfortable.

College comes with freedom but also responsibility. They'll undoubtedly make mistakes (everyone does), and hopefully, they'll learn and grow into wiser versions of themselves.

PARENTS: LET'S TALK ABOUT YOU

If this is your first kid heading off to college, no one tells you what it feels like to lose your place in the daily rhythm of their life. It's as if someone snuck into your bedroom at night and amputated a leg while you were sleeping. I remember those final weeks before my oldest child left for school.

I allowed myself a ten-minute cry every morning, usually around 7:15 a.m. like clockwork. I'd sit at my desk, think about how he'd gone from a colicky newborn to a high school graduate, and cry. Just a little. It became my breathe-and-cry pre-send-off meditation before starting the day.

Is this your last kid leaving the nest? You might feel it on an entirely different level. The silence hits differently. The house suddenly has way too many snacks in the pantry, and no one there to eat them.

When we dropped our youngest child at college, I knew I'd fall apart if I walked within five feet of her bedroom, so my husband and I went straight to the airport. We flew to Banff for five days of glorious hiking and enough distraction to feel like we were moving forward. (Of course, she called a few times—okay, at least a dozen—with freshman panic. Of course, we answered. But we also managed to hike most of the breathtaking trails without stopping to sob into our trail mix *too* often.)

If you're sending your final kid off to college this year, plan something for *you* that's celebratory or just plain distracting.

You've earned it.

Recently, my hairstylist was snipping away when she casually mentioned she was feeling startlingly blue about her youngest graduating. Next thing you know, we were both reaching for the box of tissues, she with her scissors still in hand.

There's overwhelming joy. But there's also a silent, unexpected ache. After all, you've spent years organizing life around this human: driving to and from dress rehearsals at 10 a.m. or 10 p.m., packing approximately 1,800 school lunches per child, scheduling doctor's appointments, filling out permission slips, and showing up at games, tournaments, and performances in snow, sleet, sideways rain, and everything in between. I vividly remember one drive home from my son's debate tournament in central New Jersey—three exits on the turnpike in a blizzard. It took two and a half hours. My husband was driving, and although I'm rarely known for being quiet, I bit my tongue the whole way (while clenching the door handle) so he could focus on the salt truck in front of us.

You've been there, too. Remember schlepping in pajamas to Michael's five minutes before closing for the emergency, last-minute poster run? That full-time job of raising school-aged kids suddenly winds down, and we're left wondering: *Now what?*

Turns out, this isn't an ending. It's the start of something else. Not only for them but for you, too. It's a chance to reinvent or rediscover the parts of yourself that may have been pushed to the side (in between the crumbs of Goldfish crackers and the forgotten lunch bags).

You're still a parent, and that never changes. But your role is evolving. Like any good transition, it comes with a little uncertainty and a lot of potential.

This transition isn't just theirs. It's yours, too.

Part of your next steps? Pulling back.

This can be the hardest part, especially for parents who've been deeply involved in every piece of their child's lives up to and through the college process. But now it's time to adapt your role. Not to let go entirely. But to loosen your grip enough for your child to hear the message: *I trust you to do this.*

Let them register for classes themselves. Let them text the roommate first. Let them figure out which orientation session they're supposed to attend. You can stay close but give them the thrill (and occasional panic) of steering the ship on their own.

A QUICK PRE-COLLEGE CHECKLIST

(For Parents Who Want to Help Without Helicoptering)

- MEDICAL Make sure they know how to refill prescriptions, book a doctor's appointment, and carry their insurance card somewhere they can find it in the abyss of their backpack.

- FINANCES Set up a bank account or debit card and help them track spending before shelling out $59 at CVS just because they're stressed about a midterm.

- ACADEMICS Encourage them to check out the course catalog and plan a balanced schedule so they won't feel lost on day one.

- A SENSE OF BELONGING Suggest they explore clubs, reach out to a roommate or advisor, find a great spot for coffee, and know where to go for help whether it's academic or emotional.

- THE BASICS Take them shopping for the basics like weather-appropriate clothes, Twin XL sheets, a mattress topper, and a cute shower caddy.

- ENJOY THIS TIME Let them do regular kid stuff: late nights, unlimited ice cream, summer jobs. Soak up the little moments together.

One OTHER THING *That* NO ONE WARNS *You* ABOUT

The goodbyes start long before move-in day.

Some friends leave early for orientation, sports, or pre-college programs, while others stick around until right before Labor Day. The result? A slow, disorienting trickle of goodbyes. One day you're buying a desk lamp at Target; the next, their friends are disappearing, one by one, like a reverse graduation.

It's strange and bittersweet. It's also kind of beautiful. Make the time for it. Stay up too late watching old movies. Take the goofy, slightly blurry photos you'll both be grateful for someday. Hug your kid like you mean it, including when they roll their eyes and try to squirm away.

Then, out of nowhere, move-in day arrives...

MOVE-IN DAY: WHAT NO ONE TELLS YOU

I will not sugarcoat this: move-in day is *weird*. It's sweaty, hectic, and emotionally (and physically) draining. You'll be carrying boxes, untangling cords, folding clothing into impossibly small drawers, and trying to figure out how to insert bed-risers without pulling out your back.

My advice? Be helpful, not hovering. Let your kid take the lead. If they want help setting up their room, great. Make the bed. For most parents, it's a rite of passage, and hopefully, the last time you'll wrestle with a fitted sheet on their behalf. If they'd rather unpack solo and send you out for the eighteenth forgotten item from Target, that's fine, too. Either way, being present counts, especially if your only job is holding the door open or pretending to clean every surface with those vile disinfectant wipes.

I still marvel at how fast it all went—from diapers to dorms, from cookie crumbs to full-grown adults. Honestly, I still feel like I'm playing house with my husband, and yet, we've miraculously managed to raise three actual humans (two with college degrees and one on the way). Gulp.

Eventually, it'll be time to go. The goodbye might feel harder than you expected. Hug them. Say something simple and loving even if it comes out shaky. Whatever you do, try not to burst into tears or shout their name across the quad in front of their hall-mates! (Full disclosure: I've done both. With all three of my kids. Despite writing an entire book telling other parents not to. Yep.)

Then leave. Don't drag it out. Don't circle back for one more hug. It doesn't mean you don't care; it means you trust them.

If you do shed a tear in the parking lot, you're in good company. If you don't? Totally okay. Either way, you're doing it right.

Say a quiet prayer for them if that brings you comfort. Maybe thank God, or whoever you turn to in moments of faith or hope, for getting them to this point. I whispered "Baruch Hashem," which means "thank God" in Hebrew. It was a small way to express appreciation and take in the weight of it all. However you do it, the point is to stop and honor the moment. You've given them roots, and now it's time to give them wings.

When it's time to drive away, do it with love and some yoga breathing. Ten minutes later, your kid might be calling to ask how to connect to the campus Wi-Fi. They're ready. You've done your job. And even if your heart needs a minute to catch up, trust that it will. It always does.

Big Picture, Bigger Ideas

Our BIG WISH LIST *For* COLLEGE ADMISSIONS REFORMS

Chapter written by:
Beth Gelles and Nancy Stuzin
(Co-Founders of Acceptance Ahead)

Throughout these pages, I've shared the stories, the laughter, and the lessons I've learned in the trenches. But for this final chapter, I asked Nancy to join me. Together, we wrote our wish list of changes we most want to see—recommendations that could make this process fairer, saner, easier, and more humane for students, parents, school counselors, teachers, and the admissions officers navigating the craziness from the other side.

If you want to understand what's broken, you don't need statistics—just a single Monday-morning text.

It was 7:00 a.m. Neither of us had touched our coffee yet when our phones buzzed with this message:

"James is applying to twenty-eight schools. We know the Common App has a twenty-school limit, so we're using the Coalition App for the extras. So far, he's adding Oberlin, WashU, SMU, and maybe Bates. Thoughts?"

Thoughts? Oh, so many.

First: Why are students applying to twenty-eight colleges? Would you audition for twenty-eight different roles in the same Broadway show?

Second: What exactly does James love about both Oberlin and SMU? Two schools that have basically nothing in common except for existing in the United States?

James' mom was a sharp, level-headed woman and well-respected in our town. But the college process had unraveled her. And she's hardly alone.

THIS CHAPTER IS OUR BATTLE CRY

The college admissions process was never perfect, but over the past fourteen years, we've watched it sink to new lows. What was once a somewhat sane system that usually worked has mutated into a machine fueled by misinformation, panic, unpredictability, and levels of bureaucracy that defy common sense.

Students are drowning in essays and contrived attempts to "stand out." Parents are losing sleep. Counselors and teachers are suffocating under paperwork. Colleges keep adding hoops to jump through. Less transparency. More confusion. "Likely" schools turning into heartbreakers. Strategy now outweighs substance. Sometimes luck does, too.

IT DOESN'T HAVE TO BE THIS WAY

We've spent years in the throes, witnessing the madness unfurl. So now we're stepping in with real solutions. Some of our ideas may sound bold, but each one addresses a piece of this process that has veered from frustrating to downright absurd.

1. LIMIT THE NUMBER OF APPLICATIONS PER STUDENT

There is zero reason for students to apply to twenty, twenty-five, or heaven help us, thirty colleges. Not only does this overwhelm high school seniors, but it also throws high school counseling offices into mayhem and stretches admissions officers to the brink.

Let's also not forget the financial toll. College applications aren't just an emotional roller coaster: they're an overpriced one. Fees range from a reasonable $40 per pop (thank you, University of Northern Iowa) to an astonishing $100 (Stanford, are you serious?). Some schools, like Colby and Macalester, graciously let you apply for free (probably because they know you'll be spending a fortune later).

Back in the good old days (when the anxiety was still there, but at least *manageable*), we recommended students apply to eight to twelve schools that were strategically chosen and well researched. With a balanced list, kids always had strong options, and we could predict results with much more accuracy.

Let's not lose our minds here. Twelve schools, *max*. No more sending out twenty-seven applications in a blind panic. A hard cap, whether imposed by the Common App or individual high schools, would push students to be more thoughtful and strategic. Blindly applying to twenty-eight schools doesn't make anyone a stronger candidate. A student with a 10% shot at each school has a 10% shot at each one. All that extra effort makes the process more tiring and expensive.

Ideally, fewer applications would also give admissions officers the breathing room to slow down and spend more time with each file. While it wouldn't erase the randomness entirely, it could reduce the number of last-minute decisions made in a haze of fatigue and junk food. The difference between a yes and a no should never hinge on who had the most caffeine or the fewest essays left in their pile.

Instead of treating applications like lottery tickets, students would be far better building a smaller, more intentional list of schools where they'd be thrilled to enroll.

2. LIMIT THE NUMBER OF ESSAYS STUDENTS NEED TO WRITE

If colleges want students to write meaningful essays, they need to stop drowning them in prompts.

First, there's the 650-word personal statement: a Common Application staple.

Except that's just the beginning.

Then come the supplemental essays, which vary dramatically in number, complexity, and word count. Some schools ask for one. Others? Two, four, sometimes six or more. These aren't just throw-away check-the-box responses.[60] These prompts can range from 50 to 500 words. Some prompts are thoughtful, engaging, and open the door for students to share their story.

Others sound like they were written by a group of overenthusiastic adults trying a little too hard to be creative:

- *If you could be any fruit, which one would you be and why?* (Occidental College) If a kid answers with "banana," are they boring? Is "pomegranate" more mysterious?

---

60 While we've included examples of terrific and not-so-terrific essay prompts, colleges frequently update their applications. Be sure to check each school's website and the Common Application for the most current prompts.

- *What theme song best represents your life?* (University of Southern California) As if every seventeen-year-old has already compiled their own Oscar-worthy soundtrack. One of our students enthusiastically chose Marvin Gaye's "Let's Get It On." Let's just say...we suggested a remix.

- *We're in your hometown. Where should we eat and what should we order?* (Elon University) How is anyone supposed to describe their town's best food experience in thirty words? Plus, how can a kid pick between their favorite pizza slice or the yummy omelet they crave from the late-night diner? What if they live in a rural area and the only options are an Applebee's or fast food that's nine miles away?

- *Think about how you would describe your approach to learning. Now, select an everyday object that you feel represents you as a learner. For example, this may be an object in the room you are writing in, something you see on your commute, or something reserved for special occasions.* Fifty words. (Drexel University's First Year Honors Research program.) Would a student be better off posing as a stop sign or as a refrigerator?

Let's turn ridiculous essay prompts into meaningful ones.

Somewhere in an admissions office conference room, we imagine a group of well-meaning but extremely exhausted admissions officers slumped around a large conference table, tossing out essay prompt ideas.

They're too burned out to say no to anyone's idea, so they mash together every idea that lands on the table. That's how we end up with the overly engineered essay prompt that feels like a cross between a TED Talk and a chemistry experiment.

Take this monstrosity from the University of Rochester:

"The University of Rochester benefactor, entrepreneur, photography pioneer, and philanthropist George Eastman said, 'The progress of the world depends almost entirely upon education.' In what ways do you envision using the curricular flexibility and co-curricular opportunities at the University of Rochester to promote progress and change within the communities you inhabit?"

Great question. For a doctoral dissertation. But for a 250-word response? It's like catering a Bat Mitzvah for 150 guests with only two dozen bagels. Good luck fitting it all in.

Then there was the University of Miami's infamous "ibis" prompt:

"The University of Miami's official mascot is the ibis. Folklore maintains that the native marsh bird is the last to take shelter before a hurricane hits and the first to emerge once the storm passes, making it an apt symbol of courage and resilience. Considering your ability to control your

own motivation and behavior, how have past experiences helped build your courage and resilience to persist in the face of academic and life challenges so that, once these storms pass, you can emerge in continued pursuit of your goals?"

First of all, most students don't even know what an ibis is. I certainly didn't. Second, if you want to ask about resilience, then ask about resilience. No need to drag National Geographic into it.

To their credit, the University of Miami finally retired the bird. This year's prompt was a breath of fresh air:

"Reflect on a community that has influenced you—be it your school, neighborhood, club, team, ethnic group, or any other group that has played a role in shaping who you are. What significance did that community hold for you, and in what ways did you contribute to it? How will you bring those experiences, values, and insights to enrich our campus community at the University of Miami?"

Now that's more like it. Clear, human, and welcomes students to reflect on something real. Progress!

Not all essay prompts are awful. Some colleges ask insightful questions that make students want to sit down and write. When a prompt is clear and invites reflection, students are far less likely to freeze or turn to AI in a panic.

Here are a few of our favorites. A quick note: prompts shift a bit from year to year, but what stays consistent is the type of questions that genuinely engage students.

1. HARVARD COLLEGE: THE ROOMMATE LETTER

Write a letter to your future college roommate introducing yourself and sharing things they might not know.

Why it works: It's fun, informal, and invites students to show their personality without trying to impress.

2. UNIVERSITY OF CALIFORNIA (ALL CAMPUSES): PERSONAL INSIGHT

Every person has a creative side. Describe how you express yours.

Why it works: It gives students room to define creativity on their own terms, whether it's painting, coding, or organizing a perfect Spotify playlist. There's room for interpretation.

3. UNIVERSITY OF PENNSYLVANIA: LETTER OF GRATITUDE

Write a letter to someone who has had an impact on you. How have they shaped your life?

Why it works: It's heartfelt. We're suckers for anything that reminds teenagers to say thank you.

4. WILLIAM & MARY COLLEGE: OVERCOMING OBSTACLES

Tell us about a challenge or adversity you've faced and how it has shaped you.

Why it works: It's a classic, but always a great way for students to show growth and resilience.

5. NEW YORK UNIVERSITY: BRIDGE BUILDER

Tell us about a time you encountered a perspective different from your own. What did you learn—about yourself, the other person, or the world?

Why it works: What a great way to show empathy and openness—skills every campus community needs.

6. UNIVERSITY OF NORTH CAROLINA (CHAPEL HILL): ACADEMIC CURIOSITY

Discuss an academic topic that you're excited to explore and learn more about in college. Why does this topic interest you?

Why it works: It allows students to geek out about what genuinely excites them.

7. BOSTON COLLEGE: DANGER OF A SINGLE STORY

Reflect on a time someone defined you by one narrative and how you overcame that.

Why it works: It pushes students to show depth and resilience against stereotypes.

Here's our simpler, saner approach to application essays:

Keep the 650-word personal statement. That one makes sense.

Ditch the endless supplemental prompts and replace them with a universal set of six to eight standardized essay questions. Every student must answer the same ones with a substantial but manageable word count. We recommend 250 to 300 words each.

Students write their essays once, upload them to the Common App, and they're done. Colleges could then pick which ones they want to read.

Most important: Say farewell to the dreaded "Why Us?" essay.

This is a ridiculous exercise where students scour the internet to manufacture fluff about specific classes, professors, research opportunities, and study abroad programs. Many of these essays end up sounding like an infomercial.

Applying to college is stressful enough. Instead of forcing students to perform intellectual gymnastics in 250 words, let's ask questions that matter: who they are, what they care about, what they want to change, and how they think. Isn't that what colleges want to know anyway?

3. BRING BACK STANDARDIZED TESTS AND USE THEM SMARTLY

Before COVID upended the world, only a handful of colleges were test optional (Bowdoin, Wake Forest, University of Chicago, and a few others). However, when test centers shut down and students couldn't physically take the SAT or ACT, waiving test requirements became a necessary and compassionate response.

Now, years later, testing access is back, but many colleges have stuck with test-optional policies. Why? Because more applicants mean lower acceptance rates, which leads to higher rankings.

Is that what's best for students? We're not so sure.

Colleges are starting to question it, too. Schools like Harvard, MIT, Dartmouth, the University of Miami, Purdue, Stanford, and the University of Alabama and Penn State (starting in 2027) have already brought back testing requirements, recognizing that GPA alone is not always a reliable measure of readiness. A 4.0 at one high school doesn't necessarily mean the same thing as a 4.0 at another. And with grade inflation rising nationwide, GPAs have become a much murkier data point than they used to be.

Test-optional policies have added layers of stress and second-guessing for students, parents, and counselors. Should they test at all? Should they send the scores? High-scoring students with less than perfect transcripts agonize over whether submitting them will help or hurt, and students with different academic profiles wrestle with their own version of the same question.

Colleges are starting to see the flip side: in trying to level the playing field, they may be missing out on high-potential students—the very ones they hope to admit. Sometimes, even a slightly lower score can add helpful context or tip the balance in a student's favor.

A study from the National Bureau of Economic Research (NBER) found that:

- Low-income students who submitted scores more than tripled their chances of admission (from 2.9% to 10.2%).
- First-gen students who submitted scores more than doubled their acceptance rates.

Rather than scrapping standardized tests, colleges should use them as a tool for social mobility: a way to spot promising students from underserved backgrounds who might otherwise be overlooked.

Ironically, the students who might benefit most from submitting scores, including many first-generation and low-income applicants, are often the ones told not to bother. Without clear guidance, many skip testing altogether, not realizing that admissions officers review scores in context. Without that extra data point, they're at a disadvantage compared to wealthier peers who can highlight academic potential through private tutoring, summer programs, and access to AP/IB/Honors courses.

What started as an effort to level the playing field may now be secretly widening the gap.

Rather than walking away from testing altogether, colleges should use it to help strong students from all backgrounds stand out and make it clear that scores will be reviewed in context. A 28 on the ACT from an underserved student shouldn't be weighed the same as a 28 from a well-resourced one.

Here's the bigger picture: diversity is what makes a campus feel alive. Hearing different stories and perspectives pushes us to think in new ways and experience the world with more compassion. College should feel more like a place where students genuinely learn from each other and less like an echo chamber.

The Issue of Grade Inflation

Grade inflation has landed a leading role in college admissions. We've worked with students who had seemingly solid transcripts, with grades mostly in the low-to-mid 90s, only to see them face-plant on state exams and standardized tests in those same subjects.

One case still plagues us. A public-school student had a transcript full of A's, including in biology. Then, her dad called us in full freak-out mode after she had bombed a required state exam, the kind meant to assess subject mastery. Her score? A 54. Oy. Either the teacher wasn't teaching the material, or the grading was so inflated that her transcript became a hot air balloon—soaring high until reality hit.

This isn't a fluke. We've seen A+ English students struggle to write a coherent essay and tank on the verbal/English portions of the SAT or ACT.

The mismatch is impossible to ignore.

Standardized tests aren't perfect, but they were designed as equalizers. With grading policies all over the map, a solid test score can help colleges gauge who's genuinely prepared, especially when GPAs alone don't tell the full story.

That's why having your child take the SAT or ACT is a smart move, unless testing really isn't their thing. Skipping it shouldn't be the default just because they don't feel like spending a Saturday morning answering multiple-choice questions.

If practice tests go well, why not give it a shot? A strong score remains an asset, even at test-optional schools. If the results are disappointing, they don't have to send them.

One student summed it best: "I didn't even know whether I should be prepping. Some friends were taking it three times, and some not bothering at all. It felt like a guessing game."

We don't push every student to test. Truly test-optional colleges exist, but skipping testing may narrow options. Wouldn't it be better if testing were one clear, consistent option that was available, contextual, and fair?

4. AP CLASSES & EXAMS: MORE DISCONNECT

We've believed for many years that if a student takes an AP class, they should be expected to report their AP exam score to colleges. Right now, however, students can take the class, skip the test, or choose not to share the score—no questions asked. Most colleges don't require them to submit it.

We've seen a mismatch too many times to count: a student earns an A or a 98% in AP U.S. History, and then eeks out a 2 or a 3 on the AP exam. That's grade inflation at work, or there's a gap between what's being taught and what's being tested.

If a student takes an AP class, it seems fair for colleges to consider both the course grade and the AP test score. Together, those pieces tell a fuller story.

Since colleges don't require AP scores, students who earn high grades but perform poorly on the exams just don't send in their scores. And colleges? They accept that A or 98% as if it accurately reflects what the student learned.

Now here's where it gets more complicated. According to Summit Prep, "the average AP score is higher now than it was in 2019 for 29 of the 38 total exams." That raises new concerns that the AP exams themselves may be inflating too, especially after College Board shortened and modified many of the tests during and after the pandemic.[61]

So where does that leave us? Caught between two kinds of inflation: course grades that may not reflect accurate rigor, and exam scores that may not reflect true mastery.

We're not dismissing the value of APs. Many students work incredibly hard in these classes. But if colleges see APs as a sign of academic strength, they should look at all the data—not just the part that paints the rosiest picture.

5. THE EXTRA TIME EPIDEMIC: LET'S MAKE IT FAIR FOR EVERYONE

Standardized testing accommodations exist for a reason. Thanks to the Americans with Disabilities Act (ADA) and Section 504 of the Rehabilitation Act, students with documented learning challenges rightfully receive extra time. That's how it should be.

But over the years, we've seen the number of students receiving extra time skyrocket, especially in well-resourced communities where parents are hyper-aware of the competitive stakes. More and more families pursue evaluations early in high school, hoping that extra time will provide a needed boost.

We don't get involved in testing accommodations. That's between families, school counselors, and specialists. But we can't ignore what we've seen. There's been a surge of students, many from privileged backgrounds, suddenly receiving diagnoses for ADHD,

61 Summit Educational Group, "Are AP Exams Inflated?" *Summit Blog,* July 11, 2024, https://summitprep.com/blog/ap-exam-scores-are-inflated/.

processing issues, test anxiety, or executive functioning challenges right before testing season. However, accommodations are rarely approved if they are requested too late and there is no documented history of using them in school.

We don't want to judge. Most families are advocating in good faith; they're not scheming villains. They love their kids. They see how brutal the college process has become, and like any parent, they want to give their child every possible advantage.

Extra time shouldn't be a Band-Aid for kids who don't need it. It should be a critical support for those who genuinely do.

In fact, some experts question whether extended time even helps all the students it's meant to. Gregory Fabiano, a psychology professor at Florida International University, told *Education Week* that for kids with ADHD, "they have a hard time paying attention for the typical time that they're supposed to do the task. Why would giving them another 20 minutes...help at all?" Research shows that extra time doesn't always improve outcomes. It's just easier and cheaper for schools to offer than true behavior-support programs.[62]

The extra time on standardized exams becomes a real problem when colleges are unable to distinguish between students with lifelong, well-documented learning challenges, and those whose parents rushed to obtain a "diagnosis" after disappointing practice scores right before junior year.

We've worked with students who have had an IEP or 504 plan since middle school. They've always needed extra time. That's fair. What no one talks about is how this growing trend hurts the very students accommodations were designed to support.[63]

This is where things start to feel really out of sync: one student we worked with was diagnosed with dyslexia and granted four full days to take the SAT. Another received two full weeks to complete the ACT in segments.[64] Meanwhile, most students are racing against the clock on a Saturday morning, trying to finish in under three hours.

How is that standardized?

There's another side to this conversation that deserves a moment of reflection: what message are parents sending their kids when they suddenly take them for a neuropsych evaluation and push for extra time when the student doesn't need it?

---

62 Elizabeth Heubeck, "Experts Question Extended Test-Taking Time for ADHD Students," *Education Week*, October 13, 2025, https://www.edweek.org/teaching-learning/does-extended-time-on-tests-actually-help-students-with-adhd/2025/10
63 An *IEP* provides special education services and supports for K–12 students with disabilities. A 504 plan offers accommodations (like extended time) for students with disabilities who do not need special education. 64 According to official accommodations guidelines from both the College Board and ACT, students with documented disabilities such as dyslexia may receive testing accommodations that allow the SAT or ACT to be administered over multiple days. In some cases, students may complete the test over the course of a full week or, for the ACT, within a special two-week testing window. See College Board, *Services for Students with Disabilities (SSD) Accommodations Manual*, 2023; and ACT, "ACT Special Testing: Information for Examinees," https://www.act.org/content/act/en/products-and-services/the-act/registration/accommodations.html.

We once had a student sit in our office and tell us, point blank, that he had been diagnosed with dyslexia, but then hesitated.

"I was told I have dyslexia, but I don't," he admitted softly. "My parents just wanted me to get extra time."

Our hearts broke. Think about what it feels like to be in his shoes and believe your parents don't trust you to succeed on your own. That kind of message can slowly erode a child's confidence.

Parents want the best for their kids. But sometimes, in the effort to help, we forget to step back and ask the hard but loving questions:

What is this really teaching my child?

How does it feel for a child to hear that their natural ability isn't enough?

That's not the story we want our kids to believe.

Why Not Make the SAT and ACT Untimed For Everyone?

If extra time is such a game-changer, why not just give it to everyone?

What if we eliminated timed tests completely?

Let's just make all standardized tests untimed. For *everyone*. Problem-solved!

- Redesign the SAT and ACT to eliminate the mad dash against the clock.
- Let kids take as long as they need to complete the test whether it's two hours or an entire day.
- No more whispers about whether some students have an advantage over others.
- No more stress over securing a diagnosis just to level the playing field.

Imagine a world where students could simply think about answering the questions, instead of frantically calculating whether they have thirty-seven seconds left to decode a passage about the blue-footed booby.[65]

We should also think a little more carefully about what the SAT and ACT are trying to test. How often, in adult life, is preparedness and competence measured by how quickly you do something? Isn't that what machines are for? In adult life, we rarely have to read and summarize what we understand about an essay we've read in thirty seconds.

At the end of the day, not every student is a natural test-taker. Some struggle with processing speed and others with test anxiety. Even worse, there are kids with palpable panic because they believe their entire future is being determined on a random Saturday morning. If we're going to keep standardized testing, let's make it 100% standardized.

---

65 Blue-footed booby (*Sula nebouxii*) is a marine bird found in the eastern Pacific Ocean, known for its distinctive bright blue feet and elaborate courtship dance. These birds are skilled divers and primarily feed on fish. They are commonly found on islands off the coasts of Central and South America, especially the Galápagos Islands—as well as in SAT Reading Comprehension questions.

6. DITCH (OR RETHINK) EARLY ACTION

Speaking of systems that don't work, let's talk about Early Action (EA).

Every year, we work with students who bleed Michigan blue. They live and breathe maize, have memorized every word of *The Victors*, and would trade a younger sibling for a spot in Ann Arbor.

But until recently, there was one major problem: Michigan didn't offer Early Decision.

Instead, they offered non-binding Early Action, which often felt like a polite brush-off. "Thanks for your application! We'll get back to you..." EA didn't offer much of an advantage, didn't help colleges predict yield, and mostly led to disappointment. Our hunch? Schools like Michigan and Wisconsin have been drowning in applications and end up deferring hordes of strong candidates.

In fact, EA at many big-name state schools should come with a warning label: *Prepare to be deferred, even if you're an off-the-charts applicant.*

To make matters worse, EA no longer even lives up to the "early" part of its name. Once upon a time, decisions came out before Regular Decision (RD) deadlines, giving students time to adjust their lists or pivot to an ED2 option. Now? Some schools, like Michigan and Wisconsin, don't release results until late January. After RD deadlines have passed.

What's the point?

We're all for options that reduce stress and give students clarity. But if EA isn't providing answers when they matter most, maybe it's time to call it what it is: **Deferred Action.**

The good news? Michigan finally announced an Early Decision option for the 2025–2026 cycle. For students who know it's their top choice, ED is a way to show serious commitment. And for Michigan, it's a long-overdue step toward less opacity and more predictability.

7. KILL DEMONSTRATED INTEREST

Applying to college is a lot like dating.

Colleges flirt with students through glossy pamphlets, gushy emails about their "vibrant community," and eager reps making their rounds at high schools and regional events. They put themselves out there, hoping students will be intrigued.

But they also want to be pursued.

Colleges don't just want students to apply; they want them to "show them the love." They want to know that students are thinking about them and picturing a future together.

Fair enough. But tracking every little display of affection? That's when things feel a bit too much.

Not every student has the time (or budget) to crisscross the country, book hotels, attend admissions sessions, and nod enthusiastically on a campus tour led by a relentlessly energetic sophomore in the freezing cold. For some families, college visits have become a full-blown production.

Spring break? Time for a Big Ten road trip.

Winter break? Why not get a taste of Southern culture, and Duke, Wake Forest, Elon, Washington & Lee while you're at it?

Hitting the slopes in Colorado? Might as well take a peek at the schools. On the way to Napa? A quick detour down to Stanford couldn't hurt.

For families juggling tight finances, packed schedules, or multiple kids, this isn't exactly feasible. Even students with plenty of resources can't visit every school on their list, and they shouldn't have to.

Do colleges really care?

The big state schools and the Ivies? Not so much. But most other schools? Oh, they're watching.

Not just the visits. The emails. The clicks. The time spent lingering on a webpage.

Colleges utilize algorithms to determine if a student opened an email, how many times they clicked, and even how long they kept it open. They want to feel wanted. But at some point, this feels more like they need constant validation from already stressed-out, insecure high school students.

Colleges have worked hard to make themselves more accessible to all students, and we applaud these efforts. Virtual tours, online info sessions, and student panels are fantastic tools that allow families to learn about a school without booking a flight or spending hours in a car, train, or bus.

But if these resources are genuinely about equity, why are schools so focused on tracking engagement? Shouldn't applying be enough? Shouldn't students visit the schools *after* they get in before making a final decision?

Demonstrated Interest has become yet another stress-inducing, strategy-driven layer in an already overcomplicated process. If you think Demonstrated Interest is bad, just wait until we get to Yield Protection (spoiler: it's worse).

8. RETHINK THE RECOMMENDATION LETTER

In large public high schools, teachers juggle hundreds of students and are expected to write dozens of personalized letters, often on their own unpaid time. Many barely know the student beyond class participation and whether they turned in their homework on time.

Let's talk about fairness:

- The most "popular" teachers end up writing 40–50 letters, while others write none.
- Most letters are neutral. Occasionally, a standout one makes an impact, but it's rare.
- Why not rethink recommendations entirely? Instead of forcing teachers into this madness, let students submit letters from the people who know them best. The list could include:
- A coach who's seen them push through failure (and maybe wipe away a tear or two before getting back in the game).
- A boss from their part-time job who can vouch for their work ethic (and whether they mind wiping down tables for the third time and dealing with cranky customers without losing their cool).
- A best friend who can speak to their character (the honesty would be striking).
- The mom of the kids they've babysat for, who knows firsthand how responsible they are (and who still talks about how they somehow got her toddler to eat vegetables *and* take a bath before bed).

Wouldn't these perspectives give a richer picture of a student than a rushed letter filled with recycled adjectives?

Of course, if a student has a teacher who knows them well and *wants* to write a recommendation, then great. But giving students the freedom to choose who speaks on their behalf would make the process more consequential.

And teachers? They could finally get their evenings and weekends back. Maybe even watch a reality show (hopefully, one that has nothing to do with college admissions!).

9. BE TRANSPARENT ABOUT THE REVIEW PROCESS

Parents and students imagine the admissions process as a giant black box: applications go in, decisions come out, and no one really knows what happens in between.

Colleges love to preach "holistic admissions," but what does that even mean? Most families have no clue how their child's application is reviewed. Is it one person flipping through an entire profile in five minutes? Is there a full committee debate? Does an intern get to weigh in while eating leftover pizza?

These are our burning questions:

- Do admissions officers really read every essay? If so, how many times?
- Are applications sorted by geography, major, or something else entirely?
- Do less-than-stellar grades mean an automatic rejection, or is there wiggle room?

- How do colleges compare a student from a well-resourced private school with one from an underfunded public school?
- Are these essays being read by actual humans, or is AI taking the first pass?

That last question is no longer hypothetical. A recent report described how some colleges are already using artificial intelligence to help review applications and essays. At Virginia Tech, for example, an AI "essay reader" now scores short-answer responses alongside a human reader, and at Caltech, admissions officials have acknowledged experimenting with AI tools to summarize transcripts and application materials in order to move faster through tens of thousands of files.[66] Families rarely hear about when or how these tools are used, which makes the whole process feel even more secretive.

We ask these questions every time we visit colleges and meet with admissions officers. They usually respond with confidence, reassuring us that **every application is read**, essays are evaluated thoughtfully, and students are reviewed in context. But given the crushing volume of applications, it's hard not to wonder if this is entirely true.

The question every student (and parent) really wants answered is: why didn't they get in?

Obviously, colleges can't explain every decision. Still, even a short note or coded response could make this process feel less arbitrary. It would help to know a few things:

- Was something missing from the application? Maybe their extracurriculars, their choice of major, or the fact that they didn't end their supplemental essay with a profound yet original closing line?
- Did they fall short academically, or get edged out by someone stronger on paper?
- Did they ever *really* stand a chance?

Colleges insist that "it's not personal." But to students (and, understandably, their stressed-out parents), it absolutely is. Kids have poured their heart into their application, and when that rejection email arrives, they're left with nothing but unanswered questions, and probably an overpowering urge to crawl back into bed and watch all ten seasons of *Friends*.

Imagine if colleges gave a *sliver* of feedback. It wouldn't erase the disappointment, but it would make the process feel less like a guessing game.

Sharing general patterns or offering feedback broadly would go a long way toward building trust. When students and parents understand the "why," even the bad news would hit more softly.

When Dr. Nicholas B. Dirks, the 10th Chancellor of the University of California,

---

66 Jaweed Kaleem and Jocelyn Gecker, "A.I. Is Scoring College Essays & Conducting Interviews," *Los Angeles Times*, January 2, 2026.

Berkeley (2013–2017), launched his book *City of Intellect: The Uses and Abuses of the University*, we talked about this very gap between universities and the public. He didn't hold back.

"Nowhere do universities fail the transparency test as badly as they do in admissions. I have long believed that the black box of admissions should be addressed not least by being clear that these decisions are (or should be) driven by two fundamental things: first, predicting which applicants will be best suited for the educational opportunities and challenges of any particular university; and second, admitting a 'class' made up of different students with a wide range of skills, aptitudes, and interests (from history to physics, violin to tuba, and crew to football)."

I agree. Families deserve to know what criteria matter and how a class is built, instead of guessing at what goes on behind closed doors. Transparency in admissions is about letting families feel like they're part of the conversation—not standing outside *the room where it happens*.

Once upon a time, interviews played a meaningful role in admissions. Now? They've devolved into something unhelpful and wildly inconsistent. Back in the day, applicants met with admissions officers: the people who literally worked at the college. These days, students are more likely to be paired with alumni who haven't set foot on campus since the early 2000's and have zero formal training. Some are fantastic. Others? Not so much.

We've seen it all: well-meaning but clueless grads turning interviews into lectures about their own glory days. Alumni who ask wildly inappropriate questions ("So what will you do if you don't get into Yale?"). One student handed over his resume, only to watch his interviewer crumple it up and toss it in the trash. For real.

To make things even more chaotic, some schools now offer student-led interviews. Friendlier? Yes, but they aren't truly evaluative. Students now go through the motions with no impact on their application. Lovely chat. Zero impact.

Then there's the dreaded video submission requirement, which is arguably even worse. Many colleges now strongly "recommend" (read: subtly pressure) students to submit a short video highlighting something not already in their application. Sounds harmless, right? Except that filming, editing, and perfecting a one-minute clip is yet another hoop that students with the resources and video-production skills feel obligated to jump through.

We've seen students agonize like they're Steven Spielberg over these videos. They spend hours perfecting the lighting, camera angles, wardrobe, and scripting every word. The results range from effusively sentimental monologues about a childhood teddy bear to fast-paced skateboarding montages featuring their town's best coffee spots, to full-blown (hopefully unintentional) displays of privilege. We bet that no one in admissions is watching these for more than a few seconds.

And right when this process couldn't get any more theatrical, along came the dialogues portfolios. Beginning in the fall of 2025, a growing number of elite schools, including Columbia, MIT, Northwestern, Johns Hopkins, Vanderbilt, and UChicago, accept recordings from Schoolhouse.world, a peer tutoring platform co-founded by Sal Khan. In these sessions, students log onto Zoom, debate complex topics like immigration or climate policy, and rate each other on traits like curiosity and empathy. The more sessions you attend, and the more virtue points you rack up from your peers, the stronger your dialogue portfolio.[67] Please note that this is a recent development, and we have not seen much about how widely it is being used in practice. We are hoping it quietly sails off into the sunset.

I mean, what could go wrong?

As of now, there's no indication that colleges plan to scrap these videos or dialogue-style assessments. If anything, they seem increasingly willing to experiment with more performance-based add-ons, not fewer.

But let's be honest. These new gimmicks like interviews, videos, and now dialogues, are mostly distractions. They end up rewarding the kid who can put on a show instead of the one being real.

If colleges want to evaluate students fairly, they need to stop rewarding those with the best iMovie skills or the highest empathy score on a peer-reviewed Zoom call.

Ditch the interviews.

Ditch the videos.

Ditch the dialogues.

Everyone wins.

11. STOP WORRYING ABOUT YIELD AND ADMIT THE BEST STUDENTS

It's time for colleges to stop playing yield games and start admitting students based on merit and not enrollment projections.

Right now, admissions offices are so fixated on protecting their yield rates (the percentage of admitted students who end up enrolling) that they turn down strong applicants for one reason: they suspect they'll say no. This practice, often called **yield**

---

67 David Deming, "We've Been Thinking About College Admissions All Wrong," New York Times, July 15, 2025, https://www.nytimes.com/2025/07/15/opinion/college-admissions-essays.html.

protection, means some students are rejected or waitlisted *not* because they aren't qualified, but because colleges worry that they're using the school as a backup. Instead of prioritizing the most qualified students, they zero in on the ones most likely to say yes. It's defensive and unfair. Our kids deserve better.

Early Decision has made this even worse. At some schools, more than 60% of the freshman class is locked in through ED and ED2, filling spots before students get to see all their options. Sure, yield numbers look great. But is this about admitting the best students, or just gaming the system?

The obsession with yield is often attributed to college rankings, particularly *U.S. News & World Report*. While admit rates and yield have not been direct inputs in the rankings methodology for many years, the culture surrounding rankings continues to reward the appearance of exclusivity and selectivity.

Schools are, in fact, evaluated on far more telling factors: student-faculty ratios, financial resources, student outcomes, research opportunities, and graduation rates. Yet families and institutions alike remain fixated on headline numbers that are easy to compare but are far less telling.

Why let a narrow perception of selectivity—rather than student fit and success— dictate decisions that shape students' futures?

Admissions should be about finding the right students for the right schools and not playing a numbers game to boost rankings. If a student is an incredible fit and academically qualified, they deserve to be admitted. End of story.

By stepping away from the hysteria around selectivity rates, colleges have the power to set a healthier tone. Students will follow their lead. So will parents. Maybe, just maybe, the process could start to feel a little more human again.

12. STANDARDIZE THE PROCESS ACROSS ALL COLLEGES FOR EVERYONE'S SAKE

We do this for a living, and even we can't always keep up. We belong to several chat forums with counselors across the country, and every single day, experienced professionals post questions about application requirements that are confusing or constantly changing. Each college seems to have its own quirky, slightly different, completely maddening set of rules.

It's draining.

For context, the most seasoned counselors spend hours calling admissions offices and scouring university websites just to make sure students don't miss a tiny but critical detail. If it's this complicated for us, consider how overwhelming it is for a seventeen-year-old and their family.

If we professionals who do this full time are racing to keep up, how are students and parents supposed to?

Here's a small sampling of the madness:

- **The "Courses & Grades" Maze:** Some colleges make students retype every single class and grade from high school into the Common App Courses & Grades section—a painstaking exercise that can take hours of precious time. For instance, the University of Washington and the University of Minnesota explicitly require students to complete this section in full. Meanwhile, other colleges push students into a separate system called STARS—the 2025 version of the **SSAR** (Student Self-Reported Academic Record), where you enter the same transcript data all over again. Penn State requires a STARS record. Same idea, totally different format. And University of Wisconsin–Madison? They've created their own process entirely; students must self-report their courses and grades directly through the UW portal. Why make anything easy? If a student applies to all of these schools, they could end up reproducing their entire transcript three separate times in addition to the official transcript their high school sends.

- **The Teacher Recommendation Shuffle:** Some colleges require multiple teacher recommendations, while others only want one. A few have baffling restrictions on which subjects count (Caltech doesn't consider foreign language a core subject. Seriously?).

- **The Test Score Blackout Mystery:** Some colleges suppress the SAT/ACT score section on the Common App, so students can't see whether their scores were successfully reported. Others don't. This leaves students guessing, and, in some cases, frantically emailing admissions offices to confirm whether their scores even made it through.

- **The Expanded Resume Requirement:** Some schools, like UT Austin, ask for an additional, multi-page resume detailing every activity, leadership position, and job, far beyond what the Common App allows. It's great for students with extensive extracurriculars, but once again, the requirements are all over the map. No wonder families feel lost.

We're not saying every college needs to have identical requirements. But can we at least agree on some basic standardization to preserve everyone's emotional well-being?

Let's Fix This Mess Already

College admissions shouldn't be a game of strategy, privilege, and extraordinary stress, but that's exactly what it's become. Students are applying to thirty schools, churning out essays about which historical figure they'd bring to dinner, filming Hollywood-level videos, and jumping through hoop after hoop to stay in the game.

Parents are losing sleep. Kids are losing time to be kids. Everyone's losing their minds.

Meanwhile, test-optional policies, yield protection, and a tangle of inconsistent requirements have turned the process into a three-ring circus.

We've spent years guiding families through this, trying to reassure them, translating the confusion, and reminding students that they're more than a GPA or an essay. We've watched brilliant kids doubt themselves and thoughtful parents wonder whether they're helping or making things worse. Each year, the pressure ticks up another notch, and more families start believing that gaming the system is the only way to win.

Why does it have to be this way?

It doesn't.

If colleges prioritized authenticity over strategy, trimmed the essay load, asked better questions, and stopped obsessing over rankings, we might finally give birth to an admissions process that makes sense. One that lets students breathe. One that values honesty over performance. One that gives kids a little room to be high schoolers. And human.

We don't have all the answers. But we do know this: everyone, including students, parents, teachers, counselors, and admissions officers would benefit from a process that feels saner, clearer, more streamlined, and kinder. We know admissions teams are under enormous pressure as they sort through thousands of applications. Our goal isn't to make their jobs harder; it's to make their work better, so they can concentrate on what counts the most: admitting students who will bring energy, curiosity, and a willingness to show up for that 9 a.m. class.

Ultimately, that's what this process should be about: students finding the schools where they'll flourish.

And despite everything, we still believe that's possible.

Let's fix this together.

Acknowledgements

In fourth grade, my teacher praised a small stack of short stories I had written and invited me to read them aloud to the class. Their polite applause felt like a standing ovation to nine-year-old me. From that moment on, I imagined writing a book...someday.

For years, my family and friends echoed that same voice I had in my own head, insisting I should write a book. But putting together a book about college admissions while running a counseling practice, shaping hundreds of essays, tending to a marriage, and trying to keep up with my own three kids, felt overwhelming and slightly insane. I *wanted* to write it. I just had no idea where to begin.

Nancy, however, did.

Somewhere between our first "can you believe this parent's expectations?" conversation and our ninety-ninth college road trip, the stories started piling up. Nancy would either gasp or grin with me after each meeting and exclaim, "Write this down for your book!" Eventually, I listened. Then I did what any overwhelmed, fifty-something woman flirting with a midlife crisis and perpetually immersed in college angst might do: I signed up for memoir-writing classes. From there, everything took off. The stories. The humor. The wisdom. The heart I had been pouring into college counseling finally found its way onto the page (or the computer screen).

Writing this book became a long, unexpected, joyfully chaotic, and often crazy process, and I never could have done it alone. To everyone who encouraged me, laughed with me, or simply said "keep going" when I wasn't sure I could, thank you for helping me finally put this book into the world.

To my Scarsdale sisters, Julie, Tracey, Erika, and Erika's husband Bob (my lawyer-turned-literary-expert friend), thank you for letting me talk on repeat about this project for months, never once suggesting I take up pickleball instead. You are my daily laugh track and my much-needed sanity check.

And to my California mom-friends, Maria, Devon, Marni, and Wendy, thank you for cheering me on from three time zones away, for believing I'd actually write this book, and for sharing the fun and exhausting work of parenting, from celebrating our kids' college acceptances to the chapters that came after.

To Irv Cruz, my wonderful trainer and friend, thank you for letting me talk in endless loops about this book. You pushed me, physically and mentally, on the days I wanted to quit and helped me see I was capable of more than I thought. I appreciate you more than my Bosu.

To my friends who were published authors long before I ever was, Linda Rottenberg, thank you for telling me to "put my tush on the cush" and for letting me know how often this book made you laugh even in its infancy. And to Linda's brilliant husband, Bruce Feiler, thank you for asking exactly the right questions at exactly the right moments. My friend Darren Gold, thank you for cutting straight to the chase and helping me understand why writing this book mattered. Thank you for pushing me to dig deeper and think bigger. And to my local Westchester author friends, Lynda Loigman, Jackie Friedland, and Barbara Josselsohn, thank you for your generous sharing of book-world wisdom and for the encouraging emojis—those thumbs-ups and lady-in-the-red-dress-salsa-ing texts actually gave me a bigger boost than Diet Coke and pretzels at 4 p.m.

To my editing goddesses and crew, Julia Case-Levine, Suzanne Kirsch, and especially Robin Nabi, thank you for your early and thoughtful reads, discerning eyes, smart ideas, and honest feedback, even when it meant cutting paragraphs (and chapters). Robin, your edits strengthened this book at every stage. Without you, it might still be 600 pages long. A special thank you to Betsy Thorpe, who read the earliest full draft and offered ideas and direction that helped me broaden this book for a wider audience and to Julie Mazur-Tribe for making the introduction.

To my writing teacher, Janet Pfeffer at Sarah Lawrence, who inspired me and served as my writing muse (and therapist!) long after class ended, thank you. Your wisdom and patience kept me moving forward, especially when I wasn't sure what came next. And to my early readers in that class, including Kerry, Jen, and Linda, thank you for convincing me that the very first piece I ever read aloud was worthy of becoming a first chapter.

To Jim Rowe, my first mentor in marketing (and becoming an author!), thank you. This idea began as a single chapter ("Just Talk") and grew into something real because you believed in this book, and in me.

To Jenn Tuma-Young, my publisher and fellow Jersey girl, who had me at "hello," thank you. From 6 a.m. texts to late-night messages that proved sleep is optional when you care this much, your creativity, energy, and relentless guidance turned me into one very "Inspired Girl." Thank you to the entire crew at Inspired Girl for believing in me, and for your unwavering commitment to getting this book into the hands of every parent navigating the high-school-to-college maze.

To my college roommates, Alisa, Alexa, and Melissa, thank you for reading early drafts. I didn't need any proof to understand why our friendship has lasted all these years, but you gave it to me anyway. And to Pam, my closest friend from business school, thank you for cheering me on through every stage of this book while trusting my advice about your own daughters' college journeys.

To my oldest friends, Andrea (Migie) and Deborah, thank you for letting me send chapters from our childhood. I hope they help us all remember where we came from, and why those early memories and inside jokes will always matter.

To my friend Mayra, who walked into my life next to a copy machine on July 1, 1992, my first day at Grey Advertising, thank you for showing up again and again for me and for my entire family. I am forever grateful. You are one of the most extraordinary humans I know, brilliant with words, and continually reminding me that the best ideas come from the heart. You couldn't be more right.

To my closest friend Hilary—my daily 7 a.m. (PST!) phone call, my pep talk from the West Coast, and my California book-signing hostess—thank you for answering every panicked call from my house, my car, or the produce aisle in the grocery store, and talking me off the ledge every time. You've been the friend I count on and adore every step of the way.

To every student who has ever let me into their unfiltered, earnest, stressful, heartfelt college journey, thank you. You didn't just provide the material that made this book possible; you gave my work meaning. And to the parents whose children I've worked with, thank you for your trust, and of course, sharing the madness.

To my mother-in-law, Rolly, who encouraged me for years to write this book and has saved every email, card, and text I've ever sent her, thank you. You devoured every piece I wrote in my memoir class and became my own little book club, always ready for the next chapter. The way you treasure my words and stories has buoyed me more than I could possibly put into print.

To my mom, who spent my high school years schlepping me to play rehearsals, marching band, Model UN, and every activity imaginable (often after she taught a full day of kindergarten), and miraculously never complained, thank you. Since first grade, you've been convinced my writing was one step away from a Pulitzer Prize, and you've spent my entire life kvelling to anyone within earshot. I love how you jump up and down for every one of my successes as if they mean more than your own.

To my three kids, who agreed to be "featured" in this book even though I drove you crazy about college long before this title or any manuscript existed, thank you for giving me stories, perspective, patience, love, encouragement, and an infinite supply of material. Thank you for putting up with my triumphant screaming (often louder for other kids' acceptances than for your own) and for tolerating the way I turned every embarrassing or mundane moment of your lives into potential college essay fodder. You've taught me more about what it means to feel supported and successful than any admissions cycle ever could. I am ridiculously grateful and proud to be your mom every single day.

Then there is my husband, Jeff. Thank you for loving me for almost thirty years, living through chaos and joy, ignoring my dramatic tantrums, encouraging my writing classes, raising three terrific human beings, and cheering me on through every draft, firmly saying, "Just write the book." Your faith that this might one day be a bestseller always makes me chuckle on the outside and glow on the inside. Thank you for being the calmer half, for letting me wake you at 3 a.m. the night (or nights!) before our three kids got their college decisions, and for listening tot me spiral about every student I've ever worked with, as if they were our own. Thank you for dreaming big with me. I love you for the life we've built together and for being all-in on this book from day number one.

Finally, to Nancy, my business partner, my lifelong friend, and the sister I never had, thank you. Without you, this book simply wouldn't exist. You are the only person who truly understands every detail behind every story, every student, every parent, every SAT score, every late-night text, and every Hampton Inn free breakfast. Visiting more than 160 campuses together has made this work meaningful and, dare I say, fun. Thank you for devouring chicken salad sandwiches with me on road trips, for editing this book so many times you could recite it by heart, and for laughing every time I blurted out, "Look what we did! We started this business from scratch!" I am incredibly grateful for you, for our students, for our partnership, and for that first conversation in a nail salon—proof that the best things often begin in the most unexpected places. I guess we really are *Crazy for College*, and I wouldn't want it any other way.

ABOUT *the* AUTHOR

BETH HELLER GELLES is a sought-after expert in the field of college admissions. As co-founder of Acceptance Ahead, she has visited more than 160 college campuses and has guided hundreds of students and families over the past fourteen years. Known for her clarity, humor, and warm presence, Beth helps families make thoughtful decisions and move through the admissions process with confidence and far less stress.

Beth is a graduate of Harvard College and Northwestern University's Kellogg School of Management. She and her husband live in Westchester, New York, and are the proud parents of three children who made it through the college process with minimal tears—and who have (mostly) forgiven their mother for turning nearly every family moment into a potential college essay.

bethhellergelles.com